EROS and the
WOMANLINESS of GOD

Andrew Greeley's Romances of Renewal

BY INGRID H. SHAFER

What are the major theological themes and symbols in Andrew Greeley's popular romances, or novels as they are called? How do these themes and symbols fit into archetypal mythic structures and into the Catholic analogical universe? What is the connection between a feminine image of God and our attitudes toward the world in general and toward the religious dimensions of sexuality in particular? What can Eros teach us about God, about ourselves, our relationships to others, and to death? What, ultimately, are the radical consequences of the Incarnation and the sacramentality of the world? What kind of Church emerges from Andrew Greeley's stories?

This book is the result of Dr. Shafer's research and reflection upon these questions. While the author provides meticulous scholarly support, she writes for the educated general reader as well as for the academic and/or theological professional.

EROS and the
WOManLINESS OF GOD

About the author

Ingrid H. Shafer, a native of Austria, studied English and American literature at the universities of Vienna and Innsbruck. She came to the United States in 1960 and earned masters degrees in human relations and German literature from the University of Oklahoma and eventually her doctorate in philosophy from the same univesity. Dr. Shafer is married and the mother of two daughters. Since 1968 she has taught a wide variety of courses in philosophy and religion, and she is currently associate professor of philosophy and religion at the University of Science and Arts of Oklahoma.

✠ EROS
and the
WOMANLINESS
of GOD ✠

Andrew Greeley's Romances
of Renewal

INGRID H. SHAFER

Loyola University Press
Chicago

Loyola University Press
3441 North Ashland Avenue
Chicago, Illinois 60657

All quotations from the published and unpublished works of Andrew Greeley are reprinted here with his permission. Unpublished citations may, of course, be subject to change and revision in their published form.

William Blake's poem "The Garden of Love" is reprinted with permission from The Norton Critical Edition, Edited by Mary Lynn Johnson and John E. Grant, of *Blake's Poetry and Designs,* copyright © 1979 by W. W. Norton & Company, Inc.

Quotation from "Ash Wednesday" in *Collected Poems 1909-1962* by T.S. Eliot, copyright 1936 by Harcourt Brace Jovanovich, Inc.; copyright © 1963, 1964 by T.S. Eliot. Reprinted by permission of the publisher.

Design by J. L. Boden

Library of Congress Cataloging in Publication Data
Shafer, Ingrid H.
    Eros and the womanliness of God.   12-86
    Bibliography: p. 267
    Includes index.
    1. Greeley, Andrew M., 1928-   —Fictional works.
2. God in literature.   3. Woman (Christian theology)
in literature.   4. Sex in literature. I. Title.
PS3557.R358Z88   1986   813'.54   86-7512
ISBN 0-8294-0519-4

For Monsignor Anton Egger
who first taught me that God is Love
and the Church a Loving Mother

MAY MAGNIFICAT

May is Mary's month, and I
Muse at that and wonder why:
    Her feasts follow reason,
    Dated due to season—

Candlemas, Lady Day;
But the Lady Month, May,
    Why fasten that upon her,
    With a feasting in her honour?

Is it only its being brighter
Than the most are must delight her?
    Is it opportunest
    And flowers finds soonest?

Ask of her, the mighty mother:
Her reply puts this other
    Question: What is Spring?—
    Growth in everything—

Flesh and fleece, fur and feather,
Grass and greenworld all together;
    Star-eyed strawberry breasted
    Throstle above her nested

Cluster of bugle blue eggs thin
Forms and warms the life within;
    And birds and blossoms swell
    In sod or sheath or shell.

All things rising, all things sizing
Mary sees, sympathising
    With that world of good,
    Nature's motherhood.

Their magnifying of each its kind
With delight calls to mind
    How she did in her stored
    Magnify the Lord.

Well but there was more than this:
Spring's universal bliss
    Much, had much to say
    To offering Mary May.

When drop-of-blood-and-foam-dapple
Bloom lights the orchard apple
    And thicket and thorp are merry
    With silver-surfèd cherry,

And azuring-over greybell makes
Wood banks and brakes wash wet like lakes
    And magic cuckoocall
    Caps, clears and clinches all—

This ecstasy all through mothering earth
Tells Mary her mirth till Christ's birth
    To remember and exultation
    In God who was her salvation.

                    Gerard Manley Hopkins

contents

foreword

This book might have been called *The Academic Sins*, a meta-pun on Andrew Greeley's own finest punning title, *The Cardinal Sins*. For the secret sin that every academic dreams of committing is neither of the ones for which, as Ingrid Shafer begins by pointing out, Father Greeley has been condemned— the sins of sex and money. These concerns are, it is true, regarded as even less appropriate to ordained priests than to secular academics, but profane academics of the old school are supposed to spurn them, too, in favor of the sacred world of ideas; as Aldous Huxley once remarked, an intellectual is someone who has found something more interesting than sex. Yet the true secret sin of an academic is *fiction*, and this is what Greeley has committed in such an inexpiable scale.

Greeley is not, of course, the first scholar to have committed fiction. Some have committed murder mysteries, under their own name (Dorothy Sayers, Ugo Bianchi, and Robert van Gulik, author of the Chinese box murders) or under an alias (Michael Innes). More particularly, scholars of religion have committed novels (Mircea Eliade, Arthur Cohen) or even *children's* fiction — some again, out of the academic closet (C.S. Lewis) and others pseudonymously (Lewis Carroll). Those of

us who do not venture out of the formal gardens of academe
into the jungles of fiction envy those who do; we envy them not
merely for the profane reasons—for making all that money and
writing about all that sex, but for sacred reasons—for producing
works of pure creativity while we merely analyse such works.
Our sacred envy may also be exacerbated by our guilty suspicion that, by exorcising some of their emotional demons in this
way, fiction-writing academics may render themselves more
immune than the rest of us to the fictions of autobiography,
theology, fantasy, that keep thrusting themselves into our supposedly objective writing (just as—moving in the inverse direction—King Charles's head kept getting into Mr. Dick's autobiography).

But the infection works in the other direction, too; the
novels of academics usually carry into the jungle something of
the hothouse atmosphere of the academy; the novels of academics tend to argue a point of view, to dramatize an idea, in a way
that the novels of (non-academic) novelists do not. This is, I
think, true of Greeley, too. Ingrid Shafer argues here that Andrew Greeley uses his fiction to say something about religion
that he could say neither as a sociologist nor as a traditional
priest. Indeed, in her view, the Greeley trinity—priest, novelist,
academic—pulls not in three separate directions but all together,
like the horses of a well matched troika. She therefore attempts
to decode what he so carefully encoded, to translate back into
academic language the ideas that he so carefully translated *out of*
academic language into fiction; like Penelope, she unweaves in
the night of analytical prose the fabric that was woven in the
light of the novel. She peels back the fictive flesh to expose the
theological bones like a *memento mori*. Or, perhaps, given Ms.
Shafer's argument that Greeley sees God as female, one could
speak more appropriately of this book as a kind of inverted
vierge ouvrante: the medieval image of Mary built with a door
that could be opened to reveal, within, the image of Christ.

To the extent that the fiction does say something above and
beyond the ideas that are written into the novels, the books
cannot be entirely decoded in this way; as Isadora Duncan once
remarked when asked what her dancing meant, "If I could tell
you, I wouldn't have to dance it." As in any analysis of fiction,
when one reads the quoted excerpts one sees things that are not

in the analysis; *inter alia*, one sees the *story* itself—the dance of the lord of the dance—that is frozen in the analysis. I found myself getting caught up in reading the excerpts and sorry to be called away from them to read what was said about them; truth may be stranger than fiction, but it isn't as much fun.

But then, as with any analysis, the bones are refleshed with a new fictive world projected by the analyst; Ingrid Shafer's response to Andrew Greeley's fiction is her own fiction, her own story written into the story of the women in Greeley's books. Her fiction is not exactly the same as his, I think; her reading of his novels is different from mine (just as my reading of the myths that Greeley uses often differs from his reading of them). Indeed, Ms. Shafer insists that she wants her readers to construct their own personal responses rather than slavishly following those she suggests. Like Chinese boxes or Russian dolls, we encapsulate one another; the next box will be created by the person who reads my response to Ingrid's response to Andrew Greeley's response to the myths. For we are all circling, each in our own way, around the same magnetic images, like moths around a flame.

The magnetic core of the Greeley novels is a mythology in which the fire of sexual passion, diffused into all aspects of human emotional experience, lights the way to the grail of an upbeat grace. Greeley did not invent this mythology; no one invents a mythology. A myth is a story that many people have found meaningful for a long time. Greeley found his mythology ready to wear, on the racks of Irish Catholicism. Of course, he retells the myths in his own way, but the power is built into the story itself; the myth is always in style, even before one updates its hemline to the fashionable length. The recent Wisdom Bridge production of *Hamlet* dressed the actors in 20th century clothes, but played the final duel scene in Elizabethan costume. And at the very end, when hand-held 20th century television cameras photographed the dead Shakespearean characters in their crowns and doublets and hose, the images that they projected on the television screens at the side of the stage were the images of the characters in the 20th century clothes that they had worn in the earlier scenes. So, too, the Greeley characters live simultaneously in Chicago now and in the Celtic twilight of *illo tempore*.

And there is another way in which the Greeley novels are mythological, besides the literal ways in which myths are quoted and the less literal ways in which myths are reworked. The books reach out to our culture with a mass appeal that gives them a universal currency very like that of a myth in a more traditional culture. The very fact that damns the books in the eyes of academia—the profane fact that they are sold by the millions at airports—lends them a kind of sacred authenticity that sociologists, if not literary critics, needs must respect. Indeed, literary criticism may be irrelevant to a myth; Claude Levi-Strauss once remarked that, while poetry is what is lost in translation, myth is what survives even the worst translation. Andrew Greeley's versions of the myths are not poetry; he would be the last to claim that their primary value lies in their aesthetic excellence. But they are certainly a translation good enough to keep the myth alive in our day; the intrinsic power of the plot writes "not applicable" in invisible magic letters next to any potential critic's criteria of literary excellence. The novels' mass appeal makes them a phenomenon of sociology and, in Ms. Shafer's view, of theology. For, as Greeley himself remarks (and is quoted here by Ms. Shafer), the myth both grows out of personal experience and shapes our perception of personal experience. Millions of people respond to the mythology of the Greeley novels, in part because he touches upon a mythology that they already have and in part because he presents them with a mythology that they want to have. This being so, it is a point of considerable interest to see just what that mythology is, and what mythology is embedded in its reworked plots. This is one of the many worthwhile things accomplished by Ingrid Shafer's retelling of the myth of Andrew Greeley.

Wendy Doniger O'Flaherty
The University of Chicago

pReface

Until 1983 I knew Andrew Greeley only as the author of many articles and numerous nonfiction studies. As an intellectual omnivore, I was particularly delighted to find in him a scholar who successfully integrated such diverse disciplines as sociology, theology, and psychology, while demonstrating a keen sense of the history of ideas and the significance of literature and the arts.

Then, browsing through a University of California bookstore, I discovered paperback copies of *The Cardinal Sins* and *Thy Brother's Wife*. I read the quotation from the Song of Solomon on the flyleaf of *The Cardinal Sins*: "Stern as death is love, relentless as the nether world is passion. Its flames are a blazing fire; deep waters cannot quench love, nor floods sweep it away." This seemed like my kind of story! For as long as I could remember I had been drawn to fiction and poetry of philosophical or theological significance. As a child growing up in Austria, my favorite novelists were Franz Werfel and Sigrid Undset. In my teens I discovered the poetical works of Goethe, Dante, Donne, Milton, and T.S. Eliot. Greeley's novels seemed to fit the pattern.

I was not disappointed. I found a lively style, compelling stories, and characters with whom I could identify despite their obvious allegorical significance. Most importantly, I felt myself drawn ever more deeply into the analogical exploration of such perennial theological themes as the androgyny of God, the nature of evil, the role of mysticism and the paranormal, the pervasiveness of grace, and the sacramentality of the material world, particularly that most primordial and powerful of all natural forces, sexuality.

After reading the other four novels published at that time, I was convinced that Greeley's fiction might warrant my critical attention. I was fascinated by the skillful manner in which he managed to combine the literary forms of morality play, Romance, and contemporary novel with the scriptural mode of parable. Clearly, his works responded to a profound human need to find meaning in life. It seemed that Greeley's sensitivity to the tragic possibilities of human existence had engendered their own negation, the assurance of hope and grace revealed against the dark shadows of sin and despair. Above and beyond the chaotic jungle of errant human passions and the Church as a human institution corrupted by authoritarianism, envy, and lust for power, his words conjured up a bright, warm image of God as passionate, caring, and sustaining Presence, and the "real" Church as a community of equals, a genuine mother whose nurturing love enfolds every last one of her children within her warm embrace.

My scholarly curiosity had been aroused, and I began to survey critical responses to the novels. Surprise turned to dismay, and finally, to utter consternation. While most of the reviews I read were favorable, far too many seemed almost or completely oblivious to the rich symbolic tapestry presented in the works. References to liturgical cycles, the grand themes of the Mass and the Christian year, carefully chosen poetry and hymns, the generally metaphorical nature of the stories, were universally disregarded. None of the reviewers, for example, took note of the parallel to St. Bernard or Dame Julian of Norwich in the poignant scene of Peg nursing her husband Tom, "administering her sacrament to him," in *Ascent into Hell.* Nora's Madonna role as Christ analogue in *Thy Brother's Wife*

was consistently ignored. No one bothered to mention the recurrent theme of a sinner's return to his/her first love as symbolic of God's loyalty for Her/His people. Instead, far too many
reviewers focused on the titillating morsel of a celibate priest
actually describing moments of physical intimacy, and horror of
horrors, daring to use erotic imagery to convey theological
insights.

In their eyes and minds, works which Greeley considers
"comedies of grace" were reflected as blasphemous, steamy
sleaze, deserving of a plain brown wrapper, and his readers were
curtly dismissed as ignorant soap-opera addicts whose brains
could barely grasp the contents of *The National Enquirer*.

Could I have been wrong? I reread the novels. The religious
symbolism and theological themes seemed even more powerful
the second time around when I was familiar with the characters
and no longer distracted by fascination with a complex array of
plots, subplots, conflict and resolution. Why is it, I wondered,
that Greeley's spiritual message appears obvious to me as well as
to thousands, perhaps millions of average (nonclerical and/or
nonacademic) readers, while so many reviewers miss the point
completely? Can the same surface be transparent to some while
remaining totally opaque to others?

It certainly can. People, even critics, tend to see only what
they expect to see. Francis Bacon called this universal human
tendency the "idol of the cave" or, possibly, the "idol of the
theatre." More recently, experimental psychologists have discovered that a kitten, raised from birth in an environment
marked exclusively with contrasting vertical lines and kept in
this artificially manipulated "world" for several months, will be
permanently unable to respond to horizontal patterns. This unfortunate feline will be condemned to a life of falling off tables
and colliding with the bottom edges of beds and couches. Its
perception of reality, the way external stimuli are processed and
transformed into useful information, has been unalterably affected. Could it be that a similar process is at work as far as
critical responses to Greeley's novels are concerned?

The problem is not only or even primarily the fact that
Greeley employs highly charged and often erotic religious symbols, nor the fact that reviewers know that he is a priest. The

"blinding effect" occurs at the juncture of sexual imagery with the author's special status as a celibate priest, particularly a priest who is enormously successful in financial terms. A bona fide priest actually portraying moments of sexual encounter! Red lights start flashing . . . Blasphemy! Pornography! Filth! Judgment has been passed before the first page of the book is read. Merely glancing at the cover might have sufficed. Never mind that the erotic scenes are depicted with sensitivity, taste, and tenderness, and are understood as such by most nonclerical readers. The mere fact that they were hatched in the mind of a priest warrants their condemnation. To add insult to injury, the works have been commercially successful and thus, claim the critics, must have been written for the appallingly unChristlike purpose of acquiring wealth.

Imagine those critics alive in ages past. Would they have shrunk in disgust from the Song of Solomon (offended by the word "vulva," which by means of an unbloody interpretative "operation" has been so miraculously transformed into "navel" in modern translations), and would they have censured the ecstatic visions of Richard Rolle, Teresa of Avila, and St. John of the Cross? Would they have banned Wolfram von Eschenbach's *Parzival* (for, after all, the questing hero appears to enter the married state without benefit of clergy) and demanded that Chretien des Troyes expunge the sacramental-though-illicit lovemaking scene from his *Tristan and Isolde*, that Petrarch forget Laura (as he finally tried to do, "inspired" by reading the Church Fathers), and that Dante expel Beatrice, that glorious, fully female, and even married sacrament of divine love and grace, from the *Paradiso*?

It seemed obvious to me that Greeley's fiction functioned as a literary Rorschach test of metaphoric multicolored inkblots designed to elicit stock responses from the Catholic elite's unconscious. This kind of irrational critical reaction would be no more than a harmless inconvenience if it only affected its source. Unfortunately, however, published reviews tend to encourage or discourage potential readers.

In an effort to get at the bottom of this puzzling phenomenon, I put on my social science hat (there are advantages to a broad academic background) and conducted a small-scale national survey of clerical reactions to Greeley's novels. One of the most intriguing patterns which emerged in that initial survey was finding that three-fourths of those who were most hostile toward Greeley and most critical of his fiction had read none of the novels. An irate monsignor wrote, "I do not read anything by Greely [sic]. I consider him a desgrace [sic] to the Church." Another extremely hostile respondent put it bluntly, "His novels have been reviewed and read by people whose opinions I respect, and he has been judged by them a waste of their time and therefore mine."

In contrast, over one-third of those who had read two or more of the novels had actually recommended them to their congregations, and almost two-thirds might recommend them. Thus it appeared not only that clerical opinions concerning Greeley and his work were extremely polarized, but that a great deal of hostility supposedly engendered by the novels themselves was in fact the result of entirely unconnected and possibly prior factors, which may themselves have been responsible for the decision to read the works, and attitudes toward them and their author. What other explanation is there for such antithetical reactions as Father Bill Smith's published estimate of Greeley as a priest with the "dirtiest mind ever ordained,"[1] and one of my survey respondent's insistence that "without Andrew Greeley, the American Church would be even more dishonest, boring and irrelevant than it is. He loves his ecclesial family so deeply that he is willing to serve her with courageous independence and fierce love"?

In this context it is interesting to note that a nonjudgmental, gracious, and "grace-full" God-image appears to be more and more prevalent among diocesan priests. Among respondents to my initial "Clergy on Greeley" survey, slightly more than half of those ordained before 1955 opted for a maternally tender God-image. This proportion rose to two-thirds of those ordained between 1955 and 1969, and to almost three-fourths of those ordained after 1970. The shift is most pronounced for the categories of Mother/Father and Spouse/Master. While still slightly less than one-half of the younger priests thought of God primarily in terms of Mother, this is proportionately more than twice the number of those ordained prior to 1955. In the category of Spouse/Master the break occurs later. Those ordained before 1955 and between 1955 and 1969 scored 63 and 65 percent respectively in favor of a Spouse-oriented God-image. This proportion rose to 89 percent among those ordained after 1969.

Four-fifths of the respondents ordained after 1960 (a little over half the total) with a "graceful" God-image did not consider Greeley's novels a threat to the faith of young people and would not discourage their congregations from reading them, while only about two-thirds of those with low scores on the Grace-scale were rejective of repression. Among the older priests no such correlation emerged.

Thus it appears not only that priests are envisioning God more and more in traditionally feminine terms but that this graceful God-image is increasingly being internalized leading to a more positive view of human nature and a greater tolerance in general. One might speculate, based on these findings, that Greeley's Church represents, indeed, the future, a vision to be realized by an as-yet-unborn generation of priests.

A number of supportive respondents specifically asked to remain anonymous. "I am afraid that several bishops would no longer invite me to speak to their clergy," wrote one, "if they knew I had *great respect* for Father Greeley!"[2]

These findings, combined with my survey of Catholic reviews, tend to support Greeley's contention in "Who Reads *Those* Books"[3] that he is the victim of a group mythology/neurosis "which dominates the reactions of the Catholic elite, a mythology which 'yuks' about the alleged sexual steam and cannot see the theological theme."

I began to sense an exciting topic worthy of careful consideration. What are Greeley's major theological themes and symbols, and how do they fit into archetypal mythic structures and the Catholic analogical universe? What is the connection between a feminine God-image and our attitude toward the world in general and the religious dimensions of sexuality in particular? What can Eros teach us about God, ourselves, our relationships to others, and death? What, ultimately, are the radical consequences of the event of the Incarnation and the sacramentality of the world? What kind of Church emerges from Greeley's stories?

This book is the result of those deliberations and reflections.

introduction

Religion . . . is the transition from God
the void to God the enemy, and from God
the enemy to God the companion.[1]

this book is about the God-Who-Is-Love, as mysteriously
alluring as Juliet and as passionately pursuing as Romeo—
only infinitely more so; a God who is at once the Holy Grail and
the Questing Knight, the Magic Maiden and her Prince, the
Shekhinah and Yahweh, Mother Earth and Father Sky. A God,
in short, like ours.

The central Judeo-Christian insight consists in recognizing
the personhood of God, in acknowledging that the ultimate,
ineffable, totally other creative ground of being is simultaneously "someone" very much like the best we can be, a genuine
"Thou" Who relates to us the way we relate to one another.
Among the ancient Hebrews, this personal God was experienced primarily as a creator, king, and judge, a passionately
pursuing but often terrifying Presence, demanding absolute
obedience to the divine will. Jesus not only put God's father-
hood into focus, but by using the familiar term *abba* (daddy)
invited all of us to approach God in a far more intimate manner
than had been the Old Testament pattern. He thus psychologi-
cally prepared the way for our understanding, accepting, and
internalizing the Incarnation, the final reconciliation of God and

humanity, spirit and nature. Almost all the officially-sanctioned Judeo-Christian God-images, however, are masculine in keeping with the androcentrism of the Western (and Jewish) tradition. This accounts, one suspects, through the dialectical dynamics of opposites generating one another, for the increasing importance of Mary in popular Catholic piety. Thus little if anything new can be said about divine masculinity. It is part of every Christian's analogical imagination: God, the Creator; God, the Judge; *Pater, Filius, Spiritus.*

The twentieth century, however, is marked by an emergent consciousness of the feminine contribution to individual and corporate human life and a theoretical if not always practically implemented insistence (at least in the West) on the civil and legal equality of men and women. Thus we are granted the unique opportunity to explore the "other side" of God, His womanliness (as real as Her masculinity), which has been largely disregarded in official Judeo-Christian speculation. Woman God (to be distinguished from the feminist Goddess) as I have decided to call Her, can be recovered for all Christians out of the Old Testament Wisdom tradition, a number of Psalms, and the Song of Solomon. She refers to Herself in New Testament passages as a nursing mother and brood hen, and emerges in the gentle, caring, feminine (though *not* effeminate) character of our Lord Himself. She figures prominently in the mystic tradition and lurks, for Catholic and Orthodox Christians, in the marvelously multivalent presence of Mary, whose youthful beauty and maternal tenderness have inspired countless songs and stories, poems, paintings and prayers. She is the fervently adored and deeply beloved *Virgo, Mater, Theotokos,* the Immaculate Conception and indefatigable miracle-worker whose body, so the Church insists as an article of faith, was taken up to heaven upon her death. She represents, nevertheless, only a minor motif in the composite portrait of the Judeo-Christian God, particularly the portrait "painted" in official magisterial pronouncements and theological disputations. She is an ancient and fundamental strand of popular mythic imagination largely buried beneath countless layers of androcentric propaganda, but so strong, so vital, so essential that three thousand years plus the combined forces of rabbinical and patristic scholarship have been unable to keep her down. Spirit, sprite, Lady Paraclete. She lives.

This book, then, is about the womanliness of God. Woman

God for short. It is also about the sacramentality of the sexual experience (another topic thrust upon us for serious consideration and open discussion by the lived reality of the post-Freudian age) one of the most powerful natural symbols for the way God relates to us and wants us to relate to Her (or Him) and each other. Passionately, honestly, totally. "Sexual morality," writes Gregory Baum, "must not be understood as a fixed code of rules but rather as the revelation of the role of sexuality in human life and the initiation into a new consciousness, out of which people are able to deal with their sexual gifts in a constructive and reconciling manner."[2] It is finally, about a new-old vision, a re-vision of the Christian message as an invitation to love, to love not with dispassionate, desiccated, "safe" *agape,* but filled with the blazing fire of divine *eros.*

When I mentioned the womanliness of God theme to a fundamentalist Protestant university administrator (cunningly refraining from any reference to the sacramentality of sex) the reaction was immediate and predictable:

"Why do you people insist on making God into something He obviously is not?"

Me: "How do you know that God is a He?"

"*He*" tells us so in the Scriptures, or are you one of those (shudder, gulp) who consider the *Word of God* a meaningless myth?"

Me: "Well, myth, of course. But certainly not meaningless. Quite the contrary: myths and symbols aren't lies, they reveal the most profound truths, the kinds of truths we can't capture in the net of literal and verifiable language."

End of dialogue, (if something can end which has never truly begun).

Beginning of an extended sermon on the inerrancy of the Scriptures.

This discussion is illuminating for at least two reasons. First, it demonstrates the extent to which neither the cognitive claims of contemporary physical and life sciences nor the results of positive historical exegesis or dialogical-hermeneutical interpretation have managed to shake the rigid fundamentalism of scriptural literalists, even of those who, like my acquaintance, hold doctorates and/or positions of authority. To them the Bible does not communicate the word of God, it *is* the Word of God.

Secondly, the response is typical for a mind-set shaped in

the image of what we generally (fairly or unfairly) associate with masculine characteristics: a combination of judgmental aggressiveness with rule-governed ideation drawing on fixed codes and organized information. My colleague's God is a dictatorial father, master, and judge, who permits no deviation from eternal, unchanging Truth and equally eternal, unchanging moral laws.

This approach is antithetical to what David Tracy and other contemporary theologians consider the central task of theology, "the dramatic confrontation, the mutual illuminations and corrections, the possible basic reconciliation between the principal values, cognitive claims, and existential faiths of both a reinterpreted post-modern consciousness and a reinterpreted Christianity."[3] It fails to comprehend the essential Christian emphasis on manifestation, proclamation, and prophetic action, grounded in belief in the eternally present event of Jesus the Christ, disclosing Himself in ever-changing identity for each new generation. It exists in reactionary, artificial isolation from the living context of ongoing history and secular culture and refuses to accept the most important implication of incarnational thinking: faith in the ultimate significance of our lives, faith in a God who loves us and became one of us to take away our sins (not our minds), faith in the sacramentality of the world, faith in the radical graciousness of Reality. It does not only constitute cognitive, moral, and psychological cowardice and inauthenticity, but by confusing part of the truth with the whole, it constitutes a particularly insidious and destructive form of idolatry, as Paul Tillich would be quick to remind us.

In the epilogue to his thoughtful exploration and spirited advocacy of religious pluralism, *The Analogical Imagination*, David Tracy writes:

Fundamentalists, traditionalists and dogmatists in every religion . . . need not trouble with a messy pluralism. They already know the truth—a truth, it seems, that sets them free from the world but never for it. In their comfortable isolation, they can continue to preach a truth that can ignore all the truths disclosed in the classics of other religions and secular cultures, save the one truth the despised "world" has taught them all too well—the truth of power in its myriad forms, from the sword of religious wars to the bureaucratization of the spirit in contemporary fundamentalist and dogmatic empires.[4]

This book is about God. Not so much about the God of philosophers and theologians as the God encountered by ordinary people doing ordinary things. Like wiping a kid's nose. Or being the kid whose nose is wiped. Like storming out of the house after a fight with your wife, and remembering, suddenly, how you spilled a coke all over her jeans the evening you met, and how mad she was and how absolutely gorgeous she looked with her eyes flashing blue lightning and her hair a lion's mane . . . Like smelling the steaming earth after a summer storm. Like feeling that funny fluttering within your belly and realizing, *really* realizing for the first time that, by God, "it's a baby, a human being, and it's growing inside of me!" Like going up to the teacher after class to tell her that you cheated to get that A. Like getting a phone call at 4:12 in the morning informing you of your mother's death and suddenly remembering how she used to sit on your dad's lap on that wooden chair with its cracked and yellowing white enamel in that tiny kitchen of long ago. Like making love . . .

Buried deeply near the root of institutional Christianity and threatening the soundness of its foundation there lurks a fatal flaw, the ever-recurring and never-resolved challenge of metaphysical and ethical dualism which not only severs spirit and nature, male and female, autocracy and egalitarianism, *agape* and *eros*, God and the world, but also insists on pronouncing one-half of each pair good and the other evil. Ironically, it was precisely this kind of split, this primordial wound, which the Incarnation was meant to heal. In no way can this dualism be traced to the message of Jesus or the event of the Christ. It was caused, instead, by the subtle ways in which both were twisted and turned by the early interpreters and apologists who insisted on molding them according to their own preconceptions and metaphysical commitments and refused to acknowledge the truly radical, transformational nature of the Christian story.

The Gospels themselves are already somewhat infected with the dualistic disease, and the Acts reflect an early power struggle between the autocratic misogynist Pauline and egalitarian Jerusalem communities. The Church Fathers further obscured the genuine and radically new Christian vision of the sacramentality of the world and the discipleship of equals by their redaction of Christianity into something dangerously close to Manichaeanism with its insistence on the corruption of matter and the evils of sexuality (concepts alien to the Judaic heritage and to the teachings of Jesus). It seems that as soon as Christianity turned into a body of official teachings, many of the doctrines were consciously or unconsciously adapted to the prevailing pessimistic philosophical and counter-cultural religious mind-set, a life- and world-negating ideology, reflecting the death throes of a culture which, paradoxically, had never learned to deal with mortality. On the other hand, among rival religions and philosophies Christianity was the least dualistic (which may well have contributed to its historical success). Throughout its evolution the Christian tradition as a whole, and the Catholic vision most specifically, has never entirely abandoned the conciliatory kerygma of God's passionate love for the world hallowed by the Incarnation, that central mystery, that ultimate paradox, that affront to reason, of the Christ as *both* one hundred percent human *and* one hundred percent divine. The Christian theological self-understanding reflects an ongoing process of synthesizing opposing visions of reality, and of allowing popular undercurrents to emerge and become incorporated into the complex fabric of the whole. Unfortunately, however, much of the central revelation of love being stronger than death has been obscured by reams and reams of "thou shalt nots."

This kind of redaction process is not, of course, unique to Christianity. It is part of every religion with a priestly caste and was very much in evidence in Judaism. The Torah embodies the interests and biases of its authors and/or compilers. Divine revelation is invariably articulated in culturally and historically conditioned language, and the sacred texts of any religion are never more than reflections of the Truth in the doubly distorting mirrors of their respective authors (doubly distorting in the sense that authors are affected both by their individual biases and by the cultural prejudices of their communities). We can compensate, however, for at least some of this distortion by reading the texts within the context of socio-economic and ideological currents of the times in which they were composed. Vital hints concerning genuinely essential insights might be derived from the extent to which those insights *conflict* with prevailing worldviews and cannot be reduced to environmental conditions.

The dominant mind-set of Western culture (in keeping with its Indo-European roots) has been strongly androcentric, and up until recently few have even considered challenging certain fundamental assumptions directly rooted in this androcentrism (an androcentrism which is in itself largely responsible for the prevailing dualistic mode of apprehending reality). These premises include both the tradition of depicting and/or imagining God as a male and in direct consequence of this masculine God-image, the assumption that men and men alone have been "historical subjects and revelatory agents in the church."[5] The latter of these topics has been considered extensively by contemporary feminist theologians.[6]

Elisabeth Schüssler Fiorenza writes:

> Women as church have a continuous history and tradition that can claim Jesus and the praxis of the earliest church as its biblical root model or prototype, one that is open to feminist transformation. . . . The history and theology of women's oppression perpetuated by patriarchal biblical texts and by a clerical patriarchy must not be allowed to cancel out the history and theology of the struggle, life, and leadership of Christian women who spoke and acted in the power of the Spirit.[7]

> Androcentric texts are part of the overall puzzle and design that must be fitted together in creative critical interpretation. It is crucial, therefore, that we *challenge the blueprint of androcentric design, assuming instead a feminist pattern for the historical mosaic, one that allows us to place women as well as men into the center of early Christian history.*[8]

While the two topics are closely interrelated, it is the issue of the God-image which I wish to address in this book, not so much to "place women as well as men into the center of early Christian history" (which has been admirably done by others) but to contribute to the recovery for the Judeo-Christian tradition of the essential vision of divine androgyny, the fullness of God. I hope to accomplish this by exploring divine femininity, which for at least two and one-half millennia has existed primarily underground, in countercultural, heterodox, and popular (secular) traditions, and thus, paradoxically, has found itself rather frequently allied with precisely the kinds of dualistic heresies and thought systems (such as Kabbalism, Gnosticism, Catharism) which were most vocal in affirming the absolute corruption of the flesh, and whose influence tended to increase misogynism among those whom they affected.

The central insight contained in the mythic formulations of the creation reveals God, i.e. the divine original, shaping humanity in "It's" image, female as well as male, thus demonstrating that the creative source itself is not an "It" at all (though Tillich's sterile and abstract "Ground of Being" is an important philosophical concept which, in its essential emptiness, clears the way for the re-vision of God-the-Person) but rather the dynamic interplay of primal femininity and masculinity. The Incarnation implies a vision of the Christ (to be distinguished from the historical Jesus) as male/female. In both the Old Testament and the New Testament, furthermore, we encounter a God not only deeply, one might almost say foolishly or madly, in love with humanity but intensely and emotionally involved with each one of us individually. Evidence for this passionately loving androgynous personal God does not only or even primarily come from the orthodox Scriptures (subject to interpretative revision by scribes with occasionally rather androcentric axes to grind). It also emerges both in heterodox traditions and in manifestations of the popular religious imagination, most particularly in the visual arts and secular literature. Both divine androgyny and the womanliness of God can be traced from ancient fertility cults and non-Western religious traditions to the Jewish Kabbalah and Catholic Mariolatry. They also lurk beneath the epics and romances of old, as well as much of today's fiction, insofar as those supposedly secular traditions reveal the human side of the eternal dialogue between God and Her/His creatures.[9] As David Tracy tells us, we can no longer afford to hide within the ivory tower "purity of siege mentality where we alone possess the truth and we build our righteous worlds unsullied by the 'invincible ignorance' of the alien others."[10]

The justification for my approach is contained in non-dualistic Incarnational thought, and it flows from belief in the sacramentality of the world. If, as Saint Thomas insists, God truly is the source and goal of all human activity, and if, as Hegel, Whitehead, and Teilhard de Chardin (among others) agree, the cosmic process is a form of divine self-actualization and revelation, then S/He is bound to emerge not only in those records which we recognize as sacred but also in countless other places as well. It seems appropriate to begin not with preconceived ideas as to which specific texts carry religious significance, but rather to inquire what if any unique characteristics are shared by sacred texts in general. Once one or more of those qualities have been identified, we can ask whether those same qualities can also be discovered in pagan, heterodox, and secular sources. Paul Ricoeur and David Tracy present us with just such an analysis. Religious use of language, according to them, consists in what they call "limit-language" appropriate to the "limit-experience" of religion.

> Religious language, whenever it is authentically related to a religious insight of extraordinary force as in the New Testament, employs and explodes all our ordinary language forms in order to jar us into a recognition of what, on our own, can seem only a desirable but impossible possible mode-of-being-in-the-word. As proverbial, that religious language disorients us and forces us to see another, a seemingly impossible way of living with authenticity. As parabolic, that language redescribes our experience in such a manner that the sense of its meaning (its now limit-metaphor) discloses a limit-referent which projects and promises that one can in fact live a life of wholeness, of total commitment, or radical honesty and agapeic love in the presence of the gracious God of Jesus the Christ.[11]

Religious experience and religious language are prior to the text. Certain texts, by their highly concentrated and pervasive use of limit-language are universally classified as sacred. But our

God, the One Who dwells in the world, the One-Who-Ind-wells-The-World, the One-Who-Acts-In-The-World manifests Her/Himself in an infinite number of ways, speaks to us in countless voices, and seeks us out in the most unlikely places. A sudden spark of insight, a flash of lightning or love, She leaps out at us from the formulas of theoretical physics and assaults us in the privacy of our morning shower. She glows in the fragility of a spider's web, sings out in the pure strains of a Bach cantata, breaks through the innocence of an infant's smile. She lies next to us in the marriage bed and fills us with ecstasy in ever new and surprising ways. She is everywhere and anywhere at once, dancing across the cosmos and through our hearts. There is no reason to assume that in a world thus permeated by grace, Scriptures and orthodox doctrines represent the exclusive de-positories of religious vision (though the guardians of doctrinal purity, the institutional establishment, will tend to dispute this claim, particularly if the vision itself stretches existing religious categories to their limit). If, as David Tracy has so masterfully demonstrated, the analogical imagination cuts through the Gor-dian knot of the variety of Christian, non-Christian, and secular traditions, then we must intensify our journey into and through the mysterious landscape of potentially pregnant archetypal symbols (regardless of origin) in order to uncover ever new levels of religious significance. Then we are free to explore limit-language and limit-experience whenever and wherever they may occur *qua* religious significance. Then we may even discover that the deep chasm which supposedly exists between the sacred and the profane is an illusion and that the "Secular City" is now and always has been—"the City of God."

It is precisely this kind of exploration which I propose to undertake in this book. It grows out of the conviction that our longstanding, culturally ingrained custom (rooted in meta-physical dualism) of portraying the divine *qua* person almost exclusively in masculine terms does a grave injustice not only to human females but also to God in whose image we appear in *two* complementary editions neither of which is complete without the other, and that this misogynism has seriously impaired our ability to come closer to an adequate understanding not only of divine Reality but also of ourselves and most particularly our sexual natures. God-As-Woman, Woman God, the femininity of God must be confronted before we can truly yield to the *X* mystery of the Incarnation. For two thousand years we have automatically repeated certain formulas which, properly understood, contain exactly this insight but which, partly due to their androcentric language, have tended to convince us of the exact opposite. Since Jesus the historical person was a man (as biological primates, after all, except for rare abnormalities, each of us has to be either male or female), maleness was presumed to be the standard of perfection; and the central message of the Incarnation, that the Word had become Flesh (not male flesh or female flesh but simply *human* flesh), was interpreted in those terms.

My methodological starting point is the assumption that valuable and valid insights concerning the nature of divine reality can appropriately be derived from religious and secular, Christian and non-Christian, orthodox and heterodox sources (including works of scholarship, literature, and the representational arts), as long as the God-image revealed by this method is consistent with non-dualistic Incarnational theology and can be reconciled to the central Judeo-Christian revelation of a passionately loving, personal deity.

If the fullness of God is to be recovered for the twentieth century, that recovery must involve an engaged conversation with current scholarship, literature, the arts, and popular sentiment. It is for this reason that I have chosen to develop my paradigm in and through a process of reflection and meditation upon the literary works of poet/priest Andrew Greeley, who has sounded the themes of the womanliness of God and the sacramentality of sexuality more vigorously than any other contemporary writer, and who stands, as one of his fellow priests indicated to me, squarely in the tradition of the "bards of old." Greeley's thought is of particular relevance to the present situation precisely because he is not only an exceptionally well-educated priest with impeccable academic credentials, but also because he is Irish-American. His New World perspective puts him into the democratic and pluralistic circle of those secular forces with which the Church has to come to terms if she is going to impact the future in a meaningful way. His Celtic roots allow him to transcend the androcentric and even gynephobic mind-set which has dominated Western civilization since the Romans imposed their patterns upon subject peoples. His novels are carefully crafted "Parables of Grace" and "Romances of Redemption" whose conscious use of limit-language teases, provokes, shocks, and even compels readers into taking second, third, and fourth looks at themselves, their lives, and their relationships to God—a God whom Greeley insists loves us as tenderly as our mother and as passionately as our mistress, wife, husband, or lover. Greeley's vision transcends the conventional existential despair of the intellectual elite and the selective cultural critique of liberation theology. He delights in the currently rather unfashionable kinds of "happy endings" (in the sense of allowing for the possibility of renewal and redemption) which are firmly rooted in the Judeo-Christian tradition of love overcoming death. Variations on this major theme, first sounded in the enchanted fantasy world of *The Magic Cup,* lie at the heart of each of his subsequent novels. In addition, despite their occasionally shocking imagery and language (deliberately designed to shock the way Jesus shocked), Greeley's stories are grounded in the Catholic imaginative universe, spinning out the motifs of liturgical cycles, and the grand themes of the Mass, while incorporating carefully chosen poems, hymns, and a wealth of symbolic allusions.

Methodologically, this study presents an experiment. I have no intention of limiting myself to analytical arguments. I propose, instead, to use the analogical imagination in order to communicate a *sense* of Eros and Woman God by appealing to images and archetypes which are already dormant in the reader's preconscious. I will appeal to what Michael Polanyi has called the realm of "tacit knowledge" which speaks (if at all) in figurative language telling stories and painting pictures which, in their imaginative immediacy, are ontologically prior to the theoretical propositions of philosophy, theology, psychology, and even the natural sciences. I see myself in the role of a guide who takes her readers through the landscape of Greeley's fiction in order to discover beneath and beyond the surface stories deeper levels of significance which will, I hope, serve to illuminate my twin topics, Eros and the Womanliness of God, and inspire others to set out on their own explorations in their own private analogical universes. Accordingly, each chapter will begin with a few carefully selected citations from Greeley's work (both published and unpublished), appropriate to the topic of the particular section. Those passages, occasionally supplemented by others inserted later on, will present the major texts to be considered and interpreted. My interpretations will be deliberately subjective, based on my academic and personal background, which spans two continents and happens to be a rather unusual patchwork quilt of Catholic theology, Hegelian philosophy, Jungian psychology, Oriental religions, comparative mythology, German and American literature, human relations, and eighteen years of teaching courses in world civilization and the history of ideas (in addition to marriage and motherhood).

The first part of this study introduces the basic themes of an androgynous God-image and archetypal divine femininity, Woman God, as discovered through the analogical imagination. The second part explores various religious implications of sexuality, compares the analogical universes of Christianity and the Romance, and identifies the "baptized" Eros symbol as the driving force of rebirth and renewal which fuels the human pilgrimage toward psychic wholeness and the knowledge of God. The third part focuses specifically on the goal of the journey, Jesus/ Mary, the Holy Grail, the "Magic Princess," passionately seeking as well as passionately sought, represented on earth by the maternally loving and supportive presence of the Church.

pART ONE

the RELIGIOUS
imagination

one

STORIES OF GOD

She remembered lying cold and hurt on the asphalt, unable to move and scream for help. But the Courts were still a kind of sacred place. . . .

The rain had stopped, and the clouds were racing rapidly across the sky, the way humans raced through life. The naked trees seemed to be twisting toward heaven, begging God for the life and covering and beauty that spring would give them. And maybe even for the kids on whom the trees had looked down for so many years.

In the story Jesus told, the man who found a treasure buried in a field had to give up everything to buy the field and gain the treasure. He was forced to choose between the old and the new. . . .

You must lose your life to find it. That's what this next week was about.

That includes you too, Mary Noele.

All right.

Noele Marie Brigid Farrell!

I said all right. All right?

All right.

Stop laughing at me. You're as bad as Moms.

All right.

Well! *You* can laugh at me if you want.

All RIGHT!

Then Noele saw a broad beam of sunlight move lazily down Jefferson Avenue, like a sophomore girl slouching home from the Ninety-fifth Street bus on a warm, Indian summer afternoon, daydreaming about a senior boy to whom she had never spoken a word in her life. Dark clouds moved ahead of the sun as though running from it, and Jefferson Avenue was bright all the way to Ninety-fifth Street.

Noele knew the demons from hell could still touch her, perhaps even hurt her. But they would never prevail against her. She heard in her memory Mary O'Hara's voice and imagined the little Irish kids dancing on the Courts with the Lord of the Dance.

"We can go home now," she told Patrol Officer Day.[1]

Revelatory experience discloses to us that in the final analysis our relationship to Mystery is gracious. Despite everything, we know and feel that we are "held, held fast by love." We cry God. But our lives are no safer for it. Nor are we now "in the know." Although we interpret every aspect of life from the conviction of ultimate love, no explanation of all the non-love is forthcoming. All we have is the faithful presence of the powerful God. His energy suffuses us, enabling us to undergo and overcome all that life brings. Bonded to God beyond all breaking we become people of courage, humility, humor. But to have this God as companion on the journey means we must also take him as path. Our passion is to move with God and he wants us to walk the road which he is hacking out of the wilderness. Our faith is not the still point of the turning world but a force which makes the world turn faster. Our journey is not the way of adjustment in order to survive but the way of struggle in order to transform.[2]

The word, then, is personal. *Cor ad cor loquitur*: love speaks to love and its speech is powerful. The religious leader, the prophet, the Christ, the apostle, the priest, the preacher announces in signs and symbols what is congruent with the gift of love that God works within us.[3]

It is impossible to separate Andrew Greeley, the novelist from Dr. Greeley, the sociologist, or Father Greeley, the parish priest. The material in his fiction flows directly from his sociological findings which confirm the continued power which God exerts upon the religious imagination of contemporary human beings and chronicle the American Catholic experience from the "Garrison Church" beyond Vatican Two. In sharp contrast to the prevailing fashionable assumption of the secularization of the contemporary world, Greeley insists that "the basic human religious needs and the basic religious functions have not changed very notably since the late Ice Age."[4] He has persistently and eloquently advocated this position in such nonfiction works as *Unsecular Man*, *The Religious Imagination*, and *Religion: A Secular Theory*. The novels themselves represent a conscious attempt to tease the Christian comedy of grace out of the new-old symbols presented to us in contemporary life. As a sociologist he views religion as a symbol system which mediates our encounter with the ambiguities of life, while disclosing at least some reason for hope, some justification for assuming that human life has significance, and, in the Catholic perspective, the presence of a living, gracious, personal God who passionately cares about each and every one of us. Like the theologian John Shea, Greeley realizes that "people are interested in their own personal stories. We must begin with contemporary stories and bring forward the story of Jesus, the premier sacred story of Christianity, to interpret the depth of what is happening."[5] It is for this reason, one presumes, that Greeley not only introduces "spiritual guide" characters into his tales to help make the connection, but also (to the inevitable chagrin of art-for-art's-sake purists) insists on providing introductory remarks and/or postscripts. Greeley consciously uses the novel (or, as I am going to argue, the Romance[6]) in order to convey the theological message, also proclaimed by Shea, of the "Experience named Spirit" the "in-rush of divine love mediated by human love" into our hearts which are generally "living in either rejection or envy,"[7] but which nevertheless are capable of hope and renewal. In *Religion: A Secular Theory* Greeley writes:

> The propensity to hope, the need for validation of hope, the capacity to experience goodness in external realities, and the perception of that goodness as ambiguous are all functions of that dimension of the organism which is called the prerational or preconscious; these capacities and experiences are primarily a function of that aspect of the organism (brain?) in which free-floating images, pictures, stories exist independently of direct control by the conscious self.[8]

Greeley constructs his religious paradigm by combining the pragmatic notions of religion as experience of the sacred developed by Rudolph Otto and William James with the sociological theory of religion as a set of fundamental models or templates which both determine our understanding of ultimate reality and give shape to that Reality. Religion thus represents a constitutive element in the worlds we create. The image precedes theological reflection and analytical reduction. Fundamentally, religion is not something to be learned and rationally assimilated. It is rather a different way of seeing, the gaining of a new perspective, a form of enlightenment which allows us to commit ourselves to a special kind of world-transforming action, rooted in a special kind of world-understanding vision. It is exactly this kind of limit-experience which confronts Noele at the tennis courts, allowing her to see her own torment, the thrust of her life, within the context of the grand pattern of alienation and redemption, death and rebirth, appropriately placed within the liturgical season of Holy Week. While Greeley does not, to my knowledge, use that analogy, one might argue that the universal human preconscious proclivity to hope presents something like an empirical proof for the ultimate graciousness of the Really Real. The human organism is born with an innate desire for oxygen, water, and nourishment—a desire which, while easily frustrated, is nevertheless directed toward fundamental, preexistent elements present in the ecological environment to which the physiological unit is inextricably linked. Analogously, human consciousness yearns for order, meaning, goodness, and love, revealed most immediately and directly in our relationships with other human beings, and generally made conscious as contrasted with their absence. War affirms the reality of peace; violence the reality of gentleness; egotism the reality of altruism; competition the reality of cooperation; death the reality of life; meaninglessness the reality of meaning. "The principal sacraments in our lives are other human beings or, more precisely, our relationships with other human beings."[9] We encounter grace and hope in others as they encounter it in us, and from that proximate experience we are inevitably drawn toward the assumption of divine graciousness. It makes less sense to assume that this intuition of a meaningful presence at the cosmic core of things is no more than self-deception, than to assume that "at some deep level in our personalities we intuit the truth about reality, and then, under the influence of this intuition, seek to ask the questions that will enable us to 'surface' our insight as an articulate answer to the question."[10] It is at this point that our religious imagination taps the creative depths of our preconscious and sets out to give symbolic shape in the form of stories and myths to the reality which we have experienced. "Religion as story leaps from imagination to imagination, and only then, if at all, from intellect to intellect."[11]

I have chosen to illustrate some of the characteristics of religious storytelling by referring to *Lord of the Dance*, not because the novel presents the Catholic analogical imagination more clearly than Greeley's other fiction, but because it is at this time Greeley's only published novel in a contemporary non-clerical setting with a strong Woman God protagonist (or, one might argue, Woman God in Her three Celtic incarnations, as virgin, spouse, and crone); because it allows the introduction of almost all the motifs which appear in various combinations in the remaining novels; and because it represents a work of transition from Greeley's initial preoccupation with the Church as experienced from within the organization to a growing emphasis on the Church as revealed through and in the community (a concern, however, already anticipated in *Death in April,* which combines a non-clerical setting with a strong Woman God figure and the fire-water symbolism so pervasively present in *Lord of the Dance*).

Noele, teenage heroine (and Virgin archetype) of *Lord of the Dance* visits her "sacred grove" (reminiscent of her Celtic heritage) of the tennis courts, a space at once terrifying, holy, comforting, *and* due to her recent rape, demonic. It is there that she must renew her personal covenant relationship; it is there, her private Mount Sinai, that she "hears" the voice of God and encounters the Mystery, not, like Moses, in a burning bush, but in the form of a cheerful sunbeam lighting up a familiar street. Like the people of Israel, she has experienced slavery and violent defilement, and, like Moses (or Christ), she must be true to her secret parentage and bring her family out of spiritual bondage. Hers is a new-old story, a story of sin, despair, and redemption through faith in the ultimate graciousness of Reality. The theme of laughter is sounded. Noele's God, like Nora's God[12] in *Thy Brother's Wife*, is a God-Who-Laughs, a God who loves her like a mother. No explanation is given for evil and pain. None is needed. The images are enough. We see ourselves in a world in which beauty and ugliness, sin and grace are next-door neighbors, each revealing the other, a world which would be absurd if it were not for our wisely foolish pervasive faith in love and the ultimate graciousness of Reality, which does not cause or condone evil but allows it to exist as a void or absence of goodness in order to grant us the gift of freedom.

Divine revelation is disclosure of the hidden, gratuitous, positive forces which challenge us to confront evil and enable us to move creatively into the future. God is present within our lives as a call, a beacon, a horizon. Grace skips or slouches down Jefferson Avenue in the shape of a giggling sunbeam. Instead of conceptualizing God as a remote, distant agent over and above history who intervenes at His convenience, or a hidden and numinous Ground of Being residing serenely in abstract isolation, Noele encounters divine reality as the innermost dimension of her life, the eternally creative and benevolent Matrix-Mother out of Whom she, her father, mother, the entire Farrell clan, and ultimately every human being, every bird and bug and blade of grass came into being. Noele interprets her experiences in terms of the Catholic religious paradigm reinforced by the presence of a warm and loving family context (paradoxically, strengthened rather than weakened by tension and conflict) and a supportive, joyous church community symbolized by Father

Dick McNamara, Ace, Ph.D. in psychology, ex-marine chaplain, and college teacher. Noele is able to transcend her defilement, the radical confrontation with Evil, due to the particular manner in which the religious dimensions of her life have been formed by her relationships with her friends and family. The religious imagination, writes Greeley,

> which contains in free-floating imagery and story the religious subplot of our life, will, on the one hand, have considerable effect on how we behave toward other human beings and will, on the other hand, have been shaped to a considerable extent by our experiences with other human beings. The stories of grace both shape our sacramental encounters with others and have been shaped by prior sacramental encounters with others.[13]

Noele is at once a deftly drawn, believable American teenager and an allegorical figure out of an ancient myth or a morality play, described as

> a Celtic goddess in the nineteenth-century illustrations of Irish folklore books, strange, unreal, almost unearthly. Her long bright hair, contrasting sharply with her pale buttermilk skin, swept across the room after her like moving fire. Her green eyes absorbed you as if you were a glass of iced tea on a hot summer evening; they were neither soft green nor cat green, but shamrock green, kelly green. She seemed a pre-Christian deity, a visitor from the many-colored land of Irish antiquity.[14]

Like the Church, which she represents, she was conceived at Easter and born at Christmas; like the Church, she is the future while remaining solidly rooted in the past and present; and like the Church, it is her mission to challenge each deeply beloved member of her family to stop playing games, to stop concealing and twisting the truth, to stop being afraid of taking the "leap of faith," of going through their private deaths and resurrections for fear of facing themselves in their psychic nakedness. As in two previous novels, *Thy Brother's Wife* (Holy Thursday), and *Ascent into Hell* (Good Friday), *Lord of the Dance*

(Easter Sunday) moves within the analogical universe of Holy Week, adding to the themes of commitment and crucifixion, the theme of resurrection, the consummation of Christ's marriage with the *Ecclesia*, symbolically recalled in the Easter Vigil liturgy of blessing the baptismal font by plunging the lighted candle into the waters, in a "baptized" version of the ancient pagan fertility rite of joining fire and water to ensure fruitful fields, livestock, and wives. Both themes, that of the womanliness of God (in the figures of Noele and, to some extent, Irene) and the sacramentality of sexuality (in the relationship of Brigid and Burke, and Irene and Daniel) are brought into clear focus.

In terms of literary character type, there is something of Oedipus and Antigone in Noele, but unlike Oedipus her quest for the truth does not result in the kind of destruction inevitable in the fatalistic vision of the ancient Greeks. Unlike the doomed protagonists of Attic tragedy, she is not a plucky human fly caught in the web of capricious, petty, and envious gods. She is, instead, a child of a loving and gracious God who respects independence and wants her (and us) to become the best she (or we) can be. The truth/Truth literally sets her and her family free. Noele, like Persephone, is defiled by the powers of evil, alien and extraneous to herself. Rigid rule-oriented thinking might consider her forever stripped of innocence since her virginity was technically violated. Greeley recognizes the absurdity of equating innocence or "virginity of the spirit" with an intact hymen, and he presents in Noele an image of genuine purity which cannot be ripped from us even by the most violent actions of others. Noele is at once the ancient virgin-goddess (whose "virginity" consisted in her independence from male control, *not* an intact maidenhead) and the "new woman," no longer at the absolute mercy of men who have it in their power to preserve or "undo" her (to use the term made immortal by Samuel Richardson in his *Pamela*). She is mistress of herself, and an appropriate symbol both for the Church and for Woman God.

Her spectacular grandmother, Brigid, exemplifies the pervasiveness of sin and the prevalence of lack of faith. She is a twentieth-century version of the Counter-Reformation morality play *Frau Welt* (Mrs. World), damned, she believes, because of her countless transgressions. Yet her name is Brigid, reminiscent of the great Irish saint and pre-Christian triple goddess, and, despite her failings (of which her perversely proud insistence on her own utter depravity and her concurrent unwillingness to consider herself worthy of forgiveness are by far the most heinous) she shows herself capable of courageous and genuine love.

> Brigid knew she was damned. From the day of her arrival in America in 1934, her life had been nothing but sinful—lust, deceit, adultery, even murder. She was beyond forgiveness. Death would mean an eternity of blackness, not the hellfire of the catechism class of the west of Ireland, nor the hell of frustrated self-fulfillment—about which her son the monsignor was probably talking with the pious young actress on Channel 3 at this very moment—but the hell of black nothingness reserved for those who are so profoundly evil, they can be put nowhere else by divine justice but in a dark and bottomless abyss.[15]

Brigid represents the counterpart to Noele (who recognizes their special kinship). In symbolic language she is the "old whore," a Greek *hetaira*, haunted, however, by a sensitive Christian conscience. The Noele/Brigid combination reveals the Virgin/Harlot manifestations of the Church. In the archetypal code, Virgin and *hetaira* are two sides of the same coin, both free spirits, independent from the bonds of male domination, revealing the sacramental and demonic possibilities of unattached femininity. If Brigid is married, she has accepted that condition out of choice, it is not something forced on her by convention. As whore she exists primarily in the mode of negation, of deception, manipulation, betrayal, and sexuality in the service of greed and selfishness. Ultimately, she, too, learns that she is the child of a loving God who is revealed for her in her erstwhile lover and present husband, Burke Kennedy. Brigid and Burke are "two pirates, saved from ugliness only by their attraction for each other,"[16] as Noele observes astutely. Both she and Burke are redeemed precisely by allowing, almost despite themselves, lust to fuse with genuine love.

The Covenant tells us that God loves us. In Jesus we come to understand that divine love consists in loving our fellow humans. The biblical revelation allows us a vision of the dynamics of history other than the blind necessity of fate (whether that fate be visualized as Greek pantheon or a Darwinian struggle for survival). In faith we can find the strength to go on despite our weaknesses and recalcitrant hearts, knowing that we are not alone, that our struggle to make order out of chaos is a reflection of the gracious mystery called God who loves us as passionately as the most ardent lover and as steadfastly as our mother.

Greeley presents, in the guise of novel and Romance, the Christian symbolic universe, recovering for the present age the parabolic language of the past. In *The Great Code: The Bible and Literature*, Northrop Frye distinguishes between three kinds of language which he calls the hieroglyphic, the hieratic, and the demotic, respectively.

In hieroglyphic usage, words are signs assumed to be imbued with at least semimagical power. Subject and object, emotion and intellect are not separated and verbal abstractions are rare. It is language which grows out of an experience of the cosmos as intimately an inextricably connected with and possibly affected by the one who tells the story. With Plato we find a clear example of the second, hieratic or metonymic use of language which focuses on boundaries, limits, and differentiation. It separates the irrational from the rational and assumes that words are the outward expressions of a distinct and different inner reality. Third phase language intensifies this separation of subject and object, but moves the center of reality into the material world and is used for objective description of the natural order. With Einstein and the expanding field of contemporary theoretical physics, however, we have either come full circle or we have returned near our starting point on the rising and expanding spiral of intellectual history. Frye observes that at the present "we seem to be confronted again with an energy common to subject and object which can be expressed verbally only through some form of metaphor."[17] He suggests that ours may be the dawning of a new age, a transcendence of the current third-level demotic, descriptive language, and a return to a form of metaphorical language characteristic of primitive communities (analogous to Ricoeur's Second Naiveté), adding that "God may have lost his function as the subject and object of a predicate, but may be not so much dead as entombed in a dead language."[18]

This suggests an intriguing agenda for contemporary poets and theologians: the destruction of God's linguistic cenotaph by allowing those symbols to speak to us again and thus recapture for the present age the power of transforming grace. There is a crosscultural tradition which considers the secret world of God a world of language, symbolic of a dynamically unfolding divine reality. In this perspective it is through the human use of language, most particularly the kind of language involved in poetic utterances, storytelling, and myth-making, that divine self-revelation is encoded in ever new forms for generation after generation. Myth and symbols, precisely because they have their origins in a primary prerational level of nonreflective, naive thought, have the power to bring us nearer the simple truths which have been buried under countless strata of metaphysical and theological speculation. They provide us with the immanent patterns, the archetypes and preconscious paradigms which shape our religions, philosophies, stories, ways of life, and ultimately, our very civilizations.

Myths are the stories we tell in order to understand, explain, and give meaning to the primordial struggles we intuit within ourselves. They allow us to organize that preconscious chaos of amorphous desires, needs, and wants which constitutes our instinctual heritage, and which invariably comes into conflict with the demands of communal life. Thus myths and rituals serve to integrate the individual into the larger patterns of society, uniting past, present, and future into a coherent whole. Without myth, without ritual, without a symbolic life expressed through language, each one of us would be forced to create reality anew. We would be forced to pass from one stage of life to another without help, and be forced to face death without the assurance of some kind of continuity. It is at this juncture that religion, literature, and psychology intersect. Thus

Carl Gustav Jung, the great "archaeologist" of the human un-conscious, insists that myths constitute the vital links connect-ing us with the collective self.

> A sense of a wider meaning to one's existence is what raises a man beyond mere getting and spending. If he lacks this sense, he is lost and miserable. Had St. Paul been convinced that he was nothing more than a wandering weaver of carpets, he certainly would not have been the man he was. . . . The myth that took possession of him made him something greater than a mere craftsman.[19]

As long ago as 1960, Andrew Greeley, then curate at Christ the King Church and a graduate student at the University of Chicago, wrote in *Strangers in the House: Catholic Youth in America* (published in 1961), "Our young people have retreated into a world of fantasy and non-involvement because they, like the rest of Western civilization, have lost faith in the world and in themselves."[20] He attributed this metaphysical malaise largely to the failure of Christians and most particularly the clergy to provide effective solutions to a prevalent sense of despair and alienation. Yet, he argued, there was cause for optimism. "The human spirit is not defeated. The longing for meaning and significance is still very much with us."[21] The contemporary loss of self rooted in what he called the collapse of community was not an irreversible condition. "If man is not related to God," he argued, "then he cannot be related to nature and his fellow man; but on the other hand, by using natural signs, physical symbols to relate to nature and his fellow man, he can relate to God. All symbols then are some kind of liturgy."[22] After de-ploring the lack of meaningful symbols in modern society, he put the central problem in a different form:

> To harmonize the city and nature, the technical and the numinous, the profane and the religious is never easy; in the world of Einstein and Planck it is terrifyingly diffi-cult. . . . A new cosmos must be built, a cosmos in which nature and technology are seen as restored in Christ. Tech-nology will not be abandoned, the big city will not be deserted, but *both must be sanctified.* How this is to be done, where we must begin, I do not know. To suggest answers

to these problems is the work of the poet, the metaphysician, and the theologian.[23]

Little could this young man suspect, one assumes, that one day he himself would emerge as such a poet/priest, giving literary form to Karl Rahner's insistence on God's universal salvific will which indelibly stamps the human race with a divine orientation.

This kind of "sanctification" of the post-modern world can be greatly facilitated by placing it within the context of a twentieth-century equivalent of something Frye calls *kerygmatic* or "proclamatory" language (found most consistently in the Bible), a mixture of the metaphorical and the existential, which is precisely the kind of language used by Greeley in his stories.

Symbols give birth to new meanings when they are confronted by the social and individual conditions of a new age. In the frantic effort to recast the Christian message according to the alien medium of demystified pseudo-scientific language, the recent tendency has been to discard traditional symbols and rituals. This superficial and amateurish quest for "relevance" has, however, been singularly counterproductive, since it underestimated the culture-shaping power of symbols which go through countless incarnations, speaking in new modes, differently interpreted to human beings as distant in time and space as the first-century scribe at Corinth and the twentieth-century executive assistant at her IBM PCXT. We cannot afford, Greeley states in his nonfiction books and articles and implies in his stories, to tear down the bridges connecting us with the past. Temporarily silent symbols will come to speak again in a new mode; they will shed unexpected light on the ambiguities of the present; they will disclose new meaning which is important for contemporary life, and they will mediate divine redemption in the Church. The creativity of the Church's symbolic language, of the creeds and the Scriptures, assures an almost limitless fecundity of the Gospel as well as its continuity in history. Sensitive to the new experience in the Church, it is the task of the Christian not to repudiate the symbols of the past but to reinterpret them, to discern their meaning in and for a new age, to make them the key for understanding the present. This is precisely what Greeley does in his stories, as this study will demonstrate.

two

the
androgyny of god

Rarely did the Presence say anything. Rather it absorbed, bathed and soothed her. Tonight however it laughed. Not a sardonic laugh; rather it laughed the way she often laughed at Noreen when that teenage tomboy did something particularly wonderful. Everyone, sighed Nora, wants to be a mother. Even You.[1]

He took me, a country lad, from my home, and with the affection of a loving mother he has given me all I needed. I had nothing to eat and he provided food for me, I had nothing to wear and he clothed me, I had no books to study and he provided those also. At times I forgot him and he always gently recalled me. If my affection for him cooled, he warmed me in his breast, at the flame with which his Heart is always burning . . . and he still cares for me, day and night, more than a mother cares for her child.[2]

God then is above masculinity and femininity, above our human divisions combining all the perfections of both sides of our nature within His infinite simplicity. But should He appear to man always under the aspect of masculinity, the out-thrusting male, the Father who continuously "sends forth" His creative words, not only should we miss something in our apprehension of Him, we should also tend to remain "sent forth," directed from above, unhomely with God. That is why Mother Julian of Norwich, the 14th century mystic, was so fond of speaking of being "homely" with God and often referring to God as "our Mother." The mother encloses the child within her womb, and later draws him close to her as she feeds him from her breast; and always after that she provides the attractive power that draws children to the home around the hearth.[3]

. . . Laughter, not crying, is the deepest purpose that God wills for man.[4]

In a few short lines, in a popular novel, Andrew Greeley forces us to face at least three thousand years of Judeo-Christian myopia. His is not a subtle theological argument. Instead, he presents us with a deceptively simple image—the image of a mother gently laughing at her child. Hers is the laughter of parental pride and joy, the kind of laughter which shares, accepts and approves, the kind of laughter which delights in our successes and refuses to mock our pain when we fail, the laughter of maternal love which knows we are wonderful for no reason other than the fact that we are Her children.

If we allow the image to enter our minds and hearts, we might find ourselves strangely moved and changed. Have we ever, like Augustine, Anselm, Bernard, Julian of Norwich, Catherine of Siena, Teresa of Avila, John of the Cross, Angelo Roncalli (Pope John XXIII) dared think of God as our Mother, providing us with the milk of real and spiritual nourishment? Dared think of God not only in masculine but also in feminine terms? And not only in feminine terms but in powerful and positive feminine terms? A curtain tears, the windows of our mind open up to a subtly and yet radically altered landscape. The familiar is transformed, old patterns shatter and new configurations emerge. Lifelong habits of thought and language seem suddenly strangely hollow, mere pious formulas repeated for no significant reasons. *Pater noster qui est in coelis* . . . Our Father Who art in heaven . . . Our Mother Who art on earth . . . Mother . . . Father . . .

> *Mother.* And She is *laughing!*
> Mother/Father.
> Father/Mother.
> Both.

In the Catholic tradition we are surrounded by ready-made images of God the Creator, Father, Lord, and Judge. Sitting upon His golden throne amidst the trappings of supreme authority, He looks down at us from thousands of cathedral walls and ceilings, His right hand raised in a gesture of reproach, not stretched out to grasp our hands in friendship and support. This image of God is only partially supported by Old Testament evidence (the result of interpreting the Sinai experience, whether passionate encounter and/or empty aleph, in terms of theocratic, authoritarian thinking) and is antithetical to the vision of the Father expressed by Jesus who transformed once and for all the caricature of Yahweh as a petty, vindictive tribal deity into the New Covenant God of passionate love as described by Greeley in "Godgame.":

If you're exuberant, you're exuberant, and by all signs and accounts Whoever is behind it all is nothing if not exuberant. Reread the parables of Jesus, stripped of their later allegorical interpretations; a father who forgives a spoiled brat of a son before the clever little fraud even has a chance to deliver his phony speech, a farmer who pays loafers a full day's wage for at most an hour of grumbling effort, a judge who dismisses a capital charge of adultery against a woman who is patently guilty without even bothering to ask her whether she has any regrets—there, my friends, you have exuberance with a vengeance. Indeed the last story was so exuberant as to be profoundly shocking to the early Christians and hence was cut from many texts of the Bible, not the first time Church leaders have tried to tone down Jesus' description of his experience of the Father.[5]

As revealed through Jesus, Yahweh truly manifests "exuberance with a vengeance," doing, I might add, exactly the kinds of thing a mother might do behind her rigidly and obsessively "fair" husband's back. All the proper Old Testament categories are preserved. Jesus speaks of a father, a lord, a judge. But his father forgives, his lord refuses to tally wages against effort, and his judge passes sentence according to a law not engraved in stone but upon the heart. God is revealed as Love, literally entering through the Incarnation into fellowship (*koinonia*) with us, described by Karl Rahner in terms of "conjugal relations."[6] The Incarnation, the Event of God in Christ, "is the event in which God's innermost life is communicated to men, in his love for them, fully and without restraint."[7] Rahner continues, "God, as Person, freely wished to love us; and in the knowledge of this truth the entire reality of Christianity is contained."[8] If we take the image of either maternal love or conjugal love seriously, if we wish truly to experience the full impact of divine love, then it seems essential that we not limit our God to the masculine mode. Heterosexual males, in particular, should find it far easier to relate to Woman God than to God the Father, as Greeley notes in *The Religious Imagination*:

> . . . In principle we men ought to have more invested in the image of God as someone like Jessica Lange than women might. God we are told, is love. Our relationship to God is a love relationship. Normally, the most powerful love experiences we have are cross-sexual relationships. It is hard to fit these experiences into an imagery of God which is predominantly male.[9]

By now it should be obvious that both the androgynous God image and Woman God are inextricably linked to the Incarnation, the Christian vision of God as passionate lover, and the sacramentality of the world. Alas, despite Jesus, despite the spirit of egalitarianism and nonjudgmental, joyous, kinetic love which lies at the very core of the Catholic experience, the message was simply too revolutionary, too much at odds with dominant ideologies, to be allowed to pervade the emerging institution; and to the extent that it did prevail, it did so in a distorted manner. Try, even today, to imagine God the Father, or Jesus really laughing. You will find it difficult, if not impossible. The very suggestion seems vaguely or not so vaguely disrespectful or even blasphemous. A wan and sweet smile maybe, as Our Lord tells stories to the kiddies, but honest-to-God laughter, never! Jesus does, in a way, represent certain feminine attributes of divinity. Those characteristics, however, in keeping with deep-seated assumptions of the supposedly weak, suffering, and yielding nature of women, are almost exclusively limited to actions and behavior consistent with those preconceptions. There seems no middle ground between Jesus, the man of sorrows, the ultimate victim (woman stereotype), meekly submitting to the Father's will, and Jesus, the warlord (macho stereotype), brandishing a sword dripping with the blood of his satanic foes who inspired such atrocities as the sack of Jerusalem, July 15, 1099.

The official version of Christianity has tended to connect passion to the stereotypically masculine characteristics of aggressive value-judgement, a crusading spirit which rejects that which it perceives as "other" (and by implication "wrong") and perversely delights in the zealous punishment of transgressors. This mind-set encouraged the severance not only of masculine and feminine qualities but also of passionate and supposedly dispassionate versions of love; since passion connected with love came to be identified with sexual desire; and sexual desire (in keeping with the life- and world-negating spirituality of a dying culture and despite Paul's acceptance of the nuptial encounter as sacramental) was regarded as demonic. Passion divorced from love yields the fruit of death. Love divorced from passion is barren. Both are demonic perversions of genuine Christian love, the kind which lives in the parables of Jesus and which is *both* passionate *and* non-egotistical.

But, it may be objected, the kind of gentle, nurturing, accepting and, yes, passionate, foolish, and unconditional love captured in the Greeley passages is a universal human attribute and certainly not limited to the females of the species. From an ideal perspective this is correct, and is, as a matter of fact, one of the subsidiary themes of Greeley's fiction, which presents paradigmatic men and women who combine tenderness with strength. Unfortunately, however, our preconscious assumptions of what constitutes masculine and feminine patterns of behavior are shaped by the dominant mythology of our culture, and until fairly recently that mythology tended toward strict distinction of supposedly male and female ways of being. While purists may rage against the inaccuracy of stereotypes, those same stereotypes largely control the ways we think and act. They literally provide basic patterns or models which we unconsciously use to make sense of our experiences. As such they have at times resulted in disastrous instances of mass hysteria and crusading fervor to annihilate those who were perceived to fit a particular negative stereotype, as millions of death camp victims of irrational Nazi rhetoric mutely but eloquently testify.

Nevertheless, while the insidious danger of all kinds of stereotyping must be recognized, and stereotypes need to be distinguished from archetypes, it must be recognized that precisely by focusing on caricature-like extremes, stereotypes can serve to reveal archetypal structures. Archetypes generally appear in positive (constructive) as well as negative (destructive) versions. In their negative aspect, women have traditionally been associated with deadly eroticism, dishonesty, cunning, and manipulation. Dante's most despicable sins of fraud, worthy of the lowest circle of hell, for example, belong to the feminine category, while his slightly less reprehensible transgressions of violence are of the masculine type. In their positive aspect, women have been experienced and depicted most universally as mothers, gently nurturing givers and preservers of physical life, yielding and passive rather than aggressive and passionate.

Christianity developed a strangely inconsistent and self-contradictory medley of values. While preserving the common Hellenic and Judaic androcentrism, the new faith designated pride (kin to Aristotle's highest virtue of "great-mindedness" and a stereotypically masculine quality) as the deadliest of all deadly sins while simultaneously raising "feminine" humility to the pinnacle of virtue, and advocating a general attitude of meekness and submission, producing the sort of transvaluation of values Nietzsche found so distasteful and intellectually dis-honest. In addition, the human soul (both of the mortal male and female) was envisioned as feminine, to provide, one as-sumes, an appropriate "bride" for Christ. Thus, from the dualist flesh-negating perspective, one might be able to argue that the *noblest* human "part" came to be considered feminine precisely to provide the appropriate (though imperfect) complement to the (perfect) masculine deity. Coupled with a pathological fear of sexuality and women as sexual beings (from the male clerical perspective) this reorientation produced an ideal of celibate males (whose celibacy, however, was *not* interpreted as becom-ing like women, since masculinity continued to be considered the standard of divine and human perfection) and virginal fe-males (whose virginity *was* interpreted as bringing them as close to the masculine ideal as possible). In a paradoxical twisting and turning of Christ's radical acceptance of this world (if you are God, you can't get much more radical than to allow yourself to be born a human being!) the Christian message came to justify widespread violence done to human nature *qua* nature.

Thus, any consideration of the feminine aspects of divinity must first acknowledge that the terms *feminine* and *masculine* are themselves encrusted with stereotypical associations which may or may not reflect reality accurately. Furthermore, from the naively democratic perspective which seeks to level all differ-ences and loathes even archetypal distinctions among groups, any suggestion that there might be real and innate differences between men and women is tantamount to scientific heresy and blasphemy. For the purposes of this study this issue will remain unresolved, and I will simply grant that much of what I call feminine characteristics may simply be based on the stereotypes of our culture. Whatever they are and whether we approve of them or not, it must be admitted that they exist and continue to exert their influence over our lives as they have for millennia. In addition, regardless of our dedication to the equality of the sexes, we must acknowledge that there are radical physiological differences between men and women. Women have the poten-tial of childbearing. Men don't. Modern science might make women capable of parthenogenetic procreation. Men, however, will not be able to reproduce without women until *Brave New World* type "bottles" have been perfected, which, I suspect, will

take quite a while. Besides, why would anyone want to eliminate sexual reproduction? It is certainly much more enjoyable
than donating eggs and sperm to baby factories. Men and wom-
en *are* different, and from that difference (once we cease insisting
that difference implies value distinction) emerge infinite possibilities of variegated delight. Genuine equality (as opposed to
uniformity) allows each individual to develop his/her nature to
the fullest. Men and women are also complementary opposites.
Together they constitute humanity. Paradoxically, as Jung recognized, it is precisely by allowing the contra-sexual characteristics to develop within our psyche that we become most fully
ourselves.

The premise of this book is not, of course, that God can be
adequately described in terms of any finite category, whether
that category be male, female, straight, gay, young, old, fat,
thin, benevolent, malevolent, a white-haired king counting
sheep and goats upon his golden throne, surrounded by ten
thousand male virgins,[10] or a multi-brachial Hindu temptress
gyrating voluptuously across the cosmos, eager to embrace everyone and everything.

God transcends and explodes all the fancy coffers within
which we might seek to confine Her/Him. At the same time, the
Judeo-Christian God is a person, and can best be approached in
personal terms. I am more than my blue eyes and my big
mouth. The real "me" no other human can ever truly know.
Still, insofar as I am known, it is through those eyes and that
(unfortunate) mouth, plus various other portions of my anatomy. Analogously, except for those rare birds among us who are
given to ecstatic mystical communion with divine essences, we
can know God only in and through the world in general and
human beings most of all. As one of my friends put it, "Who has
ever heard of anyone having a love affair with Tillich's Ground
of Being, or writing a poem to It?" Well said, friend!

Yet, whatever the image we hold of God (our "ultimate
concern"), that image is going to provide the basis for our
thought-systems and actions. Whether we know it or not,
whether we choose to admit it or not, we cannot escape the
power of our preconscious metaphysical commitment. It will
shape and organize our individual and corporate lives. The

agnostic may straddle the fence; the atheist may deny; the biblical literalist may confine; the Existentialist may speak of *Angst* and leaps of faith. They all, in their own unique and inimitable manners, have God as their point of reference.

Thus whether we think of God primarily in traditionally masculine or traditionally feminine terms—that is to say, whether we emphasize transcendent rational righteousness or immanent passionate graciousness—this concept is going to lie at the basis of our relations to others and the institutions we form and support.

Through faith we know that we are created in God's image. Reason tells us that we create God in our image. Both beliefs support an androgynous God-image. God is the Great Unknown, the Mystery. If we seek to know God, we must first understand ourselves. The Socratic maxim "know thyself" thus takes on transcendent significance. Psychologists and psychiatrists such as Carl Gustav Jung, Abraham Maslow, and Eric and Joan Erikson, tell us that men and women, despite genuine somatic differences, are essentially androgynous beings. "In the second half of life," states Jungian analyst Jolande Jacobi, "the goal is above all the psychic *coniunctio*, a union with the contrasexual within one's own inner world and with its image-bearer in the outer, in order that the 'spiritual child' may be born."[11] The "spiritual child," of course, is none other than the realized self. Animus and anima must be assimilated before full maturation can occur. "Each sex," Erikson writes, "can transcend itself to feel and to represent the concerns of the other. For even as real women harbor a legitimate as well as compensatory masculinity, so real men can partake of motherliness—if permitted to do so by powerful mores."[12]

Even arch-chauvinist Paul, preceded by Jesus and anticipating Saint Bernard, not only uses the metaphor of "father" but also that of "mother" and "nurse" to describe his relationship to the communities he founded.[13] His self-understanding, however, is primarily in terms of paternity which he associated with baptism and rebirth. The very idea of rebirth, of course, tends to set up an unfavorable contrast between physiological maternity and spiritual paternity, the naturally born in need of being *re*-born versus the perfected ones, untainted by matter.

Contrasting modes of apprehending reality, which partially mirror the male/female typology, have recently also been connected with studies in cognitive lateralization of the brain. While initial claims concerning our "two brains" (verbal-analytic and metaphorical-holistic) may well be overly simplistic, leading to pop-psychological generalizations which have little or no foundation in fact, there is general medical consensus that our two brain hemispheres are specialized and do function in a complementary manner and that exclusive dependence on one or the other hemisphere (as studies with "split-brain" patients have demonstrated) results in severe dysfunction.

An analogous polarization of modes of thinking and being can be observed throughout the history of ideas and has, at least for the West, been identified with classical versus romantic worldviews. Classical thinkers emphasize reason, clarity, order, categorization, analysis, permanence, control, and objectivity. They distrust the world of the senses which they tend to dismiss as illusory or at least as a realm of appearances concealing the reality beneath. Thus they seem driven by a dispassionate passion to know "how" something works and tend to develop magnificent abstract theories to account for causal connections. One might say that by focusing primarily on distinction, on the boundaries which separate one bit of reality from another, making it unique, they exist in the essential mode of negation. Classical thinkers are obsessed with splitting reality into identifiable, nameable components. At their best, they learn to use the "knife of reason,"[14] with such consummate skill that they can literally dissect reality into atomic units, revealing the underlying structure. Beauty, to classical thinkers, consists in harmony of lines and the simple perfection of mathematical formulas or geometric shapes. Classical thought is inherently dualistic (not to be confused with pluralistic), and it tends to envision God as radically separate from the world. The Greeks, preconsciously aware of this mode of apprehending reality, called it Apollo, mighty god of reason and order, driving his sun-chariot across the sky, chasing away night and shadows. In its extreme form, absolutized or idolized, this kind of logical, linear cognitive paradigm, which abhors ambiguity, degenerates into coldly rational formalism and perfectionism, hostile to everything it cannot explain or contain and prone to intellectual unilateralism.

Romantic thought emphasizes intuition, dream-images, fluid boundaries, synthesis, transformation, adaptation, and subjectivity. Romantic "thinkers" care less for the "how" and more for the "what" or "that" of reality. They accept concrete reality at face value and thus seem to be prone to remain content with appearances instead of seeking to go beneath the surface. They focus on connections and interrelationships, and they delight in the unusual, paradoxical, and ambiguous. They see no need to consider opposites as contradictory or mutually exclusive, and they can accept complexity without attempting to reduce it to simple, intelligible structures. Beauty, to the Romantic, consists in nature untamed by human hands, wild, mysterious, and unintelligible. Romantic thought is inherently monistic (not to be confused with monolithic), capable of appreciating identity-in-difference or non-duality, and prone to imagine God as identical with self and nature. The Greeks called this mode of apprehending reality Dionysus, Apollo's half brother, the mysterious god of dreams, drunkenness, and procreation. In its extreme form, absolutized or idolized, this kind of intuitive, even irrational cognitive paradigm degenerates into a morass of blind, chaotic, and orgiastic enthusiasm, hostile to disciplined reflection and any kind of civilized community.

Even though those two fundamental ideologies (in Erikson's sense) coexist in individuals and societies, they tend to alternate in their relative importance throughout history, each calling forth the other after it has been dominant for a while. In addition, classical patterns have generally been the accepted elite paradigms in the West ever since Plato and Aristotle, leading to widespread dualism, specialization, and emphasis on understanding and controlling nature through science and technology.

A study of non-Western modes of apprehending reality reveals the intriguing possibility that something surprisingly similar to what I have called "romantic" or "feminine" thought may well be the preferred cognitive paradigm among Chinese Taoists and in India. Professor Nakamura, in his monumental *Ways of Thinking of Eastern Peoples*,[15] points out that the Indian model of the universe shares many features with the worldview of the European Romantics, listing such common characteristics as fluid boundaries between categories such as self and other, subject and object, reality and illusion, philosophy and mythology, as well as a fondness for poetical forms of expression, a pervasive spirit of tolerance and conciliation, no concept of "heresy," and philosophical monism or non-dualism. Archetypal "feminine" modes of thinking, by the way, do *not* by themselves encourage equality for women or democratic patterns in society.

The Western world, on the other hand, from its Judeo-Hellenic roots to the present has been dominated by God the Father, Yahweh/Zeus, benevolent or not so benevolent tyrant, a *paterfamilias* in the classical sense. Long before Yahweh, however, long before Zeus, long before Uranos, there was non-differentiation, oneness, prime slime if you will, or dark-winged *Nyx*, impregnated by the wind, laying her silver egg (concealing golden-pinioned Eros) into the void, the gently enfolding cosmic womb, an inchoate continuum, a dream-like state of fluid boundaries where humans, animals, plants, and even minerals all were mysteriously connected and no genuine distinction between the I and the Thou, self and world, had yet occurred.

Even monotheistic and patriarchal Judaism with its insistence on the radical gulf separating the creator and creation, found itself unable to eliminate all traces of a primordial androgynous deity, creating the universe through procreation. This ancient tradition, though vigorously combated by the priestly elite, and largely deleted from official texts, continued to emerge among the Jewish people, and it surfaced in medieval Kabbalistic mystical speculation. This speculation considered God as a process manifesting Him/Herself in and through the ten *sefiroth* (primordial images of beingness *per se*) flowing into creation which gives form to God's inner dynamism and is symbolized by the mystical tree which constitutes the union of all opposites. "Nothing" (a feminine archetype) is the first and highest of the *sefiroth*. The second is the the primordial point, or "world sperm," the initial departure from the divine nothing. It is deposited in the the third *sefirah*, the primordial womb, product as well as counterpart of the original point. Their union in turn yields the remaining seven *sefiroth*, causing continued mating of pairs until *yesod*, the ninth *sefirah* or male potency, consummates the *hieros gamos* with the tenth *sefirah*, his *shekhinah*,

female potency envisioned as mother/wife/daughter. Gershom
G. Scholem remarks:

> Often regarded with the utmost misgivings by strictly
> Rabbinical, non-Kabbalistic Jews, . . . this mythical con-
> ception of the feminine principle of the *Shekhinah* as a
> providential guide of Creation achieved enormous popu-
> larity among the masses of the Jewish people, so showing
> that here the Kabbalists had uncovered one of the primor-
> dial religious impulses still latent in Judaism.[16]

At the dawn of history, all across the globe, cosmogonic
myths envisioned an original state of primal androgyny, followed by the separation and procreative reunion of the world
parents. Those myths identified the masculine principle with
consciousness and reason, and depicted the feminine principle as
the intuitive bearer of the subconscious, thus positing for the
future a cleavage between the feminine and the masculine, between the passive and the active, the *yin* and the *yang*. Two
thousand years ago in a remote corner of the Roman Empire a
carpenter's son shared his experience of a God of Love rather
than Law, and taught the revolutionary "good news" of full
human emancipation. Six hundred years ago Dame Julian of
Norwich wrote of God our Father *and* our Mother while Jewish
Kabbalists celebrated God as primordial *hieros gamos*. Contemporary historians of ideas distinguish between "romantic" and
"classical" modes of apprehending reality and being in the
world. Economists, such as E.F. Schumacher insist that Western
humanity can learn from the less aggressive Buddhist ap-
proaches to technology and the environment. Twentieth-century psychologists distinguish between right and left brain
hemispheres and insist that both are necessary for optimum
mental and emotional health. Wherever we turn we are confronted with the need to build bridges and seek reconciliation. In
a perspective which envisions the masculine and the feminine as
correlatives, it becomes clear that if either is allowed to dominate and exclude the other the natural balance is disturbed and
fruitful interaction is rendered barren.

The time has come to consider the fullness of God.

three

woman god:
from astarte to mary

Magna Mater

The temperature in the tent rose, his guests were crowding him, their faces and bodies close to his. Sammy rested her head on his chest. He hurriedly started to think something comic, she put her hand over his mouth and laughed softly. The other two women were watching avidly. Sammy began to stroke his face with the tips of their fingers. Her eyes were round and large, her figure passive, available, inviting. With the three lovely bodies gleaming with sweat and pressing against him, O'Neill felt himself drifting slowly back toward a primal unity with all things fertile and creative.

Just before dawn he was suddenly awakened by a powerful incense odor. As he struggled awake, he could hear Sammy's voice, as from a great distance. "The narcotic is taking effect. Soon, sisters, he will be quite powerless." Then he sank back into the world of sensation, arousal, heat, passion. He gave himself up to it: the salty smell of women, the vision of a naked Sammy, his lentat unceremoniously ripped away, hands exploring his body. Unbearable passion. Sammy's mouth hot and eager on his, all over him. Helplessness. Delight. Surrender.[1]

31

In the distance the sound of voices, songs, music, and neighing horses blended together. They were starting the fertility dances now, she thought, imagining the ancient rite of naked bodies. She stretched out on the soft grass, her eyelids heavy with lost sleep of the night before. . . .

She felt herself melting into the warm sun and blue sky. The hard green turf beneath her was becoming soft, the harsh festival music turned into gentle strings. Someone was humming. She was dressed in the richest of saffron tunics, laden with gold jewelry. She was a bride on a wedding bed. The beautiful woman was standing over her smiling complacently. "Did I tell you that you would be Queen of Ireland? Will you take care of him for me? Was it Queen Ethne? No, it was someone else, someone even more beautiful.[2]

Finally, as the orchestra's music swelled to the mad crescendo of the sacrificial dance, I lost the remnants of my self-control and claimed her completely. My brain was clogged with insane images of her body swelling with the shape of my child within. Spring, fertility, love, life all rushing together to create unbearable pleasure. Ciara by then was able to reply, an aroused, passionate woman as out of control as I. Our own rite of spring was accomplished. We drained the holy grail together.[3]

Peg was sitting next to the bed, Hugh in her arms. A light was radiating from them, soft and misty and very bright. She had slipped the straps of her nightdress off her shoulders and the baby's skin and her own cream white body seemed to blend into one. Her eyes were afire with infatuation, possession, delight.

She saw him watching and smiled at him too, inviting him into their communion. "I've saved some of my milk for you."

"What . . . ?" he stammered.

"You've wanted to taste it and were afraid to ask." She drew his head firmly to her nipple. Her milk was sweet and warm, like Peggy herself. She was administering her sacrament to him. The light crept around him too.

"I have enough love for both of you," she said complacently.

No longer a child bride with a live doll, Peggy was age-old woman, mysterious, absorbing, life-giving, totally captivating. She put the sleeping Hugh back in his crib, patted Tom's head, turned off the light, and cuddled next to him. Father and son had both been nourished. Mother and wife could sleep. . . .

He brushed his lips against hers and touched lightly the breast from which he'd drunk as if it were a chalice from which a priest might say Mass. She continued to sleep.[4]

These passages peel away the layers separating the experiences of contemporary men and women, sophisticated inhabitants of the so-called "secular city," from archetypal mythic understandings and projections of the struggle between the forces of chaos and order, the mysterious connections of fertility and decay, the sacramental and demonic potential of sexuality, and the limit-encounter with the primordial powers of femininity and procreation in all of their ambiguity.

Archaeological and anthropological evidence indicates that before the idea of the primal pair as cosmic parents emerged (which presupposed at least some rudimentary understanding of the connection between intercourse and reproduction), early humans believed that prior to birth they inhabited the waters, rocks, plants, or animals of their environment from whence they were mysteriously inserted into their mother's womb after she had come into contact with some anonymous and holy natural source of their being. Thus they were in a sense excluded from the truly significant aspect of the procreative process and naturally considered themselves far more intimately related to the earth-mother, the "cosmic womb" than to their physiological mothers who had done no more than serve as passive containers for their early development and received them into life.

Men, in particular, knew of no procreative bond uniting them and the children of the community, and they saw themselves at best as "adoptive fathers" called upon to legitimize offspring. Thus, early humans truly considered themselves parts of the ecosystem, connected with Earth and Nature in ways almost inconceivable to twentieth-century humanity.

The imagery of the first quotation takes us back into those most ancient of all ancient memories, the at-one-ness with primordial chaos, the annihilating ecstasy of being totally possessed by and absorbed into the life-death feminine principle, experienced not as fusion with an *individual* other, but rather as merging, melting into the *universal* other, the ultimate womb which is simultaneously the primal tomb, an orgy to end all orgies, the falling into the material equivalent of Tillich's spiritual Ground of Being. In a process analogous to hypnotic age-regression, but far more radical, O'Neill falls back through the eons into Gaia and Nyx and "all things fertile and creative." As "self" and "other," "I" and "thou," subject and objects cease to exist, so does, in a sense, everything. He *is* the *tao*, the primal sea, the primal clod. Shakespeare's "weird sisters" are evoked, the *Eumenides* of the past. He is absorbed into the ancient Celtic "cauldron of rebirth" whose mysterious agency allows dead warriors and high kings to be resurrected after a night of being reduced to bubbling primordial stew.

In keeping with the ways we experience nature as both benign and capricious, the Earth Mother or Primal Mother tends to be paradoxical, appearing both as nurturing/protective *and* potentially terrifying/destructive. "As the womb of all forms of life, she has a cherishing and nourishing aspect; as the tomb of all forms of life, she has a menacing and sinister aspect; as the manifestation of an unending cycle of life, she has an inscrutable and elusive aspect,"[5] remarks Northrop Frye.

To members of primitive agricultural societies, storms, droughts, and floods, the demonic forces of chaos, seemed locked in an eternal struggle with divine and human labor to hold them at bay. Plowing and planting, sowing and reaping, digging irrigation ditches and building homes, granaries, tombs, and temples represented the human effort to join the gods in their battle to transform chaos into order. The "wild

kingdom" of beasts preying upon one another in a fierce struggle for survival is transformed into a pastoral setting of peacefully grazing flocks. Swamps and jungles are transformed into
cultivated fields and gardens yielding abundant harvests. Forests, plains, and mountains, the physical universe, are transformed into villages and cities connected by a web of roads.
Streams and rivers are dammed and tamed, their destructive
floods contained and channeled to serve life rather than death,
their flow serving agriculture, commerce, and transportation.
The destructive powers of fire are yoked to the demands of
technology. The chaotic forces of nature are harnessed in the
service of organization. The raw power of chaos is domesticated
and turned (however tenuously and temporarily) into the very
force which allows us to establish order. But beneath our carefully designed structures there lurks, as the Mesopotamians,
subject to the caprices of two particularly recalcitrant rivers,
knew so well—chaos. The process is never complete, the work
never done. One way of producing the desired results involved
placating the mysterious forces envisioned as alternately demonic and divine. In a cosmology which knew no distinction
between magic, religion, and science, the rituals of fertility
cults, considered anathema by the Old Testament prophets,
represented the human effort to tap natural energy so that the
wild forests and treacherous swamps might be transformed into
orchards. Archaeologists tell us that fertility goddesses were the
first to be worshiped by human beings, representing a stage of
imitative magic which equated human and agricultural fertility.
Many vestiges of these ancient cults can still be observed all over
the world.

I will never forget the first time I saw the tiny Venus of
Willendorf at the Vienna Kunsthistorischen Museum. An ugly
faceless little thing, large, pendulous breasts, exaggerated pu-
denda, a belly swollen with what appeared to be at least triplets.
Hardly my ideal of feminine beauty. Was this the portrait of a
woman or the portrait of a womb? The latter, one suspects. The
word *Astarte,* after all, means womb.

Still, even then at age seventeen, I could not help feeling
that the anonymous neolithic artist who left us this particular
example of his or her craft was part of a culture which surely

must have experienced the impact of the mysterious powers of procreation far more profoundly than they could ever be encountered by us, the jaded children of the scientifically sophisticated twentieth century. I recalled my own private moment of awe at coming face to face with the mystery of life. It was during the war. I was about five, when early one morning, in my parents bed, our grey cat gave birth to her first litter of kittens. For weeks I had petted her expanding belly, probing for signs of additional life and delighting in occasional rippling motions across her tiger striped flanks. Finally the moment had come, I watched her twist and turn and scream in pain, and saw the first little one emerge still enveloped in a glistening membrane, dead, I thought, surely dead. And then, wonder of wonders, the mother licked it clean and it began to mew and wriggle, blind and helpless and yet heading directly for a teat.

In a similar way, I too had come into existence, and I too might one day allow life to grow within me and thus bring another human being into the world. That morning, quite unaware yet of the mechanics of reproduction, I dimly experienced myself as a woman, the end of a chain leading back into the beginnings of time, and potentially a link connecting those coming before me with the future. I looked at my mother, and I tried to imagine what it might have been like to live inside her belly, warm and safe, all wrapped up in wet cellophane, not having to breathe, not having to eat, just being within her, part of her like her tongue or her heart or her stomach. Was it like sleeping, I wondered? Surely not, because my sleep was filled with exciting and scary adventures. Then I tried to go back to my beginnings, to the time my mother had told me, when I was smaller than the head of one of those brightly colored glass-headed pins I loved so much, and tinier still, way back before . . . What would it be like to be nothing? And how great, how wonderful, how absolutely marvelous that I was not nothing any more, and that some day, maybe, in and through me another nothing could be transformed into *someone*.

In *Motherhood and God*, Margaret Hebblethwaite reflects on the value of imagining ourselves within the womb of God:

There could be no closer image of warmth, security and

protection. There we have all our needs provided for in perfect measure, as the baby receives oxygen and nourishment without deficiency or excess through the umbilical cord. In God's womb we can stretch and turn in every direction, just as the baby, suspended in water, is as happy upside down as the right way up, and in the early months can exercise its limbs freely. Wherever God our mother takes us, we will be safe and provided for; whether in cold or heat, storm or drought, we will be protected. Wherever we journey we will still be at home, for the presence of our mother's body is closer to us than our geographic location. God is closer to us than the ground we stand on. Even though we have never seen our mother, perhaps are quite unaware of her, or even deny her existence, she is in perfect and constant intimacy with us; and when we are born into the light of her presence, we will recognize that she has been with us all along.[6]

It seems significant that this theologian, out of her personal experience as an expectant mother developed exactly the same images for divine femininity/maternity which emerge in Andrew Greeley's novels, including not only the safety of the primal womb but also the journey leading ultimately to our original home, which is eventually recognized as having been with us all along. These motifs will be explored in detail in subsequent chapters of this study.

The second and third quotations remind us of the ways in which Christianity grafted itself onto existing beliefs, transforming, converting, "baptizing" the archetypal symbols and rituals of the past into meaningful symbols and rituals for the present. Since time immemorial, human beings have intuitively sensed divinity manifested in and through the mysteries of fertility as they observed the barren winter earth clothing herself in spring and summer finery, and as they yielded to the great seasonal cycles of birth and decay, coming to be and ceasing to be. Mother Nature, the "Great Mother" is at once the source of life and the goal of life which is death, the one who gives birth, who nourishes and protects, as well as the one who destroys and devours.

Genuine acceptance of the sacramentality of the world demands that we should expect to find already in primitive religions expressions of that instinctive yearning for Her Who was to enter time and space as Mary the Mother of God. "And if we look," writes Conrad Pepler, "we shall not be disappointed, for at every turn we come across the "divine Mother" presiding over the rites and ceremonies of these primitive religions."[7]

Deeply buried within our collective unconscious there lies the image of a Mother bearing a son (often through parthenogenesis) who in due time becomes her lover/spouse. Hesiod sings of Gaia (Earth) first of all giving birth to Uranos (Heaven), her equal, who "could overspread her completely."[8] As Mircea Eliade has so masterfully demonstrated, this primeval divine couple represents a universal theme of comparative mythology, engaged in incestuous, incessant, and sacred begetting from Oceania, Indonesia, Africa, the Americas, the Far and Middle East, to northern, central, and Mediterranean Europe.[9]

Much later, in a typically Christian transformation and transvaluation of pagan symbols, the Virgin Mary would appear as Queen of Heaven and (implicit as well as chastely incestuous) Bride of Christ (symbol of the triumphant Church) as the doctrine of the Assumption (celebrated annually on the fifteenth of August) worked its way up from popular legend to officially sanctioned dogma (culminating in Pius XII's encyclical *Ad coeli Reginam*, October 11, 1954). Thus, Brigid's vision of the "beautiful woman . . . smiling complacently," while nearby naked bodies are coupling according to the ancient customs of fertility magic, captures the moment of symbolic translation, of the not yet fully acknowledged "changing of the guards" from the pagan gods to the Christian God in Her manifestation as Mary, a Mary who knows that Her time has come and who thus can afford to smile contentedly and benignly. Significantly, the vision takes place on the Eve of the Feast of Lugnasad (literally "Lug's marriage" celebrated annually around the first of August) when the wedding of Erin (Ireland) to the Sun God is ritually recalled. Many such records during transitional eras of similar "visitations" of the Virgin as semipagan figure exist in different parts of the world. According to Pepler, the Madonna accompanied by two celestial maidens is said to have appeared to the Christian swineherd Eovis in a luminous green vision near Evesham on the banks of the Avon toward the end of the seventh century (the first such visitation on English soil on record). Eovis' pagan companions insisted that he must have seen the goddess of the green forest and stream seeking to reclaim her territory. The holy Abbot himself, however, whose pigs Eovis had been tending, pronounced the vision a genuine manifestation of the Virgin.[10]

In a scenario typical of the preconscious realm of dreams and myths, Brigid, the slave/princess heroine of the *Magic Cup,* merges with both the pagan Mother Goddess and the Christian saint, thus symbolizing the actual historic fusion of roles which took place in seventh century Ireland, as the mighty pagan triadic goddess Brigid (patroness of poetry, metalwork, and healing), mother/wife/daughter of the Dagda (Celtic equivalent of the Roman Saturn) became Saint Brigid, who in turn was identified with the Virgin Mary and called "Mary of the Gael," whose abundant supply of warm, sweet milk, her hagiographers and followers insisted, nourished the infant Jesus.

Saint Brigid, abbess (and bishop?) at Kildare, Christian patroness of learning, crafts, and medicine, continued to inspire folk customs closely tied to Celtic ritual which were designed to preserve harmony in nature. Her feast day is the first of February, the pre-Christian fertility festival of Inbolc. In the thirteenth century, the poet, Giolla Brighde (ca. 1210-72) addresses both St. Brigid and the Virgin Mary in a touching poetic plea to grant him and his wife at least one child. He addresses Brigid as "faithful sweetheart of God,"[11] and Mary as "three Maries"[12] (unconsciously and innocently preserving the ancient Celtic motif of a triple goddess) which in connection with the trinity form the "six proving letters of knowledge," in the balancing of masculine and feminine forces typical of pre-Christian Ireland.

The Great Mother has not only been subsumed and absorbed by the victorious faith, but she continues on in the kind of mystic experience of primordial coupling which is described in the passage from "Rite of Spring," a ritual to be completed at the end of the book in the appropriate Celtic locale, the Strand of Inch. Inch was previously visited in *The Magic Cup,* which first sounds the motif of connecting the human journey with the quest for the mysterious holy grail, the "magic cup" and, transformed and transfigured, the liturgical chalice. In the universal religious code, the fertile womb is associated both with the image of a container or sacred vessel and with life-giving, purifying waters. Not only Brigid and Mary but *every* woman has the potential to appear as the Great Mother, of symbolizing God in Her femininity.

The final passage reveals yet another aspect of divine femininity, Her role as nursing mother, a powerful symbol sounded by Jesus himself and by St. Bernard. From the "Rite of Spring," the sowing of the the seed, literally as well as figuratively, we are following the natural cycle to harvest, child birth, and beyond. Mother's milk is a universal symbol of grace and nourishment. It connects the everyday experience of partaking of food (pleasurable as well as essential for life) with the divine banquet God has prepared for us. As the son suckles at his mother's breast, he partakes of the maternal substance, transforming it into himself. Drinking of the fountain of life, the child symbolizes all of us mysteriously joined in an act of pure giving and receiving. The cycle which was begun with the father's emission of semen into the maternal vagina is completed as the mother shares her liquid with new life. The child, while still dependent on the mother, has been born and is no longer contained within her body. As nourishment is drawn from the breast, the infant grows and develops in strength and independence. On the symbolic level, the giving of maternal milk is associated with the central Christian symbol of the Last Supper and most specifically the mysterious chalice filled with Christ's holy blood, his gift of himself to humanity. The chalice, the Greeks would say, was modeled according to a mold provided by the breasts of Helen of Troy.

Peg is Peg, the individual woman, Tom's wife and Hugh's mother, but she is also, unconsciously, transformed through the power of her radiant love, Woman God/Jesus nursing all of humanity, administering Her/His ancient sacrament. As she shares her milk with the child's father, she completes yet another cycle, becoming, for a moment, her husband's mother, fulfilling his primordial need to be joined to his mother in a beautiful transvaluation and transformation of the demonic Oedipus motif which, as we have seen, lies deeply imbedded in our cosmogonic myths (as well as, as Freud would be quick to point out, in our personal subconscious). Tom intuitively understands the moment as something indescribably meaningful, of deep religious significance, a limit-experience. By accepting the offer of his wife's breast he figuratively accepts divine grace and allows himself to be stripped of the pretensions of independence and adulthood. He allows himself to become an infant again, yielding to a power he cannot comprehend, allowing himself to be permeated by divine love passed on to him through the focusing lens of Peg's warm and maternal presence.

Mary, too, as the Madonna, is often and lovingly portrayed as lactating mother, particularly in Dominican piety. The biological function of nursing is the only physiologically feminine attribute ascribed in its fullness to that *virgo semper intacta* according to Catholic doctrine. This is possibly because ancient and medieval thought tended to associate female breasts more with bovine udders than with human sexuality and because the Judeo-Christian tradition associated milk with divine grace. Prior to the fourteenth century, the Virgin's milk stood for wisdom and paradise. During the fourteenth century, in a typical shift of symbolic significance, the fact that she nursed her son became a symbol of humility, of her acceptance of the accursed female lot. By the sixteenth century the nursing Virgin waned in popularity. Not only was she returning to her noble throne, but modesty raised its head as a result of the Counter Reformation. It was the era of Savanarola's hellfire and damnation sermons which inspired Botticelli to destroy many of his earlier works, in a reaction reminiscent of Petrarch's late-life rejection of Laura after his reading of the Church Fathers. Despite the obvious charm of the image of Mary nursing her baby, there are those who consider the suckling of the incarnate God, transferred to the sociological plane, a tool for oppression. Marina Warner writes:

> Paradoxically when this, a Christian affirmation of the created world and its processes, symbolized by the cult of Mary's milk, is applied to the female sex in particular, it becomes a means of underpinning women's subjection to their biology, and of denying them freedom to reject it or overcome it through medical means available.[13]

While this hypothesis has a certain surface appeal, it fails to take into account that genuine human liberation consists in joyful acceptance, not rejection of physiological nature. Delight in female procreative powers and the cherishing-nourishing role in general does not imply that any one individual woman should not be free to choose a different path, nor that women are nothing *but* wombs and breasts. Would-be tyrants will use any means at their disposal to ratioalize injustice and legitimize oppression. The fact that an image can be misinterpreted and inappropriately used does not, in itself, warrant its condemnation. The theory also disregards the extent to which Mary of the popular imagination inherited the powers of the ancient fertility goddesses—a fact which testifies to the immense stamina of those mythic motifs which managed to permeate Christianity as they themselves were being transformed.

In that context it is interesting to note that on the Feast of the Assumption, August 15, in rural churches all across Germany and Austria the traditional "Blessing of the Herbs" has been performed for centuries. Anselm Schott, in the official pre-Vatican II *Messbuch der heiligen Kirche* (the official missal for the laity) explains that this custom originated either in Mary's extraordinarily sweet fragrance as the "flower of the field" and the "lily of the valley" or in the legend according to which the apostles opened the tomb of the Virgin and found it empty except for flowers. He suggests that during the blessing it is appropriate to pray for physical and spiritual well-being and protection against hostile forces. The herbs blessed in the ritual should, of course, be treated reverently and preserved in a special place. Obviously (though this is not stated), they were considered to be permeated with some kind of mysterious power which, while not strictly speaking magical, nevertheless shows certain attributes connected with magic.[14]

It does not seem particularly far-fetched to conjecture that the date as well as the herbal blessing is connected to pre-Christian harvest/fertility rituals. This is merely another instance of the Virgin quietly assuming the position of the Great Goddess, becoming a polymorphic sacred image integrating maternal and nurturing qualities with her special position as mediatrix connecting the faithful to Christ.

In the past two thousand years, with various levels of magisterial approval, the Church has in practice consistently compromised with local customs, absorbing deities as well as rituals, and has symbolically converted and "baptized" both in a practical implementation of the process begun with the Incarnation which once-and-for-all hallowed the world and everything in it. "Dig deep enough under the foundations of any of those century-old lonely mountain chapels," remarked my Tyrolean friend, Monsignor Anton Egger, "and you'll find the remnants of a pagan shrine."

All across medieval Europe, consecrated virgins considered themselves brides of Christ and, analogously, monks and priests could become espoused to Mary. "The special dramatic genius of the Middle Ages, which could transform arid theology into vivid pictures and lively theatre, created the Virgin in the image of a human, approachable, supremely adorable woman who stood by humanity like a mother but loved it like a mistress."[15] In the popular imagination, Mary came to represent the feminine aspect of divinity, assuming, in a transformed and purified way, the role of ancient fertility goddesses. The Benedictine monks at Montserrat, for example, have long considered their uncommonly fruitful mountain as a symbol of the Virgin in her role as midwife. There she presides over the mysteries of marriage and sexual union, pregnancy and childbirth. In the north Italian region of the Tessin, September is dedicated to the Madonna who is portrayed as an ancient cereal-goddess, the corn maiden.

Another example of this kind of religious syncretism can still be observed in the Italian province of Naples where a modern version of the ancient spring initiation rites of Cybele and Attis attracts up to two hundred thousand pilgrims annually. Every year on the first Monday after Easter the ecstatic *Fujenti* Rite of the Madonna dell'Arco is celebrated at the tiny village of Santa Anastasia under the auspices of the Dominican friars (who reap at least some of the financial benefits).[16]

Elisabeth Schüssler Fiorenza interprets St. Paul's oft-cited injunction against unbound female hair in church as a direct attempt to curb the Corinthians' tendency to consider their charismatic worship as analogous to that of Cybele or Isis with its ecstatic frenzy (thus attesting both to the prophetic role of women in the early Church, and the tendency of early Christians to see themselves as still linked to the pagan world).[17] In the mysteries, female devotees would loosen their hair as they abandoned themselves to the dance. It seems that Paul wanted to make certain that the Christian community would establish and maintain a strict separation from certain *apparently* similar practices of the orgiastic oriental cults. If the Madonna of the Arch cult can be taken as an indicator, he was less than successful. In 1966, nineteen hundred years after that worthy apostle's martyrdom, in the spirit of Vatican II (plus a generous dose of traditional male chauvinism), the Church once again attempted to regulate the *fujenti* (operating under the auspices of the Dominican friars), requiring female pilgrims to be decently dressed, to proceed in separate groups from men, and to "avoid the ridiculous fainting spells to which their highly emotional natures may incline them."[18] The injunctions were universally disregarded by the Madonna's enthusiastic followers. In 1973 the bishops of Campagna again urged that these kinds of feasts not be allowed to become occasions of resurgent paganism. They might have been less perturbed had they realized that although there are fundamental connections between Mary and the Great Mother this does not mean that the story of Mary *evolved* from the Great Mother myths. It means, instead, as Frye points out, "that mythic structures continue to give shape to the metaphors and rhetoric of later types of structures."[19]

Those archetypal structures, however, are even more ancient than rhetoric. They precede all accessible oral and written traditions and allow us to go back to the very dawn of prehistory when human beings first emerged from unconscious submission to natural necessity and began their struggle to solve the riddle of life and death. At the basis of *all* our mythic structures there lies ineffable, mysterious divine reality revealing-concealing itself in the animal skull circles with which ten millennia ago *homo neanderthaliensis* surrounded his dead, in the sightless, pregnant stone-mothers of fifty thousand years ago, in ancient poems such as the Sumerian hymn to the "Mighty Mother, who passes across the sky,"[20] the Moon-Mother supported by the branches of the crystal-rooted tree of knowledge (already associated with the feminine principle), in gentle Nut and ferocious Ishtar, in Isis mourning the death of her brother-husband, in the Hebrew *shekhinah* and the Greek *sophia*. The Catholic figure of Mary is not defiled through her association with earlier archetypes of the feminine; she is their *fulfillment*, gathering them beneath her star-studded mantle, uniting and transforming them, in the primordial motion of Teilhard's "Eternal Feminine,"[21] whose magnetism leads beyond itself and becomes the perfect symbol of wholeness and love. Ultimately the Mary of Catholic devotion is infinitely more gracious and accessible than her ancient virgin-goddess sisters precisely because she is first and foremost—human! She may appear as sun-clothed "goddess" standing upon the moon, crushing the serpent beneath her feet, her head surrounded by the twelve stars from the Apocalypse, and she may be identified with Lady Wisdom, Yahweh's beloved from all eternity,[22] but even as the noble "Queen of Heaven," Isis-like, bejeweled and remote, she never quite loses her identity as the barefoot, simple Jewish girl, squatting on the ground, nursing her firstborn, the mother who *cares*. She is "the only feminine religious symbol who reveals a God passionately in love with his people. You can fear, respect, and even worship Kali and Tara and Nut; but for Mary you write a poem or a love song."[23]

Virgo

My mother was right. Ellen Foley was indeed a woman. Her breasts, pale white, were flawless. She was a diminutive but superbly carved idol.

I held one of her hands as I stared at the fullness of her beauty. I felt no desire, indeed did not even think of desire. Yet it was more than an aesthetic admiration. What I felt for Ellen Foley was infinitely beyond physical desire.

She slipped her hand out of mine, picked up her clothes, and arranged them neatly on a rock. Then she began to unbutton my shirt.

I was a mixture of shame, joy, pain, exaltation, enslavement, freedom. When, kneeling before me as I had before her, she removed my shorts, I felt the same sting of embarrassment and pleasure I had seen on her face. . . .

We stood there, more one than two, for a long time. Neither of us said a word, both of us smiling. Then I lowered her gently to the warm waters of the pond. She let the water spill over her body, sank beneath the surface, and then rose to float next to the rock, beckoning me to join

her. I dived in, and we swam together, at first slowly and
solemnly. Then, after she dunked my head, we began to
play, chasing each other as though this were the final act of
a ballet choreographed by some unseen power whose instruments we were.

Afterward, we sat on the rock, our bodies drying in
the sun. We did not touch each other, we didn't have to.
I'm sure it was Ellen who kept the interlude magical and
mysterious. . . .

Four more times that humid August, oblivious of
Harry Truman and Alger Hiss, Ellen and I went to the pool
and enacted our solemn, silent ritual. The last time, with
thunderclouds slowly forming in the afternoon sky, Ellen
materialized quietly on our porch in her inevitable oversize
white blouse and shorts. Already in a trance, I rose and
followed her back into the woods. On the rock, after we
had worn ourselves out with swimming, we began to
touch each other's bodies, as though we were touching the
sacred vessels in an ancient sanctuary. Then I put my arms
around Ellen and she nestled her head against my chest. It
lasted an eternity.[24]

This passage captures the essence of virginity not as violent
repression of one's natural sexuality but as celebration of a primal force as yet contained, all promise, beauty and potential. In
its root meaning, revealed by the ancient myths of virgin goddesses, virginity does not mean an intact hymen, nor (paradoxically) the absence of motherhood; it means woman at one with
and true to her inner nature, inviolate and untouched by the
male principle in the sense of not being subject to masculine
control. The matriarchal virgin archetype is diametrically opposed to the patriarchal spouse archetype which represents
woman as her husband's possession with no goal other than
union with the male and completion through service. Thus the
primal virgin can, in her negative aspect, become the ultimate
enemy of man, since she perceives herself as absolutely other
and separate from the male. In that sense the virgin is the original liberated woman accountable to neither father nor brother
nor husband, nor, by analogy, the laws of society. Thus she is
entirely free to bestow or withhold her sexual favors, and no

one can demand chastity of her since her body and her children are entirely her own, and she, in a sense, is a law unto herself. She lies at the base of the Taoist worldview which refuses to be shackled by the rules of civilized, androcentric Confucianism, and she inhabits Mount Sinai in her manifestation as Ishtar long before the children of Israel hear the thunderous voice of Yahweh and Moses receives the law engraved in stone. Thus Ellen takes it upon herself to act not according to the rigid mores of Church or society but according to the primal, inner, fluid, never to be codified or captured law of feminine nature.

Ellen, however, is more than original virgin femininity in aloof isolation. Self-contained and independent, ready to act according to the demands of her inner nature, she is *also* intuitively aware of her femininity as complementary to Kevin's masculinity. Consequently, like the spouse but without her slavish dependence, she seeks to realize herself through contact with Kevin while simultaneously allowing him to discover himself in the same process. She offers herself to Kevin, not to be possessed or "domesticated" by him, but because it is in her essence to give. She actively and silently submits to his fumbling attempts to undress her, not out of fear, not coyly protesting to escape responsibility, but freely, proudly, and yet humbly, because at some fundamental level of her preconscious she realizes that her femininity is inextricably connected to the masculine principle manifested in him. By standing and kneeling before him in her glorious nakedness, by opening herself up to his eyes and hands, she allows him to *know* her as surely as if she had admitted him to a full lover's embrace—an action which if completed would have destroyed their spiritual union by plucking and eating a fruit out of season. It would have been wrong not because the act in itself is shameful but because it would have been inappropriate to their inner natures at that particular point in time. Kevin and Ellen are children at the threshold of adulthood. In their mysterious and solemn forest ritual each of them becomes a doorway for the other as in each other they discover themselves as androgynous beings created in the divine image. Their actions are both deliberate and the results of a compulsion which neither of them understands. Both of them permit themselves to be carried by something immensely powerful and ancient and essentially nonrational, something, *Someone,* Who most generally inhabits the nether world of dreams, poetry, and myths.

Ellen Foley is an ancient Kore-goddess, a perfect bud about to unfold, yet containing within herself the mysterious secret of the universe. Like Persephone of old she is kin to meadows and flowers, a fleeting pure presence at the very edge of Hades, a transparent, pure prism meant to gather and focus the rays of divine grace. Profoundly innocent, she will eventually be thrust into the Underworld, and like Persephone she will emerge, radically and permanently changed, yet also mysteriously the same and victorious over the forces of death, destruction, and darkness.

In a twentieth-century reinterpretation of the symbol, the male narrator of the passage, Kevin, is not depicted as Eros in pursuit of Psyche, or Hades about to rape Proserpina. He does not appear as the active masculine principle plotting to invade, deflower, and possess the other. He is, instead, no less shy and virginal than Ellen, who is entirely his equal. He represents the male sexual promise as purely and innocently as does Ellen, and she perceives his still semidormant sexuality as much as a limit-experience as he encounters hers. Both catch a fleeting, yet unforgettable glimpse of Reality in their new-old relationship, a relationship reflected in the ancient myth of original androgyny which seeks to account for the common human need to over-come an inexplicable sense of existential loneliness, temporarily mended in the process of coming face to face with one's lost half (or another person who is momentarily perceived to be that missing part of oneself). There is an aura of the Marian virtues of faith, purity, humility, and silence about their ritualistic en-counter which seems in its entirety akin to a contemplative prayer as they leave the frantic activity of the world behind and in their "sacred grove" yield to the great maternal force of pri-mordial, permeating, transforming, and luminous divinity.

As the symbolic tapestry of the passage unfolds, we en-counter images of innocence, promise, joy, and the kind of liberation which comes from allowing the unconscious to emerge into consciousness and from making contact with the hidden aspects of one's self. Kevin and Ellen are children about to be evicted from the naively innocent and preconscious Gar-den of Eden, a necessary (though wrenchingly painful step) toward human maturity. But before this inevitable initiation into the adult world of sin and selfishness, of deception and cruelty and frustration, of pain and pride and broken promises, they are temporarily allowed a fleeting and yet timeless glimpse of paradise, their personal Garden of Eden in which innocence and knowledge dwell in harmony. In their encounter they experience a form of enlightenment and partake of *sophia*-wisdom, the feminine corollary of the masculine *logos*, manifesting divine providence, revelation, redemption, and creation. In this context, it seems less than accidental that the sacrament of Confirmation, a tame version of the Pentecostal pouring out of the Spirit, is administered to young people about to reach sexual maturity and thus sends them on their way with an appropriate rite of passage. Alone at the edge of the silver pond, that mysterious mirror symbolic of the feminine, Kevin and Ellen discover not only each other but themselves and ultimately God, literally, by dis- or un-covering themselves in an intriguing reversal of the Genesis account.

There is something almost pathetically naive and yet profoundly tender, reverent, and chaste about the manner in which the boy/man and girl/woman undress one another, slowly stripping away not only clothing, not primarily clothing, but symbolically taking off all the carefully constructed armor humans use to protect their soft and fragile inner core from the curious and often cruel attention of others. Living with others demands that we develop the kind of practical good sense which allows us to shield ourselves from the negative forces which are an inevitable aspect of living in nature and in society. But lest we permit the human experience to degenerate into an unstable alliance of fear and suspicion with counter fear and suspicion, we must balance this "cold war" attitude with faith in ourselves and in our fellow humans. It is imperative that we resist the ever-present tendency to hide behind and within the security of false facades and rigid walls, that we put our trust—foolishly, the skeptic will scoff—in the ultimately gracious core of reality. In overcoming the paralyzing embarrassment—largely inculcated by rigid moralism based on misunderstood "Christian" principles—of allowing another to see them without the protection of their clothing, they take an essential step in the direction of realized humanity and come face-to-face with God. As Kevin pulls down Ellen's panties, as Ellen removes Kevin's shorts, each *kneels* before the other, not in idolatry but in the assurance that they are about to unveil the sacred centers of primal, mysterious, divine creativity, that they are about to approach the holy of holies. Intuitively they understand about the numinous potential of the body, touching one another, not slaves to selfish desire but reverently, as though they were "touching the sacred vessels in an ancient sanctuary." In those moments of communion in the forest by the pond Ellen and Kevin achieve genuine spiritual union and literally become transparent to the divine mystery. They are sacraments, each for the other; they have been transfigured, transformed, and their lives will never be the same again. Though never genital lovers, they are bound to one another in deep loyalty, and they will achieve the communion of friendship in the fullest and deepest sense of the term.

The pond provides a further, vitally important clue to the symbolic structure of the episode. It is described as a natural basin formed of rocks, spring-fed, lying between two hills, and surrounded on all sides by very dark and very old weeping willows.[25] The archetypal language is clear. One can imagine the physical terrain as a vast image of primordial woman with gentle hill-breasts and the mysterious, sacred hollow of pool-vagina-womb protected by willow-pubic hair. Countless myths and stories use the motif of leaping into a lake as symbolic of intercourse, as well as of death and rebirth. Joseph Knecht, for example, in Hesse's *Glasperlenspiel* thus experiences both physiological death and spiritual transformation.[26] In a well-known Zen Buddhist *haiku* Basho presents the leap into the "old pond" as a metaphor for enlightenment.[27] Kevin imagines the pond as inhabited by water spirits. Since time immemorial, ponds and lakes have been associated with the feminine principle. Water was considered the source of all things, the inexhaustible principle of life and regeneration; and lakes, fountains, or springs were the ancient haunts of the nymphs, semidivine spirits which manifested themselves in the heat of day and were associated at once with transforming fertility, wisdom, and death. For Kevin, Ellen becomes such a nymph (primarily in her positive aspect, though in future years he may occasionally forget the lesson learned that August afternoon and come to fear her as a haunting presence and danger to his vow of celibacy). Like the primal virgin, water, particularly in the form of spring-fed ponds (as opposed to stagnant pools), represents perfect potentiality, prophetic power (thus providing the preferred site for ancient oracles), and symbolic death and regeneration. The spirit children in Porphyry's *Cave of the Nymphs* call their mother's vagina the "rock hole," the mysterious place of origins.[28]

All of those levels of meaning were not only taken over but intensified by Christianity. Christ as well as Mary are closely associated with water. Christ's mission on earth entered its public phase in the course of his baptism; and for Christians, according to St. Paul, the rite of baptism constitutes a figurative burial with Christ allowing for rebirth in the Spirit. Thus it seems in no way coincidental that the Easter Vigil blessing of the baptismal waters, as Greeley has pointed out on many occasions, constitutes the ritual reenactment of a pagan fertility ritual, which "fructifies" the water by thrusting a burning candle into its depth. The Virgin is not only depicted as Jerome's *stilla maris* (changed to *stella maris* in a fortuitous scribal error, creating for posterity another beautiful image) but Sybil-like presides at numerous miraculous springs or "sacred precincts" such as Lourdes, which are often also associated with caves or grottoes with their obvious vaginal or uterine significance. This fundamental association of the Virgin, water, and rocks—anticipated in such folk tales as the one about the fairy cave at Guernsey, accessible only during low tide, and protected by masses of rocks piled around the entrance[29]—is beautifully captured by T.S. Eliot:

> Blessed sister, holy mother, spirit of the fountain,
>   spirit of the garden,
> Suffer us not to mock ourselves with falsehood
> Teach us to care and not to care
> Teach us to sit still
> Even among those rocks,
> Our peace in His will
> And even among these rocks
> Sister, mother
> And spirit of the river, spirit of the sea,
> Suffer me not to be separated
> And let my cry come unto Thee.[30]

Thus Kevin's and Ellen's rite of passage is inextricably connected with water symbolism. They are immersed in its purifying depths; they merge with it and, symbolically, with each other. The pond has assumed a numinous quality for them and is both fascinating and terrifying (as the dark willows and the thunderclouds indicate) in its primordial, feminine, transformational potential. Still, and this is important to note, Kevin and Ellen never lose their sense of playfulness and fun. Their ritual may be solemn and serious but it also, and essentially so, allows for squeals of laughter as two healthy young animals chase and dunk one another in their private swimming hole like a couple of porpoises. The God of Love is also a God of laughter. This dimension of joyful play is yet another often disregarded aspect of virginity and Paradisian innocence.

Kevin's and Ellen's "magic forest" in its pristine and virginal perfection shows the earth as a sacrament to be treated with respect and caring. The term *ecology* may be new; the vision of the interconnectedness of all things, the refusal to abuse and destroy our physical world, to befoul our "nest" because we see ourselves not only as intimately tied to that nest, but actually to approach it with a sense of awe and mystery, is as ancient as the Great Mother and as everlasting as the loving presence of Mary.

Like the Mother archetype, the Virgin archetype is ambiguous and can be interpreted positively as well as negatively. In its positive aspect it implies primal innocence, fecundity, transformation, perfect potentiality, and an almost superhuman strength which overcomes the most powerful biological and social determinants of the human animal and thus signifies not only power over nature but power over social convention. By consciously embracing virginity women were able to take control of their lives and liberate themselves from the domination of their spouses whose children they were expected to bear. In its negative aspect, the cult of virginity, narrowly defined as a physiological state (and as such a "treasure" which could easily be taken by any passing male with rape on his mind) came to provide yet another justification not only for oppression of the female, but also for a general attitude of wholesale dualistic condemnation of the sexual impulse. Even more ominously, virginity (or the protection thereof in a valiant effort to escape a "fate worse than death") came to be associated with martyrdom, as celibate clerics and popular spinners of legends gave in to what amounts to a pathological obsession with virtuous women's torn and bleeding flesh, perversely delighting in sadistic and detailed descriptions of severed breasts (Agatha) and bodies broken and shattered on a wheel (Juliana and Catherine of Alexandria), a tendency satirized by Greeley in *Virgin and Martyr* with graphic causticity.

In the pagan tradition, virginity (of the Vestal virgins and eunuchs, for example) was associated with both power and ritual purity. During the Hellenic period and most specifically as the Roman Empire began its long and painful decline, rampant and officially condoned materialism and hedonism provided a perfect backdrop for the development of countercultural world- and life-negating ascetic philosophies and religions. There seemed to be no hope for salvation apart from the radical denial and rejection of the demonic and repulsive physical carcass confining the human spirit and keeping it enslaved to dark passions of the flesh. Joy of life and delight in the wonders of the material universe were entirely incompatible with an image of human beings as little souls carrying around fetid corpses. In such a world virginity took on an entirely new connotation. No longer was the archetypal virgin the potential source of all life on earth, a perfect symbol of natural fecundity and transformation, the seed containing within herself the tree. Instead, she came to represent the kind of barren and unnatural rejection of all things vital and fertile which was considered necessary for salvation in an utterly divided universe in which nature and matter were seen as the principles of evil, to be denied, destroyed, and transcended. This transvaluation of the Great Mother/Virgin is noted by Rosemary Ruether:

> In the mystery religions the Great Mother of springtime resurrection becomes the mother of eschatological resurrection of the soul to life everlasting. Instead of commanding mankind to release their fertility as a sacrament of earthly blessing, she orders them to suppress it as the means to a higher life.[31]

It was in this perverted form that virginity entered the newly emerging Christian consciousness. Following the pagan precedent, virginity was associated with victory over mortality and corruption of the body, just as non-celibacy was inextricably connected with death and decay. Natural birth came to be devalued while supernatural birth was exalted. Christians elaborated on the theme by making it part of a complex system of asceticism which eventually eclipsed even baptism as the prerequisite of a genuine state of grace. Thus Jovinian, who maintained that baptism, not virginity, defines the true Christian, was condemned by Pope Siricius in 389/390 A.D. Jerome quotes him as having erroneously taught that "virgins, widows, and married women, once they have been washed in Christ, are of equal merit if they do not differ in their other works."[32]

In Christianity, of course, the Virgin Mary became the symbol par excellence of ultimate virginity. In his *Answer to Job* C.G. Jung speculates that Mary, as the virginal bride of Christ, supplies the transcendent anchor of divine femininity necessary for the ontological justification of the equality of women.[33] Nevertheless, while Mary the virgin/bride/mother did appear to sneak the feminine into heaven through the back door (where it had been serenely residing since the beginning), this was done at the expense of precisely those aspects which made her a woman, her sexuality. Despite the erotic imagery of the Song of Songs, and little evidence for Mary's continued virginal state in the Gospels, loving union in the real sense was ultimately denied, since radical fusion on the physical plane was absolutely forbidden. Far from recognizing the passionate joining of man and woman in ecstatic union as an earthly manifestation of divine yearning and love, sexual union was viewed only under its animal aspect, "mere" physical coupling, totally devoid of a spiritual dimension, and actually antithetical to spiritual union.

Numerous popular stories dealt with ever more elaborate variations on the theme of the Virgin. The apocryphal Book of James, for example, tells the story of Anna dedicating the child Mary to the temple where as a prepubescent girl she is allowed to weave the golden veil of the tabernacle (10:1), despite the fact that no females of any age were admitted to the inner sanctum.[34] Pious Christians sought to emulate the Virgin who, according to Bishop Melito of Sardis and numerous *Transitus* legends, had been told by Jesus that she would be exempt from suffering dissolution of the body since she had not suffered corruption by union of the flesh. After Jesus thus addressed his dead and buried mother, angels bore her into paradise. Thus like Christ, she died, was resurrected, and ascended bodily into heaven, largely due to her permanent virginity. Legend and speculation soon became doctrine. The Second Council of Constantinople (381) announced Mary's perpetual virginity. Nine years later Pope Siricius proclaimed her officially an unspotted virgin during and after pregnancy and parturition. During the first half of the fifth century Proclus offended Nestorius by calling Mary *Theotokos* in direct violation of the Antioch tradition which distinguished strictly between Christ's two natures. From Alexandria, Cyril came to Proclus' defense, and at the Council of Ephesus (431) Nestorius was excommunicated. Finally, in 451 at the ecumenical council at Chalcedon, the absolute dual nature of Christ was formally reproclaimed and Mary was given the title *Aeiparthenos*, a Marian doctrine declared a dogma of the Church by Pope Martin I in 655.[35]

As the Virgin/Mother, Mary represents what the twentieth century would consider a feminist image: she is a mother who bears a child without male cooperation. In her aspect as *Theotokos* she becomes the Christian equivalent (in function if not in title) of a parthenogenetic goddess. Unlike pagan goddesses who were envisioned as passing through cycles of virginity and sexual activity, Mary came to be portrayed as permanently virginal, the *virgo intacta post partum*, thus setting the precedent for official encouragement of consecrated virginity. The real point of the virgin birth, however, is mythological. It is contrary to nature and as such sets Jesus apart, thus both supporting and weakening the mystery of the Incarnation. By choosing this totally unnatural manner of arriving on earth, Jesus appears simultaneously to accept and reject the processes of the world. In one sense Mary is only one among countless ancient virgins impregnated by gods (frequently portrayed as birds) who subsequently give birth to a "divine child." In contrast to a host of pagan deities, heroes, or savior figures of similar mixed parentage, however, Jesus and his mother are historical persons whose lives (though most sketchily) are a matter of public record. Cardinal Henry Newman and Hugo Rahner argue that ancient beliefs prepared the way for the acceptance of the real virgin birth, the Incarnation.

Ultimately, the concept of Virgin/Mother is the Christian equivalent of a Zen koan, a surd, a paradox, something which shatters the categories of reason, a "limit-language" metaphor, appropriate to Mary's role as symbolic of transformation, sublimation, and renewal. Thus it presents the feminine equivalent of the Infinite/Finite, the Eternal/Temporal, the Incarnation, a paradox and stumbling block to reason.

The God-images of Mother and Virgin are essential powers which inhabit Greeley's analogical universe. In its Spouse manifestation (often linked with sexual union and death), the Feminine appears encoded in such archetypal symbols as the Lake, the Boat, the House, and the City, which I shall discuss in the next chapter. Ultimately, all of Greeley's symbols of human and divine femininity are subsumed into the overarching archetype of the Holy Grail to be explored in detail in Part Three of this study.

four

aRchetypes
of femininity

The Lake

It was a hot, humid day, the kind of Middle western Sunday afternoon that only summer-worshipers like me can stand. An inviting sheet of silver, the pond always seemed mysterious to me. I imagined it inhabited by water spirits, some dark like the willows where the sun no longer shone on them, some light like the jewels that seemed to dance on the water.[1]

They could go no further. Both threw off their robes and sank into the pool with grateful relief. . . . Her naked body was flawlessly designed, perfection in its rich, supple detail. Yet he was still afraid of her. How could anything so beautiful be so dangerous? Why did she seem a trap? It was not just the weariness of their journey which blotted out his lust. Margie's haunting beauty in the moonlight warned him away, a dangerous garden with deadly flowers.[2]

57

When they hacked their way to its shores, the lake was more sinister and more depressing than the jungle. It was still and smooth, shrouded in thick mists, filled with vegetation and rubble.[3]

He stared at the rectangle of yellow light through the budding trees, drawn to it as though he were a gnat with a fatal attraction for a glowing windowpane. Beyond the trees was the motionless lake, and beyond the lake the disapproving stars . . . What was he doing here? What irresistible energies had pulled him back? Had someone else taken over his body; had a lurking presence risen from the depths of his soul and turned him into a zombie?[4]

Maria, having floated too far away, flailed in the water. "I'm not too good at this swimming thing. . . ."

Hugh grabbed her arm in the darkness and pulled her toward the pier. She brushed against him for a delightful moment. . .

"Anyway, He made the lake and the moon and this night for us—He even made this pier for me to cling to—and we should be grateful."

My countless preached sermons, Hugh thought. And when she brushes against me I think I'm going to die.

"And we should be grateful to Him for sending you to make us appreciate the night," his mother said, even though Maria's theology was foreign to her own somber vision of the Deity. . . .

Hugh tilted her chin up so he could look into her eyes, mischievous, mocking, yet so easily hurt. Wet hair glued to her head, water still on her face and shoulders. . . . In the heaviness of the summer night she seemed to promise an eternity of sweetness and life if only he would take her into his arms. . .

Hugh knew with total clarity that he had the power at that instant to decide for or against the priesthood. To envelop Maria in his arms would be to repudiate his priestly vocation.

Why did temptations have to be so pathetic and so lovely?

And was she a temptation? Perhaps after all, . . .[5]

One of the most pervasive images in Greeley's fiction is the image of water, occasionally in the form of the sea, but most frequently as a lake. Water (particularly connected with ponds, lakes, springs, and fountains) is the universal symbol of the feminine. As mentioned previously, ancient myths abound with female water spirits of benign as well as destructive nature. Nymphs are said to steal infants (archetypes of the self) and to lure sailors to their deaths with their haunting songs and beguiling forms. "The sea," writes Isak Dinesen in a contemporary tale, "had become a female deity, and Rosa herself as powerful, foamy, salt and universal as the sea."[6] The sea, in the story, ultimately claims her own, and as Peter and Rosa are swept into the icy current, "the fantastic, unknown feeling of having no ground under him in his consciousness was mingled with the unknown sense of softness, of her body against his."[7]

It is this sense of terror and foreboding which Greeley expresses in such images as "the great ugly lake" whose "twisting vegetation seemed to grasp eagerly for his soul."[8] In *Death in April* the ambiguity comes to the surface. "The lake is evil," Jim O'Neill shudders, and then, immediately and paradoxically concludes, "Lynnie and the lake. The girl is the lake and the lake is God."[9] Man quests for, desires, *loves* woman, but he also fears her demanding, limit-dissolving, ego-destroying power. She is truly his "other" and as such is alien and terrifying. The promise of bliss is never totally divorced from the possibility of annihilation. When John Donne speaks of love, he uses imagery of death, and in Elizabethan slang to die meant to experience sexual climax. "You are like a silver goddess in the moonlight," Jim O'Neill says to Lynnie (appropriately called Evelyn *Brigid* in honor of the great Irish Mary of the Gael, a major Celtic savior-figure). Her answer captures the surd: "Making up your mind whether I'm life or death?"[10] This particular theme, the inevitable association of woman and mortality, of God and finitude, emerges as a persistent motif in Greeley's novels.

Water and the infant are Lao-tze's favorite images for the Tao, that elusive and ultimately indefinable source and "mother" of all things, the "subtle and profound female."

> The great Tao flows everywhere.
> It may go left or right.
> All things depend on it for life, and it does not turn away
> from them.
> It accomplishes its task, but does not claim credit for it.
> It clothes and feeds all things but does not claim to be
> master over them.[11]

Both of those archetypes (the collective unconscious and the individual self in Jungian psychology) appear in "Rite of Spring" as Brendan Ryan tells Ciara of his Vietnam experience in the darkness of his bedroom:

> One afternoon I was poking around in the river ponds, down river from their house. I didn't permit myself to realize that I was looking for Marie, but of course I was.
> I found her, as I thought I would, bathing in one of the pools, playing in the water with the delighted Emily.
> "You shouldn't be here ma'am." I tried not to look at her olive skin, long black hair and small, high breasts—a delicate Asian water deity. "If there's an attack, you'd be in serious danger." . . .
> . . . She passed the smiling child . . . to me, revealing as she stepped out of the pool and on to the rock at the edge of the pond, her full womanly beauty.
> An innocent movement for a Vietnamese? A tease? A natural gesture? An invitation?
> Probably all four in some complex mixture. . . .[12]

Bodies of water, more than any other aspect of our physical environment, capture the feminine archetype in all its ambiguity. Carl Gustav Jung uses water (as well as the Tao) to symbolize the personal and collective unconscious. As the "maternal aspect" and the "matrix and nurse of all things" it is "an unsurpassable analogy of the unconscious" which must be appropriated if genuine self-realization (individuation) is to occur. This leap into the primal waters, however, is frought with the ever-present danger that one may drown in its mysterious depths. As Greeley's characters invariably recognize, the lake of their yearning is simultaneously fascinating and terrifying. It is the goal of their quest, but an ambiguous goal which may yet reveal itself to beckon them to their destruction. On the one hand, it is "the living spirit, . . . the perennial water, the water of life, the virgin's milk, the fount; . . . and [whoever] drinks of it shall not perish."[13] It is "the Nous, with which the divine *krater* was filled so that those mortals who wished to attain consciousness could renew themselves in the baptismal bath."[14] On the other hand, it represents the real or symbolic death of initiation into a new order of being, a radically different type of self- or God-consciousness. Initiation ceremonies, according to Jung, often involve a descent into the primal cave as we dive down into the depths of the baptismal waters and return to the womb of rebirth. In water opposites melt and merge; it represents the universal "animating principle"[15] in sacrifice and it both "kills and vivifies."[16]

The final passage quoted presents a subtle variation of the initiatory encounter of Kevin and Ellen in and next to their magic pond. Unlike Kevin and Ellen, however, Hugh and Maria are properly chaperoned by Hugh's parents and their mutual discovery is at best preliminary. Nevertheless, the association of the girl, the lake, the moon, and the heavy and fertile summer night, is clearly implied. Hugh finds himself trapped between two contradictory demands or temptations—his "vocation" to the priesthood (symbolized by his parents who had literally dedicated him to God before he was even born) and the invitation to drink deeply of the fountain of life in the form of Maria who appears to the reader, if not to Hugh, as sacrament pure and simple. Hers is a basic attitude of childlike gratitude to a loving God right out of Blake's "Songs of Innocence," a God who made the lake, the moon, the night, and the pier especially for

her and Hugh to enjoy. Maria's consciousness of a God of love
and laughter who wants us to be happy is sharply contrasted
with Peg's "somber view of the Deity," a perspective partially
(though largely unconsciously) shared by her son, and a perspective that is bound to result in years of futile struggle and
torment. That night, by the lake, looking down at a pathetically
lovely, mischievous, female Sicilian-Irish imp, Hugh rejects
genuine grace in the name of imagined duty and yields to the
insidiously beguiling temptation to suppress his real nature for
the sake of sanctity. Surely his demanding God of righteousness
and self-denial could not want him to experience "an eternity of
sweetness and life"? Surely it would be a sin to repudiate his
"vocation" and take Maria into his arms? Still, he wonders in a
fleeting moment of sanity, with an unwarped fragment of his
soul, "And was she a temptation? Perhaps after all, . . . " It will
take him a quarter of a century to discover that for him Maria
represents God.

The Boat

The days were only a little less dark than the nights.
Roaring winds and pounding waves deafened them.
Sometimes the fog was so thick they could see only a boat-
length ahead. The others prayed. Cormac was too tired. It
was all up to King Jesus anyhow. He just clung to his
steering oar and waited for the end—whatever it might be.

The clouds vanished as quickly as they had come; the
wind diminished. A roof of blue appeared again over their
heads. The waves turned into huge, gentle swells. The
curragh bobbed along, drifting slowly toward the land that
beckoned to them under the morning sunlight.[17]

The stern of the outboard was already on fire. The
man and one of the children were overboard; the woman
and the baby were in the bow, screaming. Twelve gallons
of gasoline were in the boat somewhere. . . . He watched
Lynnie swim with sure strokes to the burning craft, pull

the baby from the hands of its horrified mother, and then drag the woman out of the boat into the water. In a daze he took the child from Lynnie's arms. He somehow managed to help her get the young parents into the Higgins. Lynnie dove deeply under the surface and came up with a choking, sputtering toddler.

He was paralyzed by pleasure—unspeakable joy at the danger of exploding gasoline, a joy beyond the excitement of kissing Lynnie. He waited expectantly for the dirty orange ball of fire. Then he thought of the fire consuming Lynnie, broke out of his trance, dragged the two of them into the Higgins, and at full speed roared away from the burning craft. It exploded, a belch of black-and-red fire illuminating the summer night. Lynnie looked gorgeous— wet hair, smudged face, and bare shoulders, and a baby held tightly in her arms.[18]

He saw the wave coming, not much larger than the others, but at a different angle. It slammed into the stern, knocking Paul from the seat and smashing him against the mast. For a moment he seemed to hang free in the air; then his fingers clutched at the mast.

It was too slippery to hold. The boat spun again and Paul Cronin plunged into Lake Michigan. He was not wearing a life jacket. . . .

The pain in his body from the purple waters was like fire. He remembered the stories about Irish fishermen who refused to learn how to swim lest they prolong their death agonies.

He wished he had never learned how to swim.[19]

Now they were relaxing in the front seat of the boat, one of his arms around her shoulders, and the other at rest on her belly over the Fenwick T-shirt, . . .

"Wouldn't it be nice to float here forever?" he said contentedly.

"Marry me," she replied.[20]

Ciara stood next to the mast, one hand on the neatly fastened jib sheet, the other in her windbreaker pocket, her jet black hair tense in the wind like geese flying south in the autumn, her face exultant, her shoulders thrown back defiantly, Grace O'Malley the pirate queen of old.[21]

The boat or ship is an unusually powerful and multifaceted literary and religious symbol. As vessel/womb/house, it takes on feminine characteristics; and as means of immersing oneself into the depths of the lake or ocean, it appears as a masculine archetype—the sperm of order swimming in the waters of chaos—or else it appears as mediatrix plying between the masculine and the feminine, this world and the world beyond. Charon, an old man with a ragged and unkempt beard, takes the shades of the dead across the river Styx into the underworld. It is on a ship that Odysseus spends ten years of his journey to appease the wrath of Athena, whose prophetess Cassandra had been violated by the Achaeans when they sacked Troy. Aeneas, the valiant Trojan and son of Venus, escapes from Troy by ship, sailing toward Italy and his destiny of founding Rome. Jason and his band of Argonauts set out on the Quest for the Golden Fleece on the Argo after drinking the wine of valor from a golden goblet (the "Magic Cup"?). Ships are of immense importance as archetypes for the human situation, particularly in conjunction with the quest motif, in such allegorical tales as Sebastian Brant's *Ship of Fools* and the stories of Joseph Conrad and Herman Melville.

In Andrew Greeley's fiction the boat is one of the images which allows him to pursue his fascination with Irish mythology in conjunction with Christian symbolism. Emerging as it does from an island civilization, Irish mythology abounds with references to boats, most especially in connection with mysterious journeys toward some otherworldly goal such as the fabled Land in the West or the Island of the Ever-Living Women. In the code of mythos the Boat is inextricably linked with both the Lake and the House, and it generally appears in Greeley's stories bearing a woman's (or saint's) name, such as the Pegeen in *Ascent into Hell* or Brigid in "Rite of Spring" and "An Injudicious Affair"; and it is associated, like the lake, with such conflicting motifs as innocence, erotic passion, death or mortal danger, and renewal/rebirth. Northrop Frye quotes J.L. Borges, as saying, in a little story called "The Gospel According to Mark": "Generations of men, through recorded time, have always told and retold two stories—that of a lost ship which searches the Mediterranean seas for a dearly loved island, and that of a god who is crucified on Golgatha."[22] In the Catholic analogical universe, the two stories collapse into one. Cormac and Biddy escape to safety in their boat, metaphorically piloted by "Lord Jesus," through the dense fogs and killer waves of the Atlantic. I look at the cover of this year's (1985) monthly missalette for Holy Week, and I see a stylized boat containing two "fishes" in its hull, with a stylized crucifix/mast piercing the body of the *Ichthys*, and the waters of redemption mysteriously pouring *out* of the boat into the sea from which two more "fishes" raise themselves, each bearing a consecrated wafer in its mouth. The miracle of the loaves and the fishes is evoked, and the mystery of the Eucharist. The Christ emerges both as fisherman and fish, the One who sacrifices Himself to Himself for the salvation of human kind. The boat, in this context, is the Church, but it is also the "womb" (filled with the spiritual amniotic fluid) of the individual soul on her journey toward psychic wholeness and rebirth into divine reality beyond the space/time continuum. The boat as a symbol for the vehicle of salvation is a universal archetype and figures particularly prominently in Buddhist thought (Hinayana Buddhism literally refers to the "larger boat") where it is pictured as taking the faithful across the stream of *samsara*. The boat, in turn, is linked, as the missalette cover shows, to the fish, one of the most mysterious and multivalent symbols in existence. In the Christian tradition it stands, as I have pointed out, for Christ; but it is also, as Markale observes in his *Women of the Celts*[23], a universal symbol for woman, particularly in her sexually aroused state; and it represents in the Kabbalistic heritage a symbol of fertility. It is precisely by "unpacking" the fish/boat symbolism that the feminine aspect of Christ and the androgyny of God might be recovered.

One of the most ancient of all stories which combines a number of Greeley's themes is the Sumerian tale of god Enlil's moral transgression and subsequent banishment to the Nether World. According to Samuel N. Kramer, Enlil is described as falling in love with the virgin goddess Ninlil whose mother encourages the liaison (expecting a good match for her daughter), suggesting that her daughter bathe in a clear mountain stream.

> In the pure stream, the woman bathes, in the pure stream,
> Ninlil walks along the bank of the stream Nunbirdu,
> The bright-eyed, the lord, the bright-eyed,
> The "great mountain," father Enlil, the bright-eyed, saw her.
> The lord speaks to her of intercourse(?), she is unwilling,
> Enlil speaks to her of intercourse(?), she is unwilling;
> "My vagina is too little, it knows not how to copulate,
> My lips are too small, they know not how to kiss . . ."[24]

Enlil, however, is not about to be discouraged. With the cunning assistance of one of his advisors, he boards a boat and rapes poor Ninlil "while sailing on the stream, and impregnates her with the moon-god Sin."[25] For this infraction of the sexual code (the demonic use of sexuality), Enlil is "impeached" by his subject-gods and exiled from the city of Nippur to the Under World (a rather musty, gloomy, and unpleasant region) to which, astoundingly, Ninlil, apparently espoused to him in the sexual act, decides to follow him. This ancient condemnation of rape, apparently based on respect for women, stands in stark contrast to Renaissance attitudes (which represent a debasing of women as compared to their medieval sisters). In an age when property crimes were punishable by mutilation and sodomy by the stake, the penalty for fourteenth-century Venetian (noble) rapists of upper-class girls under twelve and marriageable virgins consisted of a small fine or a few months imprisonment. The sentence for raping a married woman or a commoner was even less "severe."[26]

The connections, in archetypal mythic form, between woman, water, boat, intercourse, fecundity, and the demonic and sacramental aspects of sexuality, are clearly established in all their ambiguity and ambivalence. This five-thousand-year-old story is strangely reminiscent of one of the more terrifying versions of Hugh's recurrent dream in *Ascent into Hell*. Hugh is still a priest, it is Christmas morning, and he has fully experienced lovemaking for the first time in his life with Liz, also a virgin and a liberated nun. Earlier that morning, after Midnight Mass, holding her close, "he had not felt so free and happy since his boyhood sailing on Lake Geneva. He would make her his own, become one with her the way he had once been one with the wind and the waves."[27] Does he recall, the reader wonders, that fateful night fourteen years before when Maria asked him to marry her, and he refused, determined to follow his "vocation"? Clearly, the physical union consummated by Liz and Hugh is neither rape nor animal coupling entirely devoid of love and commitment. Nevertheless, it contains, as Hugh subconsciously realizes, the seeds of destruction, not only, not even primarily because it involves the breaking of vows, but because Liz (though he is not conscious of that fact) is actually no more than a substitute for his real love, Maria, whom he has accidentally seen a few days earlier for the first time in years during a performance of Handel's *Messiah*. Liz as well as Hugh are *using* one another in an inauthentic and potentially demonic quest for pseudo-salvation, and are guilty of severing *eros* and *ethos* in the sense those terms are used by Pope John Paul II in his audience addresses on the nuptial meaning of the body.[28] Thus they are committing adultery not merely because they are not legal spouses but more importantly because their act disregards the sacramental value of their bodies and their sexuality, and thus violates their personal dignity. They misuse the divine call to love and physical union, Liz as a symbol of rebellion against the Church, and Hugh in a desperate attempt to recapture with Liz that lost sense of psychic wholeness which once joined him to Maria. Ultimately, their lovemaking is a lie, lust unredeemed by grace, a barren kind of coupling which results not in a genuine pregnancy, a new birth, but "no fetus, properly speaking. Just a ring of tissue cells with a hole as big as a pin. Nothing really, not after the first couple of weeks."[29] And so it is Maria, the imp/angel of his past, who appears to Hugh in his prophetic dream as he experiences both the ecstatic exhilaration of lovemaking and the terrors of the self-imposed hell of Eros misused and demonized.

The *Pegeen* was floating in a soft, warm cloud high above the earth, its sails slack, its crew blissfully lolling in the stern. Maria was naked beside him, her face smeared with raspberry juice. He began to make love to her again.

She fought him. Their struggle tipped the boat to one side. It capsized and plunged out of the cloud and toward the earth, heading straight for the smoke- and fire-belching crater of a volcano.[30]

Hugh has fallen from grace—on Christmas Eve, the feast of the Incarnation, the celebration of God's love for the world; and like the Sumerian chief of the gods, he will be exiled from his community and begin a long sojourn in hell.

In the alternate cosmos of "Godgame," a houseboat (significantly, like the Church, in need of repair) figures prominently in Ranora's cheerful plotting to arrange a permanent peace between the hero and the heroine, the stubborn rulers of two warring factions. Ranora, one of Greeley's most appealing "incarnations" of Woman God, is a diminutive imp, a sprite, a poltergeist, a "grace-full" pied piper flitting and dancing through her world seeking to transform hearts and souls through the power of music, laughter, and love. Unlike the sirens of old, she lures her "victims" not to their doom but to salvation.

"WELL," the words flew out at Concorde speed, "There is this old houseboat on a lake way into the forest AND I'm going to have it repaired today and make it real nice AND I'm going to put food AND drink in it AND comfortable chairs AND a big bed AND a nice smell AND tonight they will go to it AND fall in love with each other AND mate." . . .

So all day she presided over the rehabilitation of the "houseboat," a cheerful lemon-colored pavilion on a flat barge, . . .

Then she wandered around it, playing the Lenrau Theme and the B'Mella Theme in whimsical, mischievous, lascivious, and finally profoundly serious combinations.

Next she boarded a red and white striped skiff which was parked on the tiny beach and pulled it out into the lake. Reaching into the hull she produced a large, floating lamp, lit it by flicking a switch and carefully cast it into the water like a young nun replacing a sanctuary lamp. She played another tune, faintly comic, on her pipe, giggled and tossing off her gown, dove into the water. . . .[31]

The boat also signifies both the church building (with its "nave" from the Latin *navis*, ship) and the Church, as the ark or ship of the Lord containing the Christian community. Early instructions concerning the building of a church specified that the structure be oblong and pointed toward the east, like a ship. The insistence on the church building pointing toward the sunrise introduces yet another ancient and essential motif in Greeley's stories, that of the significance of light (and warmth) as symbol of love, grace, and forgiveness. Divine reality in its womanly and sexual manifestations is experienced as luminous and life-affirming in a conscious reversal of the cultural androcentric redaction process which insisted on banishing the original sun-goddess (still surviving in the Japanese Amaterasu) to the night sky, as Apollo took over the function of the primitive sun-goddess Artemis who was demoted to the moon. This is unlike the Celtic Brigid whose sun association continues to survive in her Christian incarnation and is signified by her swastika-like cross.

The archetypal linking of heavenly luminaries, salvation, and boats can be seen among the ancient Egyptians who pictured their gods as being raised in their boats to the heavens by Nut, the sky-goddess and life-giving woman/cow, where they turned into the sun, moon, and stars, and the great festival of the death and resurrection of Osiris which involved floating the god's image in the Neshmet-boat on a lake. During the Middle Ages wheels (feminine archetypes) were carried on chariots or boats[32] in an unconscious reenactment of ancient rituals rooted in sun worship.

Greeley's characters generally make sacramental love in broad daylight, or at least with the lights on, symbolizing the potential goodness of woman as well as of Eros. Markale points to the mythic process of debasing women (and sexuality) by changing old legends to fit the new androcentric modes. "What was good becomes evil, what was feminine becomes masculine, what was broad daylight fades into darkness, and what was on the surface of the earth disappears under the waters or down into subterranean labyrinths."[33] The new dominant patriarchal religion relegated the ancient mother goddess to the bottom of the sea and shut her away in castles, caves, and on islands. Greeley's stories release her from those cold and gloomy abodes, allowing her to ride the waves again, proudly naked, fully woman, frankly sexual, beneath the summer sun:

> His fingers relinquished her jaw, slipped down her throat and chest and came to rest between her breasts. With awkward delicacy, he slipped out the tab tie of her bikini top, gently pulled it away and tossed it to the floor of the cockpit.
>
> She was startled, shamed, exhilarated. She felt at one with the the wind and waves and the movement of the boat, the rhythms and needs of her body and her life melting into the rhythms and energies of the universe.
>
> What a strange man he is, she managed to think, half wise old sage, half silly sad little boy. Then, his voice deadly serious, like a judge pronouncing sentence, he uttered his second strange sentence. "Don't expect that I will ever let you get away, Diana Marie Lyons; no matter what happens I'll always be there pursuing you, like a bloodhound."
>
> "Hound of Heaven?"
>
> "Something like that."
>
> Brigid heaved in one direction and then tilted abruptly back. Con released her and grabbed for the tiller. "Damn jealous woman," he laughed boisterously, "She'll do anything to get my attention back."[34]

In this passage, Diana Lyons, externally beautiful and a competent Assistant District Attorney, but internally consumed by vague, corrosive hatreds and envy, emotionally battered and twisted, a bitter castrating virgin, her mind poisoned by a passively aggressive, immature father, represents what Markale considers the rebellion of the feminine in its suppressed and demonic form, emerging as Lilith, the femme fatale. As the story proceeds, she will almost destroy Connor Clarke (and herself) in a Judas-like act of betrayal; and yet, as Connor dimly realizes, she will be saved by the relentlessly pursuing and passionately loving "Hound of Heaven." She will learn to accept herself as a creature of light and capture on a presumably more permanent basis that sense of cosmic union with "wind and waves and the movement of the boat."

> "To be offered a forgiveness we do not deserve—and if we deserve it that is not forgiveness but justice—is a terrifying experience. . . . We cannot claim forgiveness, it is pure gift, pure grace, pure mercy, and, ah, there's the rub, pure love. If we have betrayed the intimate other, only absurdly foolish love can possibly forgive us."[35]

Ultimately the boat signifies forgiveness and grace. Skimming across the waves in a white-sailed blur, it allows us to rise above the forces of gravity, to take metaphorical flight, and to merge with the primal rhythms of the universe—and with God. While the boat may founder, explode, and sink to the depth of the sea if misused and turned into a demon by our recalcitrant lack of love and faith, it is also Noah's Ark, the life raft manned by Lynnie-Woman God, diving into the churning abyss to save Her children, looking "gorgeous—wet hair, smudged face, and bare shoulders, and a baby held tightly in her arms."

The House: Homecoming

> Maria.
> Her house loomed behind her— . . . A house he had never entered. Yet he knew it well enough—neat, clean, warm, unconventional furniture, and flamboyant decorations. A pleasant house, inviting, reassuring, comforting. And once you went into its light you never left. Mason Avenue, Lake Geneva, Bethlehem.[36]

He stared at the rectangle of yellow light through the budding trees, drawn to it as though he were a gnat with a fatal attraction for a glowing windowpane. Beyond the trees was the motionless lake, and beyond the lake the disapproving stars . . . What was he doing here? What irresistible energies had pulled him back? Had someone else taken over his body; had a lurking presence risen from the depths of his soul and turned him into a zombie?[37]

"After three hours of shouting we're still in the same room," he said wearily.

All through the argument his desire for her had increased. Fire yearning for water. . . .

She looked at him and smiled wanly.

"We'll always be in the same room, Danny. From now on. You know that. . . ." She rose from the couch. "I'll make you a cheese omelet. Then we'd better go to St. Prax's for the Easter Vigil. Noele will be furious if we're not there."

"Woman of the house," he yelled after her, "put some ham in my cheese omelet."

He didn't hear her angry response exactly, since she was already in the kitchen.

But she did serve him a cheese and ham omelet.[38]

Erich Neumann considers the house (sheltering structure) one of the central symbols of the Feminine under the aspect of preservation and intimately connected with two additional primordial roles of woman, as the mistress of everything which implies nourishment, and as the guardian of the transforming fire.[39] Actually, for my purposes, the neutral term *house* should be replaced by the more complex and emotionally charged term *home,* described by Kathryn Ellen Rabuzzi as one or any combination of the following: your place of origin, the place you inhabit now, your final goal. Ultimately, home "is generally considered to be where you belong, whether or not you actually attain it."[40] In this sense of *home* the image offers an important clue to the symbolic content of Greeley's writings, closely associated with the major themes (to be discussed later) of the common human journey from alienation to wholeness and the

Church as "Fair Bride," a place/spouse to come home to. From its ancient beginnings the house/home has been connected with the pervasive presence of the sexual within its enclosure, thus representing the cosmos "sanctified" by the divine *hieros gamos* of the primal parents, an encounter to be reenacted by men and women on earth.

"Much as the Cross promises Heaven, Home seems to imply Happily Ever After,"[41] writes Rabuzzi who considers this a dangerous and sentimental generalization which may "distort, trivialize, and artificially sweeten Home so that it loses its full meaning,"[42] representing for men and women alike the distorted vision of immature dependence affirmed, complete with a rescuer of appropriate sex functioning as "all-protective savior figure."[43] This caveat is entirely appropriate as long as we deal with the literal meaning of the story and real people in everyday situations. Before claiming his blushing bride, the knight in shining armor takes off his dirty socks for his magic princess to wash, and "Happily Ever After" (if thus misunderstood) is unmasked as "The Big Lie." Greeley, however, consciously uses romantic symbols as hints of an even more primary human intuition: our foolishly persistent faith against all evidence of reason in the ultimate graciousness of Reality.

In this perspective Home-as-Happily-Ever-After represents *the* central message of Christianity (particularly in its Catholic form), a message obscured by official emphasis on the Cross as exclusive agent of salvation. The universal yearning for reestablishing a state of infantile dependence is both destructive, if allowed to dominate in symbiotic human relationships, and constructive, if applied to our relationship to God. Jesus, after all, challenges us to become as little children and accept God's passionate and implacable commitment to our welfare and happiness, whether we deserve it or not. This kind of radical dependence yields, paradoxically, as Schleiermacher recognized, genuine freedom. In addition, even on the mundane level of interpersonal encounters, the possibility of building one's nest in another's heart, of being cradled in the assurance of lasting, unconditional, nonjudgmental, tender, and accepting love, and of providing in turn the same kind of safe haven for the other, of being possessed and possessing while respecting the radical freedom of both parties, opens up precisely the kind of horizon which permits us to overcome inevitable cycles of alienation and temporary abandonment and to generate a truly lasting relation-ship.

The Home-as-Happily-Ever-After becomes demonic only if the image is pushed too far and wedded to an abrogation of responsibility to do our share in creating an environment which is conducive to the kind of liberation and reconciliation which is symbolized in the Home-Where-We-Are-Always-Welcome; when it is viewed as something given, closed, and complete rather than an open-ended process tending towards the ideal. It is only when we do not genuinely believe in the possibility of the very thing we appear to seek or fallaciously assume either that perfection can be attained on earth or that we are so intrinsi-cally evil that faith in the latent goodness of human beings is itself an illusion, that Happily-Ever-After is experienced as a Disney World false consciousness bound to yield inauthenticity or disappointment.

The Home-as-Happily-Ever-After horizon thus emerges as a uniquely Catholic symbol rooted in the rejection of both naive (humanistic) optimism and radical (Protestant) pessimism con-cerning human nature, and it naturally flows from the Catholic assumption of the sacramentality of the world and the gracious-ness of the Really Real. It is also, and significantly, one of the points at which the Catholic imaginative universe intersects with the Romantic imaginative universe.

It is this kind of Home which ultimately claims Hugh Don-lon after his extended sojourn through Hell. Once, long ago he had rejected grace in the form of a lovely and wet Maria whom he mistook for a temptation sent to make him stray from the path of his priestly vocation. He has spent his entire life in a futile struggle to *earn* salvation, and for the second time is about to come face-to-face with a different mode of being and acting, ironically one which he himself suggested to his parishioners in an early sermon in which he stated that "we do not earn God's forgiveness. . . . God's love is a given. It's always there, wait-ing patiently for us."[44] Seventeen years later, a hollow, spent, and broken man, he cries out in despair:

"Maria . . . I must climb out of hell . . . I can't . . ."
"No, you don't. You can't escape that way. You should stretch up your hands to God." She recaptured his

hands. "And let Him pull you out." She pulled him back to her. "This way."

He wrapped his arms around her.

"Why do you bother with me?" he asked.

Her eyes filled with tears. She leaned her head against his shoulder. "Because I love you, you crazy so and so. I've always loved you and always will, no matter how much you hide from me."

For the first time in four decades, tears spilled out of Hugh Donlon's eyes, tears of agony and pain, of frustration and disappointment, of failure and despair. Maria's arms enveloped him. He buried his head against her chest, his tears washing her breasts, a child in his mother's arms sobbing as though his body would tear itself apart.[45]

Genuine maturity involves the ability to know when our struggles are futile, thus permitting ourselves to admit vulnerability. This is a major component of genuine humility. Being a Christian demands that we *not* automatically give in to the ever-present temptation to become so jaded by the appearances of this world and the occasionally rather dismal conditions of our lives that we lose sight of the essential truths lurking in the stories of Jesus, the dreams of childhood, in fairy tale and Romance. There is hope and love and joy in the warmly-lit stable at Bethlehem (though it may be largely a creation of the Medieval analogical imagination) inviting us to join a mother and her newborn son. It is to this kind of real Home, "a pleasant house, inviting, reassuring, comforting," that Hugh finally returns, realizing that "once you went into its light you never left." And thus, on Easter night he comes home to Bethlehem, and darkness turns into light.

Despite the earnest efforts on the part of the psychiatric establishment and the gospel according to the contemporary intelligentsia, disillusionment and pessimism are not a universal panacea. "'One of the favorite themes of American literature,'" says Jim O'Neill in *Death in April*

"is about the middle-aged successful male who returns home with a nostalgic dream of his childhood sweetheart, discovers she was much less than the woman he dreamed she was, then leaves a sadder but wiser man. . . . He learns you can't go home again, you can't become young again, you can't live your life again. So with this wisdom he passes gracefully over the bar, so to speak, and settles down to accept growing old."

"And you have learned all these things, Jimmy?" He sounded worried now.

"No way," said O'Neill hollowly. "I haven't learned a goddamn one of them—not yet anyway."[46]

This passage reinforces the message by challenging the reader to contrast the Catholic/Romantic notions with the fashionable pessimism of the intellectual elite. Greeley implies that the solution for contemporary despair and alienation may well consist in allowing ourselves to trust in our propensity toward hope, no matter how foolish and unrealistic it may appear. The dream of going home, the dream of becoming young again, the dream of a new start are precisely the kind of horizon we need to make life worth living by presenting us with images of a gracious Reality beneath and beyond the actualities of violence, hatred, betrayal, and envy which testify to the perverse joy human beings take in inflicting pain upon each other. Each of us is called upon to choose between two modes of being: life based on suspicion and distrust or life based on openness and faith in grace. Paradise/Home Lost can be Paradise/Home Regained if we resist the temptation to reject the divine invitation for fear that we are simply not good enough and that it is too good to be true. In this perspective, original sin consists in "the sin of distrust—of cosmic distrust; it is the sin of refusing to believe that the universe in which we find ourselves is trustworthy and therefore the sin of refusing to believe that the power which produced the universe and placed us in it is trustworthy."[47] Have faith, Greeley seems to say, and you can indeed go home again. The light you see in yonder window pane is not a fatal flame about to consume you; the house is not a trap designed to devour you (though demonic houses have been known to do precisely that). Your real enemy is fear, fear of letting go, fear of yielding to God's tender passion, fear of having to admit that you are not self-sufficient.

There is an exceedingly fine line between the pseudo-Christian and pseudo-Romantic "Home Sweet Home" and the genuine Christian and Romantic intuition of Home as a symbol of psychic wholeness and divine love, the twin goals of every life. One possible way to distinguish the two might be the extent to which the sacramental Home is a place/condition which allows for growth through honestly-expressed conflict and refuses to gloss over imperfections. These characteristics are diametrically opposed to the Disney World variety of illusory home symbolized by an imitation of Mad King Ludwig's Neuschwanstein, itself a tasteless, gaudy, and fundamentally phony nineteenth-century version of the lived reality of medieval chivalry.

It is this distinction which is addressed in the final passage from *Lord of the Dance*. Danny has come home, come back from the dead to his wife and daughter. This is his first afternoon after he has decided to stop running and accept the invitation. He has come home to an afternoon of "pouring out the anger and the frustration, the hurt and the pain, the betrayal and disappointment of the last two decades." But none of it matters. Primal powers are discharged in the interpersonal thunderstorm, individual tests individual, and even as they argue they relate to each other, knowing they care, because without caring there would be no point in doing battle. The peace promised within the earthly home is not the peace of stagnation but the peace of passionate encounter leading to growth and development. Danny and Irene are in love. Never mind the angry words. Fire yearns for water, and soon their passions will be spent in more constructive ways. Irene is the ancient Hesta, goddess of the hearth, mistress of the home, who transforms eggs (appropriate Easter symbols of fertility and rebirth) into a ham and cheese omelet. Danny has been admitted to the sacred precinct, and like Hugh, he will never leave.

The City

Outside, the night air was balmy and pleasant. Thousands of people crowded toward a tall pink tower located at the end of a short street that angled off the plaza. They entered the building, took an elevator down and emerged at the edge of a vast arena that appeared to be part gymnasium and part swimming pool.[48]

They descended three levels beneath the city, under the basement level of the great buildings, lower than the vast underground transportation and communication network, to the level of the old granaries, now abandoned and musty. In the floor of one of these ancient storerooms there was a rusty hatch which pulled up with surprising ease. Stone steps led down to another much smaller room which appeared to be of even more ancient vintage. Out of this room ran a network of tunnels to still more chambers. Zylong was built, like ancient Rome on Terra, over catacombs.[49]

The city and Lynnie. Lynnie and the city. Elegant, outrageous, crude, energetic, unbearable, astonishing, brilliant, shallow, captivating, and, finally, imprisoning. Two decades ago he did not know why he ran away; now he did. He had to be free; he could not go on being Lynnie's pet poodle, the great novelist as captured animal, paraded at the weddings and graduations which seemed to occupy every day as the horrors of the summer heat began. . . .

Chicago as Camelot, Lynnie as Guinevere. He looked up the massive slab of the Hancock Center, unbelievably tall and yet so carefully proportioned as to be totally unoppressive. Nice towers in this Camelot.[50]

The restaurant where they went for supper after he'd checked into his "respectable" motel a mile off Las Vegas Boulevard, was typical of the city—superb steak, a juke box affirming that what Lola wants Lola gets, and slot machines clanking in the background. Beef and money, that's our Vegas.

Las Vegas fascinated and repelled Hugh—pulsating, frantic, empty, hopeful, despairing, unsmiling, youthful, ancient. Purgatory and hell rolled into one, with perhaps a touch of the excitement of paradise.[51]

He turned his head for a final look at the green sky-scraper. It's graceful sweep was somehow similar to the graceful sweep of her [his wife's] warm and lovely breasts. "The Holy Ghost . . . with warm breast and with ah! bright wings."

That's when the Lord God intervened.

Later Red would insist to his priests and his psychiatrist that . . . he heard a "whooshing" sound in the air behind him, like someone swinging a mighty two-by-four. . . .

Then time stood still, the whole of eternity filling a single second and a single second filling the whole of eternity. He was opened up like a lock on the Chicago River and everything flowed into him, the 333 Wacker Building, the City, the blue sky, the world, the cosmos. With them came a love so enormous that his own puny identity was submerged in it like a piece of driftwood in the ocean. The invading love was searing, dazzling, overwhelming. It filled him with heat and light, fire that tore at his existence and seemed about to destroy him with pleasure and joy. Redmont Peter George Kane SAW. . . .

He SAW.

What?

The unity of everything in the universe and his own place in that unity, the certainty that everything would be all right.[52]

Then the love that had lurked behind the green glass skyscraper at 333 Wacker Drive swooped with ah! bright wing into the small studio apartment and took possession of him.

No, rather the Holy Ghost, or whatever, erupted from the emerald and from his wife's swelling breasts. Yes, of course, warm breast. Eileen was not merely the occasion of this new love which invaded their room and their bed of pleasure. She and the love were temporarily bound together in one eternal love. . . .

It was like Wacker Drive. Light, heat, fire, over-whelming, invading, possessing love; dazzling truth,

beauty and goodness; confidence, hope, joy, the promise
that all would be well; a love so unspeakably powerful that,
in the instant it possessed Red, he knew he could never
escape from it. Nor would it ever permit him and Eileen to
escape from one another. When the joy seemed so intense
that he knew he would die, the operator of this transcendental Concorde Jet turned on the afterburners and Red
thought he had died and was in heaven, a golden city
whose ivory walls were his wife's breasts.[53]

    One of the most pervasively powerful feminine images in
Greeley's fiction is the ever-present City—Chicago, in his private symbolic universe—but a Chicago which stands for the
great cities of all times, for civilization itself. She is that second
womb after the original Magna Mater of primal, raw, boundless
creative energy had been overcome and harnessed to yield ordered society. Thus Pallas Athena, Queen of the Air, the "Spirit
of Life . . . not strength in the blood only, but formative energy
in the clay . . . inspired and impulsive wisdom in human conduct and human art,"[54] is one of the second generation of Greek
gods and serves as the mighty patroness of Athens where Western civilization first burst into flower. The city is an archetype of
the cosmos, surrounded by walls in ancient times, magic circles
of defense, designed to separate "sacred, ordered space" from
the demonic chaos without, long before they began to serve the
practical purpose of keeping out greedy neighbors.[55] For civilized humanity, cities came to take on the same significance as
sacred enclosures, and temples (or cathedrals) assumed the role
of mountain summits and the closely-guarded center of the
"labyrinth."[56] In archetypal language, the feminine space of the
city surrounded (and protected) the phallic tower. Ultimately,
the city as a whole is an androgynous archetype; its power, like
that of the boat, consists in the union of the masculine and the
feminine.
    This preconscious image in its demonic aspect is brought to
the surface in Greeley's blatantly sexual symbolism presented in
the first citation (a passage from the original version of Part One
of "The Final Planet," significantly called "The City"). The

"pink tower" at the center of Zylong is the site of a particularly
bloody form of athletic contest between young men and wom-
en, an elaborate, vicious, and violent ballet performed in front
of a large and strangely uninvolved audience, in an underground
arena, described as part gymnasium and part swimming pool.
The cruelty and sadism of the spectacle is only slightly mitigated
by medical future-world "miracles" which allow for almost in-
stantaneous healing of wounds. All of this happens within the
context of a rigidly controlled, artistically and physically almost
entirely sterile society.

   If healthy, vital, positive sexuality is repressed, it emerges
in demonic and destructive forms. The forces of life become the
harbingers of death, as readers of "Happy are the Clean of
Heart" and "The Angels of September" will note. A quarter
century ago Greeley wrote that "Technology will not be abandoned, the big city will not be deserted, but *both must be sanctified*."⁵⁷ His program is still the same, and it seems that the
required sanctification takes place through a cosmic equivalent
of—sexual intercourse. The fictional future Zylong society is
almost totally alienated from its natural roots; sexuality has been
channeled into the twin metaphorical cul-de-sacs of stylized
sensuality and periodic corporate and anonymous orgiastic release, a moribund culture's imitation of ancient Celtic cycles of
extended ascetic denial punctuated by times of enthusiastic affirmation of the flesh. The force of love has been severed from
primal erotic power and both have become barren. It is a city
doomed to die unless somehow the ancient channels are restored
and the powerful rivers of passion and love are again allowed to
intermingle spontaneously. The image is terrifying, precisely
because it captures a very real scenario one might project for our
own future. Zylong represents one possible ultimate consequence of the kind of dualistic separation of spirit and matter,
agape and *eros*, which has marked official Christian teachings
almost from the beginning. It seems not accidental that Zylong
life also bears certain similarities to conditions prevailing in the
late Roman empire.

   The second passage reinforces the original image. A final,
cosmic battle is about to be waged. In a scene right out of a
Jungian dreamscape, salvation depends on descending into an

ancient, "subzylongian" labyrinth, beneath the underground abandoned granaries (another metaphor for barrenness or rejection of the feminine), the even lower "realm of the mothers" (sought by Faust), complete with false prophets and the promise of hope symbolized by an interlude of distinctly non-Zylongian (and hence illicit) lovemaking.

The third quotation introduces the symbolic association of femininity, the city, and the "magic princess" in a more contemporary setting. Lynnie of *Death in April* is compared to Chicago—"elegant, outrageous, crude, energetic, unbearable, astonishing, brilliant, shallow, captivating, and finally, imprisoning." Jim/humanity does not wish to be captured and continues his/its ultimately futile struggle to escape that alluring and powerful city deity. He seeks his Camelot and Magic Maiden, but once both are within his grasp he cannot help doing his utmost to maintain his independence and affirm his illusory autonomy. He knows that he is not complete without either but resents that imagined weakness. Ultimately, though, he comes to comprehend the real purpose of his pilgrimage. In his imagination the Hancock Center turns into the towers of Camelot, no longer the Camelot he had previously attempted to dismiss as a collection of miserable mud huts,[58] but the glorious fortress of his Celtic tradition, the earthly equivalent of the heavenly city, with structures "incredibly tall but so carefully proportioned as to be totally unoppressive." In a Christian perspective the feminine city turns into the Church, and the towers become the spires of Gothic cathedrals (such as Notre Dame de Paris), at once solidly anchored in the ground *and* pointing toward heaven, symbolizing protective, uniting, and transcending love, *not* ruthless and rigid power.

Yet, like Woman (and life), the city is ambiguous, now "Fair Bride" and now "Whore." Las Vegas represents the harlot, Sodom and Gomorrah, in her contemporary incarnation. Intensely feminine, she shimmers in the beguiling iridescence of decay, adorned with rhinestone diamonds, a *Mardi Gras*/Hieronymus Bosch scene of gilded plastic and orgiastic frenzy, the hollow promise of hell masquerading as paradise complete with the chimeric vision of instant riches/salvation. She is addictive, like heroin, the true "opium of the people," devouring her victims, and revealing the stench of decay only after they have been lulled into submission by her sweet yet deadly perfumes.

The city must be sanctified. Nowhere does Greeley express this process of sanctification more powerfully than in the two final quotations. Red Kane's Chicago is literally invaded by that Spirit of Fire and Love who transformed a motley group of first-century Jews into the vital, passionately-committed shock troops of a new faith. For an eternal instant Chicago, the earthly city, becomes the *civitas Dei* and is utterly transfigured. The categories of space and time no longer apply. Past, present, and future, civilization and nature, all of humanity melt and merge into one. Knowledge is absolute. Teilhard's noosphere has broken into the everyday of the sidewalk in front of the 333 Wacker building, a cool, carved, curvaceous, mysteriously *feminine* presence of sea green glass, the center of cosmic consciousness, which for Red Kane is inexplicably and inextricably linked with his wife's seductive image. Chicago, Everycity USA, is the New Zion, aglow with the power of love; and Red Kane, hardbitten journalist and reluctant mystic, finds himself swept into the whirlwind of the Spirit and filled with a most unexpected and at times most uncomfortable assurance of the ultimate graciousness of Reality. Subsequent chapters will deal in more detail with the Red/Eileen transcendental marriage-renewal experience. For the moment, however, it should suffice to point to the essential symbolic association of the green-glass curvaceous, contemporary architectural "goddess," Eileen's green eyes and pale, swelling breasts, and the crystalline, trance-inducing emerald with the word-transforming and mind-shattering encounter with the Holy Spirit of Absolute Love. The Heavenly City reveals itself not as a distant place but rather as a different dimension of the here and now, a state of supreme ecstasy and golden, joyous luminosity within the individual soul touched by God Herself. Red Kane's (and Andrew Greeley's) Chicago has truly become the New Zion. The City *has been sanctified.*

part two

the journey

five

the two faces
of eros

Religious Dimensions of Sexuality

And God said, Let us make man in our image, after our likeness: . . . So God created man in his own image; in the image of God he created him; male and female created he them.[1]

"You are a wonderful person. Ellen." Pat said suddenly, breaking the peace that had settled on them."

"Thank you, Pat," she said simply.

He took her in his strong arms and kissed her passionately. I like being kissed this way, she reflected dreamily.

Then he changed. He snatched the beer bottle from her hand, hurled it into the lake, and pulled her to the sand. . . . She screamed and tried to wrench herself away.

"No one will hear you here," he shouted at her and pinned her to the sand with one massive hand. She gave up, whimpering in surrender while he fondled her.

Her tears broke the spell of his violence. He released her and staggered drunkenly toward the edge of the water.

Ellen grabbed her purse and fled into the woods, dodging in terror the suddenly looming monsters that haunted the dark trees. . . .

Pat lunged into the water, ripping the surface of the lake apart. God forgive me . . . please, please, forgive me. . . . I'll drown. No one will miss me . . .

He was slipping under the water. His lungs were filling. It hurt as though they were on fire. He instinctively struggled to the surface again, felt a smooth wall against his grasping hand, clawed at it, and found a rope. He hung on, a last link with life. Why not let go? Why not let go?

He decided to live.

The rope was an anchor from a good-size sailboat moored deep in the lake. . . .

A man and a woman were on the boat. Not young, not old, they were partially undressed and relaxed in a casual embrace. . . . More temptation. He should leave before he saw anything that would make him filthier than he already was.

He did not swim away. He was fascinated by the relaxed and leisurely posture of the couple. How could something that was fever-producing in him be so sedate for them? The woman laughed, a low, soft laugh of pleasure. His stomach turned in disgust. Careful not to make a noise, Pat slipped away from the anchor and swam toward the state-park beach. Much later, he lay there naked and exhausted, gasping for breath. He thought of Ellen's terrified sobs and of the woman's pleased laugh. . . . He groaned in despair. If only God would strike him dead.

Then the strange light came, a soft bowl of light, rising up from the waters of the lake, floating slowly down the beach. It circled around him, then enveloped him. Time stood still. Peace, joy, forgiveness, love, flooded into the depths of his being. The light warmed him. It cleansed and renewed him. Ellen was in the light; the woman on the boat; Maureen, too. All the women in the world were there with him, nursing, healing, loving him.

Then they merged into a woman in a white and gold gown. She told him what to do if he were to be free of the damnation that was fighting for his soul.[2]

gain Ellen appears as a Christianized Kore, the virgin archetype of the third chapter, the mysterious primal maiden,
unconsciously bridging the chasm between light and darkness,
life and death. Patrick, like a bumbling Hades, reenacts (though
incompletely) the ancient rape, thus initiating her into the "other" world, forever beyond the gates of innocence. According to
Karl Kerenyi, Persephone "was worshiped in the most serious
manner as the *Queen of the Dead*, and the rape of the bride was an
allegory of death. Lost maidenhood and crossing the borders of
Hades are allegorical equivalents, . . ."[3] Unconsciously, Ellen
bears a double aspect. In her previously discussed encounter
with Kevin, she represents the pure, life-giving, perfect bud of
virgin femininity. In her encounter with Patrick she emerges in
her dark Demeter-Erynis association, connected with violent
and abusive, and hence demonic, sexuality. "To enter into the
figure of Demeter," writes Kerenyi, "means to be pursued, to be
robbed, raped, to fail to understand, to rage and grieve, but then
to get everything back and be born again. And what does this
mean, save to realize the universal principle of life, the fate of
everything mortal?"[4] The passage also evokes echoes of the
Eleusian mysteries in the course of which initiates passed
through initiation rites involving darkness, water, and a mysterious "sacred marriage" hoping to encounter the ultimate vision
of the original Kore unfolding into Demeter, Artemis, and Persephone, the unity of maiden, mother, and child, a being that
dies, gives birth, and comes to life again.

Beyond this archetypal core the passage captures much of
the essentially ambiguous and paradoxical spectrum of human
sexuality, which ranges from the demonic to the divine and is in
its purely physiological form (as brain research shows) closely
associated to aggression as well as to the maternal need to nur-
ture and protect. Human beings, however, while also primates,
are not merely primates. On the biological level we are distinguished by our constant preoccupation with sex in all its forms,
recreational as well as procreative. On the psychological level
we are distinguished by our use of language and our insistence
on transforming experience into meaning. Our human uniqueness seems somehow suspended between the poles of sex and
symbol. Both of these passions combine with the equally fundamental tendency toward sympathy to form this peculiar hybrid
we humans call "love," and which, Denis de Rougemont and

Anders Nygren notwithstanding, cannot be neatly separated into demonic *eros* (whether carnal or spiritual) and divine *agape*. Like all human relationships, but more radically so, love is a complex harmony sounded upon the foundation of our pervasive sexual (not to be confused with genital) potential, the universal human need to break through the cocoon of alienation, seeking to possess another and, even more importantly, to be possessed by another. While sexuality can obviously be discussed as an isolated, purely biological phenomenon, without reference to the meaning system out of which it has emerged and which it tends to posit, this kind of clinical sex-manual approach tends to be pathetically useless for men and women in concrete situations.

Patrick Donahue is a troubled teenager (destined to grow into a tormented Prince of the Church), incapable of resolving a number of interlocking battles raging within his soul. Pathologically insecure, he deeply resents a fate which allowed him to be born the son of a garbage man. He experiences his own sexuality primarily in moralistic and proscriptive terms, as temptation to sin, and as additional proof of his essential depravity. He despises himself and is consequently incapable of genuinely caring for others. He uses an erratic, fervent piety to placate his conscience after the inevitable binges of beer guzzling and sexual experimentation. As a matter of fact, his sin is not carnality so much as cowardice, the pathological fear of discovering himself and having to confront the real Patrick. An authentic sexual relationship (like all forms of friendship) involves accepting one's own androgyny and yielding to the alternating configurations of submission and dominance. Only those reasonably secure in their own masculinity and femininity can dare open themselves to the radical disclosure and commitment demanded by authentic human intimacy and respond to the limit-experience of sexual differentiation with its mysterious rhythms of giving and taking.

Prior to the incident, Patrick has been ridiculed by a social snob. He is hurt, angry, and drunk. He turns to Ellen for comfort, the way a child with a skinned elbow might run to his mother. The kiss unleashes more violent passions, a deeper need, which in turn confirms his sense of inferiority and uselessness. He is simultaneously attracted and repelled by that primal need and the vulnerability it implies.

Ellen is not a casual pickup, she is his friend, and precisely for that reason her delighted and innocent response to his passionate kiss awakens the demons within his soul. She asks him to risk being open, to risk being gentle and caring, to risk being happy. Ellen is grace, and his drunken assault on her represents rejection of grace. In his self-pity and self-hatred he cannot believe that God might call him to be happy, might expect him to take delight in those sensations and feelings which he considers symptoms of corruption. His already fragile sense of self rebels at this physiological and psychological hunger for another in whom he senses both the promise of transcendent joy and the possibility of personal, individual annihilation. It is precisely the sacramental potential of the sexual experience which terrifies Patrick who is profoundly and intuitively aware of the connection between *eros* and *thanatos*.

Like Adam and Eve in the primal garden *after* and despite having eaten of the forbidden fruit, he is both pathetically innocent—and ignorant. What was their *real* sin? Eating from the forbidden tree, which permitted them to know and through knowledge to attain full humanity? Or might it have been that first infernal lie, a lie not in words but in action, the lie of covering their nakedness, of concealing their sexuality? Two fig leaves to foster the illusion that men and women are the same, that both are complete in themselves and neither needs the other? Why did they do it? Did they really think they might be able to deceive God, the all-knowing, who had created them in the divinely androgynous image, giving them in their hunger for each other a hint of a God passionately in love with them, the Holy as active, demanding, and involved, a "Thou" calling them to respond. In and through Ellen, Patrick touches the Holy and experiences it as a demon he seeks to exorcise from within himself.

"Each man kills the thing he loves," writes Oscar Wilde in his "Ballad of Reading Goal." Wilde's love is, of course, not real love, but something which masquerades as love among those who are incapable of accepting themselves and consequently must possess and destroy others. It seems, however, that even to the extent that Ellen genuinely cares for Patrick, he must seek to destroy her, because that love, even more than his physical desire, is part of a mysterious, terrifyingly fascinating power which seeks to draw him out of himself, a white-hot flame which attracts him the way a moth is attracted, only to be consumed.

Fire and water. The flame is extinguished by her tears. His violence abates, but her tears do not cleanse him. They are not the waters of baptism and renewal. They save her for the moment (though she will never be quite the same) while casting him into the depths of self-recrimination and despair. She flees into the forest, and he descends into the pit of self-hatred and self-pity. Again his real sin, the sin which counts, is not the attempted rape (which Ellen and God are far more ready to forgive than he is ready to forgive himself) but his refusal to accept the possibility of Reality as gracious and loving. Shame at having injured another is appropriate; paralyzing, self-destructive guilt is not. Patrick cannot envision the possibility of changing precisely because, despite his occasional attacks of irrational and fervent piety, he is utterly lacking in genuine faith. Faith, hope, and love, that triad of supernatural virtues are his for the taking, but he consistently refuses to accept the invitation because he knows himself as a worthless worm. And in a strange and twisted way, it takes less courage to consider suicide than to face the possibility that he might be lovable and loved simply for himself.

The sexual imagery continues. Patrick plunges into the lake, symbolically immersing himself into the feminine principle. He is surrounded by primal woman, engulfed by her. Night and lake, universal archetypes of primordial, chaotic, fatal femininity, the merging of boundaries, death, decay, extinction. She is the "dark lady" who has haunted the human imagination since time immemorial, Lilith, Lorelei, Calypso, the one who promises return to the womb and forgetfulness. She embraces him and he almost yields to her beguiling presence.

A rope materializes providentially and just in time. God has not forsaken him. Patrick, though he does not yet know it, cannot save himself, cannot extricate himself from his private hell. He must yield to someone, he must allow others to assist him, he must admit that he is worth saving. He must respond to grace. And he does. For the moment life is stronger than death, youth and instinct provide the impetus. He hangs onto the rope, significantly attached to an anchor below and a boat above. In the boat a man and a woman recline in a casual embrace. This, too, is significant. For they provide Patrick with an alternate role model and an essential question: "How could something that was fever-producing poison in him be so sedate for them?" He has come face-to-face with the surd of sexuality. He is confronting a Zen *koan*, the unity of opposites. From that question, if he were to consider it carefully, if he were to allow it to sink into his consciousness, he might be able to draw the conclusion that the urges and fantasies which have haunted his days and dreams are not necessarily and essentially evil, that it is not only appropriate but also necessary that he come to terms with his sexual nature, that he at least try to understand and resolve the conflicts raging within his soul. He might even discover that God loves him and wants his happiness. Instead, for the moment, he simply listens to the woman's "low, soft laugh of pleasure," and in his typical manner he feels his stomach turn in disgust. Another instance of grace refused, of Christ denied.

Still, that resourceful Lady Paraclete who has been pursuing him relentlessly has not given up. Not yet. For at precisely the moment he wishes for God to strike him dead, he has a classical William James-type mystical experience, precipitated, one might presume, by the combination of alcohol, sexual arousal, and exhaustion, but nevertheless, like all such experiences, totally unexpected and gratuitous. What is this "bowl of light" he sees rising from the dark waters, which seeks him out and enfolds him in a warm, tender, forgiving, and primordially feminine Presence, the life-affirming complement to the previously encountered "dark lady" of death and dissolution?

Patrick encounters a mixture of the Eleusian vision, the birth of Aphrodite, and the Holy Grail, that marvelous complex fusion of pagan and Christian symbolism, that womanly counterpart to the masculine cross, signifying the intersection of the infinite and the finite, Spirit and Nature, the Incarnation with its promise of the Resurrection and Life Eternal. In the archetypal code of mythos and the collective unconscious, the cross can be interpreted as representing the (masculine) tree of life and the grail, the (feminine) lake of life. While the grail was never given magisterial approval as an official Christ-symbol, it has doggedly haunted our religious imagination and made its appearance in countless Romances, those secular and popular variations upon the theme of the Christian comedy of grace. The cross challenges, judges, and demands. The grail nurtures, accepts, and forgives. Both attitudes are essential to the Christian view of life and love being stronger than death.

Patrick, however, is incapable of interpreting his vision in any way other than by dedicating himself right then and there to the priesthood and celibacy. Like St. Bernard of Clairvaux, he sees two antithetical versions of love, carnal desire which disfigures and obscures the soul, and the leap of the virginal soul towards God which restores it to primal unity and purity. His precipitous decision to enter the priesthood is based on a combination of guilt and disgust with what he perceives to be the evil within his soul. Celibacy to him is not the charism of consecrated virginity founded precisely on the recognition of the essential goodness and inherent value of nongenital *and* genital sexuality. It does not represent the willing sacrifice of a treasure out of love for God. It represents, instead, the violent denial of his innermost nature, a psychic castration which must, inevitably, fail, leading either (as it will in his case) to repeated (and deeply regretted) instances of "broken vows," or (what is even more pernicious) a psychological twisting of the mind leading to self-righteous condemnation of any and all sexual practices not directly associated with procreation in marriage. In many ways both he and St. Bernard are victims of that branch of Christianity which has since the beginnings of theological reflections on the meaning and message of the Gospels identified woman and sexuality with evil. Considered in historical perspective, the early Church's emphasis on virginity and denial of the flesh seems unavoidable, and it represents the direct result of the combined forces of Jewish and Roman patriarchalism and the Greek religious and philosophical tendency toward radical dualism. Despite the clear message implicit in the Incarnation, and St. Paul's recognition of the sacramentality of nuptial sexuality (surprising and highly significant, given his strong personal bias in favor of celibacy) the early Church, in keeping with prevailing Gnostic, Manichaean, and neo-Platonic sentiment identified virtue with manliness and liberation from sin with rejection of one's sexuality. For women, in particular, disdaining the bondage of marriage and childbearing did represent release from enslavement to biology and the male power structure. This liberation, however, could only be achieved at the expense of their essential identity as women.

In the first century permanent celibacy was quite exceptional. Qumran and the community of the Therapeutae give evidence of such a life-style within Judaism, but it was practiced apart from the mainstream of Jewish culture, which considered marriage and the production of children a sacred duty. After all, Hosea had gone so far as to use the nuptial imagery of the Canaanites' fertility cult to describe the love of Yahweh for his bride, Israel, a whore at the moment but to be richly rewarded if she should change her ways. While most oriental cults knew temporary chastity, and castration was practiced in the worship of the Great Mother, Augustan legislation considered celibacy a privilege granted only in exceptional cases or to those over fifty. There is no question, however, that the immense primordial power of sexuality in all its manifestations was recognized in the Judeo-Christian tradition, leading both to official rules of conduct and to the use of highly charged erotic language to convey theological insights. It seems likely that the Old Testament custom of depicting Yahweh in passionate pursuit of his frequently wayward Bride led to such conventions as the Marriage Feast setting in eschatological writings. In the Apocalypse, for example, Christ is portrayed as united with his followers in the nuptials of the lamb after the final carnage and destruction. In such images Yahweh and Christ are identified with the bridegroom, and the Virgin and the Church with the bride. These allegories, if taken literally, might indicate that Christ was envisioned as preferring a virgin bride to one who had been deflowered by a human rival. Ultimately, however, most of the "virgo-mania" which has haunted the Christian consciousness almost since the beginnings of the faith is probably due to the dualistic metaphysics which, as I have already discussed in some detail, came to pervade early Christian thought, despite the fact that flesh-hating dualism was expressly repudiated in the doctrine of the Incarnation. On the other hand, the full significance of the Incarnation itself was partially compromised by the unnatural manner of Christ's conception and birth.

Teilhard de Chardin presents a particularly intriguing example of the extent to which dualism can influence even those who seek to transcend it. In areas other than sexuality, such as the ecstasy involved in pursuing science or the arts, Teilhard insists on the spiritual power of matter. Sexuality, on the other hand, he does not consider spiritually energizing as much as potentially confining and ideally to be eschewed once procreation is no longer a desired goal. Thus he anticipates a future in which the spiritual association of the sexes will increase while the "'reproductive' side and the physical acts which serve it"[5] will gradually yield to physical sexuality sublimated, conserved, and transformed into mutual spiritual fecundation, the radical freedom of Virginity. Thus, while he does not reject the carnal as such, he clearly follows Paul in considering celibacy the preferred state.

There are two species of creation myths: those which envision the world as proceeding from the primal maternal principle, a cosmic womb, born and nursed, and in that sense continuous with the principle of origin; and those which depict the world as created, made, by a father who is by necessity separate from his artifact. The former tend to support monistic speculation, the latter dualistic speculation. It is interesting to note that the Enlightenment concept of a clock-maker God, definitely male and essentially "other" from his creation, supportive of an extremely mechanistic model of the universe, is of the latter type; and it might be considered the ultimate perversion of the Western elite interpretation of the origin of all things. In contrast, Romantic thought tended to focus on the continuity of God and world, fusing the categories of subject and object. Monistic worldviews see no ultimate distinction between the processes of being born and dying. As Chuang Tzu stated concerning the death of his wife, why should he mourn for one who simply passed from non-manifestation to manifestation back to non-manifestation.[6] In this perspective, death is the necessary corollary of life. A universe produced by intelligence, on the other hand, is a world which at least theoretically could have been created without death, in the image of permanence. Thus the myth of the fall is necessary to explain the reality of death, *and* generation, since such a world need have no birth, either. Both death and birth are manifestations of impermanence, transience. Both are seen as inherent in the material and not in the spiritual principle. The monistic view does not distinguish strictly between the two, the boundaries merge, the realms flow into each other. Thus religions which focus on the primacy of the maternal/feminine/monistic principle tend to be viewed as threatening or demonic by those who hold the pater-nal/masculine/dualistic view. The all-encompassing womb of the former by its very nature contains the latter; the latter, however, envisions itself locked in a fierce struggle with the former. The ultimate reduction is one to a universe seen in terms of change (feminine/material) and a universe envisioned in terms of permanence (masculine/spiritual). The crucial chal-lenge presented to religions and philosophies of all ages has been to reconcile those two positions. Thus all of Western philosophy can in a sense be interpreted as a dialogue between the meta-physics of Heraclitus, representing change, and that of Parmen-ides, representing permanence. Sexuality fits into the pattern by its primal power and the undeniable datum that it reminds us both of our alienation and separateness, and our possibility of being joined to another. By its association with procreation, it is inextricably linked to the realms of both birth and death. The very fact that we come into existence carries within itself the realization that one day we shall cease to be. Having children provides both continuity and discontinuity, it constitutes, as Plato said, the participation of physical life in immortality. At the same time, it is a mighty reminder of mortality. In addition, sexuality is invariably experienced as ambiguous since it in-volves the experience of "passion" in both senses as extreme suffering and as primal, joyous, vital energy.

Patrick is incapable of allowing both the sacramental good-ness and power of Eros and the practice of asceticism to trans-form his life. One suspects that he would agree with the dualis-tic premises implied in the definition of moral asceticism given by Ries (and cited, as well as neatly demolished, by Karl Rahner):

Asceticism is the fight against all within us which comes from sin or leads to it; it is the holding down of all danger-ous urges of nature within us, of everything sensual and self-seeking, so that the spiritual man may develop all the more freely. It consists furthermore in a certain amount of voluntary renunciation of what is permitted, in accordance with the principle that attack is the best form of defense, which is applicable in the realm of human propensi-ties. . . . Anything which stirs in our lower nature as an

after-effect of original sin, anything which is diseased, cor-
ruptive and demonic in man, must be subjugated if the
noble spiritual dispositions are not to suffocate under the
pressure of the sense-life gaining the upper hand. The sup-
pressive spell of the sensual must be broken if the soul is to
rise and develop the full richness of the life of the spirit in
faithful cooperation with divine grace.[7]

Rahner points out that original sin in the Christian perspective cannot be identified with concupiscence but consists instead
in the loss of our supernatural union with God and the loss of
our primal holiness, and that genuine asceticism is never based
on the "false and cowardly minimization of the good it re-
nounces."[8] The Christian in his asceticism "becomes free, not in
order to wall up his heart but to give it away, to God and the
world."[9]

In a world hallowed by the Incarnation, sexuality becomes
one of the major means of experiencing the love of God, even
for celibates who, without engaging in genital contact, are nevertheless invited to delight in the primordial erotic call to love
and life. For those who have not received the charism of celibacy, their sexual nature allows them to experience fully the goodness of passion and the importance of commitment, that they
might shape their lives in the image of divine love and ultimately achieve a level of genuine intimacy. While Greeley does not
imply that sexual union is sacramental only when experienced in
the context of a properly blessed marriage, he does insist on
loving commitment and emphasizes the role of sexual attraction
in allowing human beings to maintain and renew long-term
relationships. It is through falling in love, not once or twice but
again and again, that we are allowed an earthly glimpse of the
divine banquet prepared for us, a vision of divine passion. "Sacramental sex is sex that is playful, sex that is fun, sex that is
relational,"[10] writes Mary Durkin, basing her analysis on that
most erotic of Judeo-Christian religious poems, the Song of
Songs. It is precisely this hidden dimension of sexuality which
the "new" Red Kane discovers after his transforming mystical
experience as he allows himself to fall in love with, once again,
or possibly for the very first time, his wife of twenty years, on
the night of All the Saints, a feast which significantly invites us

to reflect on the Beatitudes. As Greeley observes in *The Jesus Myth*:

[the Sermon on the Mount] is not a program for legislative and social reform. It is a description of a life-style by which we will know those who have accepted God's kingdom; a life-style which flows, albeit not easily, from the joy and happiness and love which one experiences when one has decisively responded to the invitation of the wedding feast.[11]

Red Kane has been invited (rather forcefully, I might add) to accept God's love, and he is about to respond in the only really appropriate manner: by loving another, by loving Eileen. Thus divine love is transformed, deepened, and in a sense consummated as it flows from us toward our fellow humans and commences that marvelous, continuous cycle of expanding and deepening love which unites us with one another and with God.

That night, however, he did not worry about his sanity. He would sort things out in the morning. For the moment, it was sufficient to know that the Lord God had entered his life like a barrage of skyrockets exploding over Grant Park on the Fourth of July and that the first order of business was to once again envelop his wife in the fire of love which had, in some as yet inexplicable way because of her, taken possession of him on the banks of the Chicago River.

As he cautiously entered their bedroom, she came out of the bathroom, glistening and glowing in a white terry robe and smelling of soap and bath oil. Her hands rested uncertainly on the belt of the robe. . . .

It was the smell of soap, normally innocent of eroticism, which slashed away the remnants of Red's restraint. Fervently he tore open the robe, peeled it off her, tossed it on the floor and assaulted her with demented caresses. Her lips tasted of mouthwash and, faintly, of old fashioned. "Dear God in heaven, how much I love you!"

The Cheshire Smile seemed to whisper a warning in his ear. Not that way, you clumsy dolt. You know better than that.

The moment was both bitter and sweet. Bitter because of his memory of the wasted years and sweet because of the anticipation of the years to come. Bitter because he would never love her enough, sweet because there would be so much pleasure in trying. Even the marks of time, the lines and creases, the folds and softness which resisted Eileen's stern self-discipline made her more attractive. . . .

"You read the bible lately, Ei?" he asked casually, folding his arms and standing, naked and powerful lord of the manor, above her.

"Good Lord, Red," she laughed, "You're quite mad."

"I came across a poem from the Song of Solomon in a book the other day. The girl says to her guy that until the sun goes down, he should roam her body like a gazelle or a young stag roams the mountain."

"Dirty book," she murmured, now soft and alight with desire.

"Interesting place to find a love manual," he sat next to her as though he were going to begin an advanced seminar on Old Testament studies.

"Please, Red," she begged.

With his index fingers he traced designs on her body, from her shoulders to her loins and back. . . . "Does that feel like a gazelle? Or a young stag, Oh Daughter of Jerusalem?" . . . .

So easy to arouse. A passionate woman who had been deprived of sex for much too long a time. Regret filled his soul like a melting river at the end of a hard winter fills its flood plain. Regret made him love her all the more. He would spend the rest of his life making up for his past failures. . . .

"Good God!" Eileen screamed, her body arching up from the bed.

Maybe, Red thought. Maybe.

At least someone very much like Him.

With his hands and his lips he took away his wife's sanity, her separateness as a person, her boundaries of self protection. . . .

"When is sunset?" she begged as in desperation she dragged him down on herself. . . .

As he held her poised precariously above the abyss of rapture, another monumental wave of love for Ellen washed over Red's spirit as healing grace. Perhaps—the thought rushed through his head—that's the way the One with the baseball bat feels about me. His lips returned to her face with infinitely delicate kisses. All right, he had failed all his other responsibilities to her. He's only been a good husband on the rare occasions when his body was driven by lust to seek entry into hers. Nonetheless, that was better than nothing. Only a coward would deprive a splendid woman of this joy which was so easily given. Only a fool would not take the risk that joyous passion might transform the rest of their relationship.

. . . "I love you, Eileen," he murmured, stroking her cheek. "I'll always love you."

Stretching luxuriously, Eileen slipped away from him and jabbed at his ribs. "The thing is, King Solomon, the daughter of Jerusalem has her own herd of gazelles, or to quote your text," she wiggled on top of him, "their own little foxes." . . .

. . . Eileen dragged him down into a primal swamp of not quite fulfilled desire, . . . inhabited by demanding kisses and gentle but persistent fingers and darting electrical impulses which exorcised his guilts and his regrets, his convictions of failure and worthlessness, his self-hatred and self-contempt. He sank into the sweet, savory, and tenaciously strong, warmth of mother earth.

Then, with giddy laughter Red Kane and his woman gave themselves over to the completion of their delightful work. Their love became an unrestrained eruption of two fire storms compelled to merge forever. . . . Finally there was satiety and peace. The naked female animal who had raced wildly down the mountainside with him was now a peaceful little girl, asleep in his arms. He drew the comforter and sheet protectively over her and turned out the lights. . . .

Did you like that?

The question was addressed to God. Since there was no answer, he continued the dialogue.

I don't know what the hell You're getting me into, besides my wife. So far I like it. Keep it up. This being mystic is fun.[12]

The episode from which these passages are taken is one of the most carefully crafted, powerful, and symbolically "pregnant" renditions of the sacramental potential of the sexual encounter Greeley has ever attempted. In their ecstatic lovemaking, Red and Eileen almost seem to reenact the cosmic process of creation and assume the roles of Yahweh and his Bride in both their alternating active and passive manifestations. Motifs introduced in other works, such as God as third party in a ménage à trois and Jim O'Neill's at least partially demonic re-absorption into the cauldron of primal femininity discussed in the "Magna Mater" section of this study, make a new and transfigured appearance as Red listens to the "Cheshire Smile" and finds himself submerged into the "primal swamp," the "sweet savory, and tenaciously strong warmth of mother earth." Once again Uranos and Gaia, Yahweh and the *Shekinah,* perform their ancient and ever-new *hieros gamos,* at once solemn, sacred ritual, violent fusion of elemental forces, and creative play appropriate to a laughing God.

It is not accidental that Red and Eileen are husband and wife, and as such present the earthly manifestation of the androgynous deity and the marriage of Christ and the Church. The human relationship with God is by its very nature "bittersweet," and for precisely the same reasons which occur to Red during that poignantly pensive moment: from the finite perspective, the sweetness of letting ourselves respond to Her love is eternally poised against our sense of regret at having refused Him for so long; the supreme joy of loving Him is inextricably wedded to our realization that we can never love Her enough. The positive and negative poles of that primordial oscillation emerge in the mystical consciousnous as the "joyful consciousness of the Transcendent Order," a sense of "Divine Presence," and the "Dark Night of the Soul," respectively.[13] Ultimately, the dualism can be transcended in the final stage of the mystic experience, genuine union which shatters (albeit only temporarily) the finite hourglass, allowing brief sojourns into the unknown beyond. "Union," writes Evelyn Underhill, is "the true goal of the mystic quest. In this state the Absolute Life is not merely perceived and enjoyed by the Self, as in Illumination, but is *one* with it."[14]

It is also highly significant that Eileen in her incarnation as "Daughter of Jerusalem" (God's people) finds Red's new personality so terrifying, his (and one suspects, her own) consuming passion so overpowering, so insane, that she eventually insists that he submit himself for psychiatric observation. As Greeley has pointed out repeatedly, the kind of divine love which emerges from the parables of Jesus is, in a purely worldly perspective, totally irrational, an invitation to break through the neat categories of time, space, and propriety which govern our mundane lives. Red has been touched by the numinous, terrifyingly attractive, agonizingly joyous, living center of reality; he has, in a sense, been charged like a battery with divine energy, and, in the marriage bed, this raw kinetic power of primordial love is discharged into his wife (paradoxically and significantly, the catalyst of the original mystical experience on Wacker Drive) who responds with the typically human, ego-protective reaction of terror in face of the unknown. Eileen manifests essential ambivalence. "We're falling in love again," she remarks. "It's your fault, woman. You've been trying to seduce me for the last three weeks," he observes. "Five actually," she admits.[15] Eileen's subtly persistent erotic campaign to recapture her husband had weakened his ego-protective shell and somehow inexplicably prepared him for that divine "takeover" on Wacker Drive. Nevertheless, she has learned to live with the "old Red," whose rarely employed skills as a lover had placated her physical needs without demanding that she open up the innermost core of her being to radical fusion. She will be terrified of this new, totally unexpected (at least on the conscious plane), "Fire of Love." Thus Moses experienced divine love in the form of a burning bush.

In "Patience of a Saint" more clearly than in any of the novels, Greeley states his fundamental theme of sexuality as sacramental agent of renewal and rebirth, allowing two individuals theoretically committed to each other in marriage to bridge the invariable chasms of habit and alienation which continuously threaten even the best of relationships. The point is not so much the original conquest, and his heroes and heroines do not simply live "happily ever after" while the curtain falls and the house lights come on. His are not the hackneyed endings of the standard romances which present sexual union as the climactic but hidden event after all obstacles have been overcome. Instead, Eros provides not only the implicit dynamics, the energy necessary to inspire the initial quest, but, even more importantly, allows for continued hope, the possibility that the Grail, the Magic Prince or Princess once attained can be recaptured again and again with passion and tenderness, and that in the light of divine love the "lines and creases" of advancing age will add to rather than detract from the beauty of one's beloved.

Being human we will fall and fail. Promises made to others, to ourselves, even to God will be broken. Regret can be both destructively paralyzing (if steeped in despair) and powerfully invigorating (if wedded to faith and hope). "Today is the first day of the rest of our lives!" How many among us really understand this deceptively simple statement; and yet, if we did, how much agony we might spare ourselves and those we love. Just as the Scriptures present the story of a God madly in love with Her/His spouse and pursuing that spouse with relentless, insane recklessness, human beings in touch with that divine Eros and willing to apply the divine paradigm to their lives are able to overcome periods of separation and barrenness and are able to defeat the demons of shame and guilt. Taking God into our hearts means to take the risk of daring to admit that we might have wronged the one we claim to love, that we might have allowed habit and boredom to starve the delicate, and yet incredibly hardy, vine of love. It means to take the chance of being rejected and ridiculed. It means to leap into the unknown. Red could not have done it alone. His armor had to be broken, his life had to be shattered to allow the gentle, caring, loving, passionate, God-intoxicated, *real* Red Kane another chance for a new life.

Fidelity, Greeley remarks in *Sexual Intimacy,* is not so much a matter of staying out of somebody else's bed (though that may well be the ultimate result of a truly loving relationship), as it is

> a permanent commitment to "reach out" for the other, a promise to persist in efforts to transcend the barriers and the distance that separate one from the other, a firm resolve to maintain effort in sustaining and developing the relationship no matter what difficulties and trials arise.[16]

A positive asceticism of sexuality allows us to develop our capacities as lovers to the utmost limits of our capabilities. It is based on the Catholic understanding of the sacramentality of the world, of the conviction, as stated by Karl Rahner in "Passion and Asceticism,"

> that the Christian religion, in the first article of its Creed, professes a God who in loving omnipotence has created every genuine reality between heaven and earth, a God who wills and loves this earth because he has created the visible just as much as the invisible and who has said that *everything* is good.[17]

In addition to providing sound advice for those seeking to establish and maintain a vital and powerful love-relationship, this particular lovemaking episode also allows for the mutual illumination of scriptural insight and sex. Not only does the Song of Solomon appear in a contemporary setting, but in a sense both Red and Eileen become transparent lenses which focus the active/passive oscillations of divine Love and communicate a sense of the mysterious passion which pervades the universe and is as potent today as it was when it started the cosmos with that mighty bang eons ago or inspired those anonymous young lovers three thousand years ago in Palestine. "The Daughter of Jerusalem," Eileen points out, with her lawyer's knack for getting to the core of an issue, "turns into a Mother from Sligo."[18] And in that deceptively simple remark, Greeley captures part of the mystery of all times, the ultimate paradox of Her Who Was, Who Is, and Who Ever Shall Be.

The Priest's Tale

THE GARDEN OF LOVE

I went to the Garden of Love,
And saw what I never had seen:
A Chapel was built in the midst,
Where I used to play on the green.

And the gates of the Chapel were shut,
And Thou Shalt Not writ over the door;
So I turn'd to the Garden of Love
That so many sweet flowers bore;

And I saw it was filled with graves,
And tombstones where flowers should be;
And Priests in black gowns were walking
their rounds,
And binding with briars, my joys & desires.[19]

William Blake

In fact, however, you are deformed material. You have been corrupted and perverted by your lives in the world. In order to make you good sisters we will have to remake you. We will have to crush the hold the world has on you and break you of your corrupt and sinful habits. . . .

It will not be easy. Most of you lack the docility for the work of destruction and reconstruction which is our task. . . .

You have left the world behind, young women—your friends, your family, your drinking and smoking, the boys with whom you may have sinned. All that is in your past. If we tolerate an occasional visit or letter from your family, that is for their sake and not for yours. . . . If it were up to me, there would be no family visits at all. They serve only to disrupt the order and discipline of community life. . . .

Above all we must strip you of your own willfulness. From this moment on you are to do God's will. And God's will is revealed to you by your superiors, who have special graces from God to know what you should do. . . . You are to become docile tools for the service of thc kingdom of God, who never question, never challenge, never hesitate and never think of disobedience. All your own self-seeking must be buried in the tomb before you are worthy to put on the Holy Habit, which will be the shroud you will wear to your grave. Your death to your old self begins now. You are preparing to die.[20]

We may not think that God does not see us when we commit terrible sins of the flesh. We may think he forgets the hideous illicit pleasures we enjoy with the sacred bodies he has given us. We may deceive ourselves into believing that there will be no day of reckoning on which we will have to pay a thousandfold in pain for every single passing moment of perverted fleshly amusement we experience. But God is just. God remembers, God punishes, God turns pleasure into pain, God uses the very organs of our sin to punish us with unspeakable suffering for all eternity. When you sin with a part of the body, which ought to be the temple of the Holy Ghost, say to yourself that some day that part of your body will become a source of eternal pain to you, so great that you will wish you could cut it off and cast it into the fire. Then it will be too late. You will suffer unbearably forever. And even if you almost escape from hell, even if you have slipped away from the raging inferno, even if you begin to climb the high hill to heaven, you will not escape. God will send the laughing demons to pursue you and drag you back, screaming with despair to the hell in which you belong.[21]

These passages illuminate the consequences of close to two thousand years of consistent failure on the part of the Christian establishment to come to terms with the central challenge presented in the Incarnation: the invitation to accept the world and most specifically the human body and the fullness of human nature as "temples of God." It is this failure which has made it so difficult for us to experience the radical inner dimensions of the

Christ event in their initial pristine and transforming power. Two thousand years of dualistic metaphysical, theological, and moral speculation obscure and confuse the lived experience of God Incarnate who referred to Himself as nursing mother and refused to condemn the adulteress because she had "loved much." No wonder the possibility of accepting woman as an analogue for God and erotic love as a symbol of divine love seems a heretical notion. No wonder we have practically no categories in our Christian consciousness for a *positive* spirituality and asceticism of sexuality, and we spend (waste) almost all our time and effort arguing essentially peripheral issues such as the sinfulness (or lack thereof) of pre- and extramarital sex, birth control and homosexuality, as though that mighty river of love and life, that primal, raw, pervasive, biological *and* spiritual "nuclear" fusion energy could really be contained and channeled by a set of narrow and primarily negative rules (the Christian versions of often bizarre primitive taboos).

Androcentrism, patriarchalism, and Hellenistic dualism combined to leave the official doctrines of Christianity saddled with a profound suspicion of sexuality and the pleasures of the body coupled with what amounts to a pathological hatred of women as sexual beings. Patristic thinking interpreted the Christian message in terms of a dualistic model of a world irrevocably split into a realm of goodness and a realm of evil, identified with spirit and matter, soul and body, maleness and femaleness, respectively. Although the Old Testament characters were generally married, often polygamous, and tended to give in to their sexual passions with impetuous abandonment (and occasionally dire consequences), and despite the use of vividly erotic imagery to illustrate the passionate relationship of Yahweh with His Bride, Israel, human sexual mores became the focal point for legalistic hair-splitting and vicious, irrational attacks. Jesus himself was hardly an ascetic. He enjoyed good food, good wine, and good company, and he was critical of the Pharisees rather than the adulteress they dragged before him. He celebrated human life as grounded in the overflowing bounty of gratuitous divine love, and he sought to liberate his followers from the strictures of the Torah, not in order to have them break all the old laws but in order to allow them to start acting in response to the passionately loving deity and out of a spirit of mutual respect and delight. He liberated us for a life grounded in a positive commitment to hope, faith, and each other. There is no reason to assume that this celebration did not include men and women equally, and every part of the human anatomy. Jesus did not challenge his disciples to go into the wilderness and stop participating in the fullness of life; he challenged them to proclaim the kingdom of God.

Elisabeth Schüssler Fiorenza makes an excellent case for the hypothesis that while women were revelatory agents and held leadership positions in the early Church, this fact was largely redacted out of the Gospels and deliberately denied in Patristic writings.[22] After all, both theological texts and traditions were produced under the auspices of a dominant clerical patriarchy which insisted on relegating women to marginal status and displacing them as ecclesial and theological subjects. Ironically, it is precisely this redaction process, combined with incensed Patristic diatribes concerning the unseemly behavior of "uppity" Christian females, which allows us tantalizing glimpses of the early Christian movement as a discipleship of equals which permitted female involvement and leadership in clear opposition to the prevailing patriarchal practices of Greco-Roman society. While the canon itself includes only scant reflections of an egalitarian, non-misogynist early Christian ethos, those distorted images still allow us to recognize that the process of patriarchalization did not begin until some time *after* the establishment of the Church, and it involved a definite power struggle. After all, there is no need to attack something which does not exist.

> The history and theology of women's oppression perpetuated by patriarchal biblical texts and by a clerical patriarchy must not be allowed to cancel out the history and theology of the struggle, life, and leadership of Christian women who spoke and acted in the power of the Spirit.[23]

> Women, looking to the most prestigious texts of the Western tradition, confront misogyny, idealization, objectification, silence. The absence of female consciousness from that tradition challenges a feminist interpretation to look beyond and through the texts. The absence anchors one

term of a double meaning. The silences, all the more difficult to restore because of the circuitous interpretation they
call for, offer clues to the willed suppression of women.
But to translate silence into meaning requires a critical
distance from tradition as well as immersion in it.[24]

Despite Jesus and his married disciples, sexuality came to
be not merely associated but literally identified with sin and
concupiscence, and it was almost universally linked with original sin. After all, the Scriptures, as translated by Jerome, told us
unequivocally that the disobedience of our primal parents
brought both sex and death into the world. Patristic and scholastic opinion concerning intercourse in the Garden prior to the
Fall is divided. St. John Chrysostom considers it anathema;
Augustine and Aquinas call it sex of a different and more rar-
efied kind, free of concupiscence (and, of course, passion, delight, and any semblance of demonic fun); Irenaeus considered
Eve, and one presumes Adam, to be virgins before the Fall.

In keeping with his Manichaean leanings, St. Augustine
discovered a perfect analogy for human rebelliousness against
the will of God in the unfortunate tendency of the male organ to
stir at the most inopportune moments (no matter how fervent
his prayers and earnest his efforts at rational control), a reaction
which one presumes was occasioned by either the physical
proximity of a luscious maiden or the memories of one.
Thoughts of women as connected with "feces and urine, the
excrement of childbirth"[25] might have helped him to purge his
mind of such unwelcome fantasies and allowed him to see what
he considered a perfectly clear connection between intercourse,
passion, and original sin.

The female of the species was consistently portrayed as
temptress, bride of Satan, the ruination of humankind. Tertullian put it succinctly: "You are the devil's gateway, you desecrat-
ed the fatal tree, you first betrayed the law of God, you softened
up with your cajoling words the man against whom the devil
could not prevail by force. . . . *You* deserved death, and it was
the son of God who had to die."[26]

Even more vehemently than Paul, such pillars of the early
Church as Ambrose, Augustine, Chrysostom, and Jerome
(who in addition to the *Vulgate* gave us that eminently quotable

quote comparing the well-proportioned female body to the whitened sepulcher) all agree that sexual abstinence is definitely more virtuous and holy than non-celibacy. After all, in the Apocalypse one hundred and forty thousand virgins stand closest to God's throne.[27] St. Paul referred to Christ as the second Adam, *pure and virginal.*[28] Justin Martyr extended the idea to Mary, making her the inviolate counterpart to the corrupt Eve, despite the almost total absence of scriptural evidence for Mary's continued virginal state. Centuries of theological haggling over a *virgo intacta post partum* followed. St. Jerome even insisted that Joseph must have remained a lifelong virgin. How could the saintly adoptive father of God on Earth have been otherwise? Particularly since there seemed absolutely no way to grant Joseph carnal experience apart from making him fall into the sins of fornication, adultery, or even more reprehensible aberrations.

The Fathers delighted in endless speculations concerning the physiological specifics of Mary's virginity and that blessed state in general. In expressions such as a "fountain sealed,"[29] they even managed to find evidence for their fixation in the Song of Songs, that graphic and powerful celebration of erotic love both in itself and as analogue for the kind of passion God feels for us. At the very root of clerical culture there lies a perverse and pathetic need to exorcise the demon flesh (some, such as Origen, unwisely going so far as self-emasculation, a custom frowned upon by the Church, while others, more sensibly, contented themselves with the castration of texts). This is coupled with the corresponding need to sublimate repressed sexuality. Suppressed libido most generally turns into hatred, envy, disgust, and sadistic "delight" in physical or psychical torture and mutilation, as Des Kenny, the psychotic priest/artist and author of the final introductory citation from *Angels of September* demonstrates. This witches' brew of perverted, demonic sexuality and corrosive, deadly envy, while alluded to in most if not all of Greeley's works, may well be the central motif (in a nonclerical setting) of the Blackie Ryan mystery with the ironic title, "Happy are the Clean of Heart."

Saint Benedict, some time after taking up the solitary life, according to the *Dialogues* of Pope Gregory I, found himself almost overcome with temptation and the memory of sweet and forbidden pleasure. He was about to

> forsake the wilderness. But suddenly, assisted by God's grace, he came to himself; and seeing many thick briars and nettle bushes growing hard by, off he cast his apparel, and threw himself into the midst of them, and there wallowed so long that when he rose up all his flesh was pitiful torn; and so by the wounds of his body he cured the wounds of his soul.[30]

While his motives were doubtlessly noble and his actions can be understood within the context of prevailing cultural patterns, it is difficult to conceive of behavior less in the spirit of celebrating the Incarnation and the glorious, liberating, love-intoxicated kingdom of God.

As I mentioned previously, this emphasis on virginity is clearly a *pagan* addition to Christianity, drawn from the (counterculture) intellectual climate of the late Roman empire. Neo-Platonists such as Plotinus, Philo, the Stoics, Gnostics, the followers of Zoroaster, Mithra, and Mani, all considered the flesh (primarily symbolized by sexuality and women) as corrupt, leading to the identification of womb, tomb, sin and sex.

Thus it is in no way surprising that almost from the beginnings of Christianity the figure of Mary and consequently the feminine aspect of God contains two contradictory analogical strands, the elite clerical tradition of the Virgin as a-sexual neuter, and the popular tradition of the Great Mother of natural fecundity. Neither is it surprising that erotic love has been the object of constant bombardment by official magisterial pronouncements for close to two thousand years. The greater part of the lower clergy and laity has ignored these pronouncements for exactly the same length of time. The real miracle consists in the persistence with which the Catholic analogical imagination, particularly in its popular form, has managed to resist two millennia of official clerical "brainwashing," insisting intuitively and stubbornly on the sacramental potential of femininity and sexuality. Readings in Church history leave the impression that a chasm developed between the members of the hierarchy and common parish priests who tended to be far closer to the pulse of the people. An interesting twelfth-century document clearly attests to those two antithetical modes of Catholic clerical life. Ordericus Vitalis relates how in 1119 archbishop Geoffrey attempted to enforce clerical celibacy at Rouen by threatening transgressors with excommunication. Ordericus describes the priests shrinking "from submitting to this grievous burden," as the archbishop flew into a rage, ordered Albert, a warm, obstinate, and obviously insubordinate prelate, arrested without being properly charged, and finally commanded his retainers to physically attack the assembled clergy "with arms and staves."

Then Hugh of Longueville and Ansquetil of Cropus, and some other ecclesiastics of advanced age and great piety, happened to be in the church, conversing together on confession and other profitable subjects, . . . The archbishop's domestics were mad enough to fall on these priests, treated them shamefully and so outrageously, that they hardly restrained themselves from taking their lives, though they asked for mercy on their bended knees. These old priests, being at length dismissed, made their escape from the city as soon as they could, together with their friends who had before fled, without stopping to receive the bishop's licence and benediction. They carried the sorrowful tidings to their parishioners and concubines and, to prove the truth of their reports, exhibited the wounds and livid bruises on their persons. The archdeacons and canons, and all quiet citizens, were afflicted by this cruel onslaught, and compassionated with the servants of God who had suffered such unheard-of insults. Thus the blood of her priests was shed in the very bosom of Holy Mother Church, and the holy synod was converted into a scene of riot and mockery.

The archbishop, overwhelmed with consternation, retired to his private apartments, where he concealed himself during the uproar, but shortly afterwards, when the ecclesiastics had betaken themselves to flight, as we have already related, his wrath subsided, he put on his stole, and sprinkling holy water, reconciled the church which he had polluted and his sorrowing canons.[31]

The point of this tale for my purposes is not to call into question the practice of clerical celibacy (though I suspect that the cult of celibacy has its origins in dualistic theories which tend to obscure the charism) but to provide evidence in support of my contention that the conflict between official, flesh-hating, legalistic, and ultimately anti-Incarnational interpretations of Christianity and a more relaxed, natural, and humane popular version has been with the Church almost (if not wholly) since its beginnings. The twelfth-century chronicler obviously perceived nothing particularly amiss about sexually active priests, two of whom are described as "advanced in age and of great piety." Their sin was at worst venial, and Ordericus saw no contradiction, at least in principle, between a priest's hands touching the body of a woman and the Body of Christ. The true sin, a sin against the loving spirit of Christ, was perpetrated by the archbishop and his goons who defiled consecrated ground and shed the blood of priests "in the very bosom of Holy Mother Church," converting the holy synod "into a scene of riot and mockery." If concubinage was so readily accepted for priests, there is no reason to presume that questionable sexual activity among the laity was condemned by the average confessor. The same dynamics which have led to almost universal clerical disregard for official twentieth-century birth control teachings can be assumed to have governed priest/congregation relationships for close to two thousand years. The people (and at least some members of the lower clergy) intuitively grasped the significance of the Incarnation and the sacramental potential of sexual love, even if the magisterium did not.

When I asked Monsignor Egger about the Austrian clergy's way of handling the birth control encyclical and other related matters such as divorced and remarried Catholics, he grinned and quoted an old saying concerning priests roaring like ferocious lions from the pulpit and bleating like gentle lambs in the confessional. "Sexual morality and marriage must be examined in context, the welfare and emotional health of the family unit must be considered, there are all those variables . . . I am not going to tell a woman who has all the children they can support that she shouldn't sleep with her traveling salesman husband the one night in a week or two that he is home. Neither am I going to suggest they produce yet another child and jeopardize the well-being of her already existing family."[32]

The true severity of the fissure concerning attitudes toward the flesh which existed in twelfth-century Christianity becomes clear when we contrast Ordericus' account with the attitude of St. Bernard expressed in a letter written in 1153 in opposition to celebrating the Feast of the Immaculate Conception:

> But how can there be holiness in conception? . . . Did holiness perhaps commingle with conception at the time of the marital embrace, so that she was sanctified and conceived at one and the same time? But this surely is unreasonable. For how can there be any holiness without the Holy Spirit, or do you mean that the Holy Spirit was a partner to the sin? Or are we to assume that there was no sin where lust was not absent?[33]

Palmer uses this passage to explain the emergence of the cult of adulterous love during the high Middle Ages. If, as Peter Lombard insisted, "every passionate lover of one's own wife is an adulterer,"[34] then it might be an act of love and respect for one's spouse to take a mistress instead. In the dualistic spirit of Augustine and Bernard, rigid medieval moralists went so far as to exclude married people from the Eucharist. While this mentality has fortunately not prevailed in the official teachings of the Church, and despite Cana conferences and the Christian Family Movement, it nevertheless continues to color opinions concerning both sexuality and femininity, and it is responsible for immeasurable and totally unnecessary human agony. If Father Greeley were to reply to Bernard's question whether the Holy Spirit is a partner to *sin,* he might well reply, "You bet your halo She is. And Herself enjoying every last minute of it!"

SIX

Christianity and Romance

"Are you grace for me too?" he asked skeptically.

Her eyes widened in surprise. She patted his hand like an affectionate parent. "Of course, dear," she said as though she were expecting the obvious. "I'm God for you." . . .

Back in his room, with the windows open to catch the soft lake breezes, he sat down to work. He hesitated as he put a new sheet of paper in the typewriter. His fantasy was the knight saving a magic princess. Once the magic princess was saved the knight might not want her. The fantasy was only a temporary energy source. Her fantasy involved grace; she took it seriously. It was a dangerous comic fantasy. He began to type, then paused and rubbed his chin thoughtfully. A *Comedy of Grace*: a title like that deserved a story.[1]

One of my predecessors in the Norton Lectures, J.L. Borges, says, in a little story called 'The Gospel According to Mark': "generations of men, through recorded time,

117

have always told and retold two stories—that of a lost ship which searches the Mediterranean seas for a dearly loved island, and that of a god who is crucified on Golgatha."[2]

The Christian Bible, considered as a narrative, has for its hero the Messiah, who emerges, as frequently happens in romances, with his own name and identity only near the end. Being the Word of God that spoke all things into being, he is the creator of Genesis, and the secret passages in Old Testament history—the rock that followed the Israelites with water, as Paul says. . . . He enters the physical world at his Incarnation, achieves his conquest of death and hell in the lower world after his death on the cross, and, according to later legend, "harrows hell," extracting from limbo the souls destined to be saved, from Adam and Eve through to John the Baptist. Then . . . he reappears in the physical world at his Resurrection and goes back into the sky with Ascension.[3]

It is not surprising that critics are increasingly attracted by the religious implications, and especially by the initiatory symbolism, of modern literary works. Literature plays an important part in contemporary civilization. Reading itself, as a distraction and escape from the historical present, constitutes one of the characteristic traits of modern man. Hence it is only natural that modern man should seek to satisfy his suppressed or inadequately satisfied religious needs by reading certain books that, though apparently "secular," in fact contain mythological figures camouflaged as contemporary characters and often initiatory scenarios in the guise of everyday happenings.[4]

In traditional romance, including Dante, the upward journey is the journey of a creature returning to its creator. In most modern writers, from Blake on, it is the creative power in man that is returning to its original awareness. The secular scripture tells us that we are the creators; other scriptures tell us that we are actors in a drama of divine creation and redemption. . . . Identity and self-recognition begin when we realize that this is not an either or question, when the great twins of divine creation and human recreation have merged into one, and we can see the same shape is upon both.[5]

Structurally, all of Andrew Greeley's stories are variations on the ancient literary form of the Romance with its polarization of action into the two worlds of light and darkness. These two worlds provide the allegorical space for the cyclical movement of descent into a realm of shadows from an idyllic world and an ultimate return to the idyllic world or an equivalent state. The paradise of unbroken perfection and vernal innocence yields to the chaotic realm of violent conflict between the primordial forces of good and evil, characterized by cruelty, horror, humiliation, alienation, and death. The night world is in turn overcome as the lower world tomb turns into a womb of rebirth and the grand circle turns in upon itself.

In the cycles of both the liturgical year and the Mass, the Catholic analogical imagination moves in a universe closely related to that of the Romance. The grand cycle of the liturgical year is actually divided into two interlocking subcycles centered around Christmas and Easter. Both cycles begin by sounding themes of alienation and despair in their religious manifestations as the sinner's yearning for redemption during the seasons of Advent and Lent respectively. The motifs of night and day, darkness and light, conflict and peace appear, for example, in the reading from the First Sunday of Advent: "And this do, understanding the time, for it is now the hour for us to rise from sleep, because now our salvation is nearer than we came to believe. The night is far advanced; the day is at hand. Let us therefore lay aside the works of darkness and put on the armor of light. Let us walk becomingly as in the day, not in revelry and drunkenness, not in debauchery and wantonness, not in strife and jealousy." (Rom. 13:11-14) The liturgy of Lent abounds with symbolic allusions to transience, sin, and death. Ash

Wednesday ashes are blessed with the traditional reminder of the human condition as dust returning to dust. Day after day, Sunday after Sunday, we cry out of the depths, are threatened by vipers, lions, and dragons, suffer the most dreadful diseases of body and spirit, and come to know ourselves as utterly incapable of escaping from hell under our own power. The descent reaches the bottom during Holy Week with Jesus' betrayal by Judas, the Passion, crucifixion, and entombment. Death, however, is overcome and provides, paradoxically (as in the Romance), the means of rebirth.

Both cycles culminate in feasts celebrating the victory of light over darkness in the traditional Midnight Mass and Easter Vigil respectively. Escape and salvation are symbolized through images of procreation and sexual union, which are also found in the Romance with its goal of marriage (representing the reintegrated or realized self). Christmas is the celebration of the Incarnation, the *birth* of Christ to a human mother; and all the theological haggling concerning Mary's perpetually intact hymen notwithstanding, the result of her impregnation by Yahweh is the radical fusion of divine and human essences. As such it indicates the perpetual sanctification of sexuality, woman, and motherhood. During the Easter Vigil an ancient pagan fertility rite provides the ritualistic pattern for the blessing of the baptismal waters as the priest lowers the burning candle (phallus) into the font (vulva) and calls on the Holy Spirit to fructify the waters, thus connecting the themes of death, rebirth, sacred marriage, and the nuptials of the lamb.

Like the annual liturgical cycles, the Mass begins with an acknowledgment of human sinfulness and a yearning for redemption, and it proceeds through the reenactment of Christ's self-sacrifice to the eucharistic banquet or comm-union celebrating the soul's marriage to Christ.

It is the purpose of this book to explore the womanliness of God and the role of Eros as a possible symbol for the way God relates to the world. While these themes are implicitly part of the Catholic heritage (surviving in symbols and rituals), they have been repressed and distorted by official teachings. Popular literature, however, and most specifically the medieval and post-medieval Romance tradition within the overarching Christian mythological universe, provides us with an unconsciously developed, and, for precisely that reason, extraordinarily direct and powerful template for the recovery of those suppressed strands of the religious imagination. Andrew Greeley's "Comedies of Grace" and "Romances of Redemption" cannot be properly appreciated or understood unless they are examined within the context of that double heritage, with which the logic of incarnational thinking ultimately reveals itself to be identical.

The Magic Cup, Greeley's first published "novel," is an almost pure Romance, complete with medieval theme and setting. It is the story of Cormac MacDermot, an Irish "Parzival" questing for his Magic Princess/Holy Grail, fair and contrary Brigid-Biddy, the first of many powerful Woman God figures in Greeley's stories. In a note appended to the text, Greeley mentions the importance of water as a central Christian symbol; and then, ostensively in passing, he points to "erotic love, [as] the symbol of divine love."[6] In seven brief words, Greeley neatly undercuts two thousand years of Christian insistence on separating demonic *eros* from divine *agape*, emerging with a powerful image implicitly present in much of the Romantic tradition: Eros transfigured and sanctified but *not* domesticated. Greeley's adaptation of the Romance form to his purposes thus reveals itself as a deliberate choice of the one literary medium appropriate to the expression of his revolutionary insight that if God is to be approached in His/Her fullness, and the radical implications of the Incarnation are to be comprehended and allowed to permeate and transform the world, if the world is to be "consecrated," if Christianity is to be the living religion for today and tomorrow rather than the embalmed fossil of yesterday, then Woman God (the loving, gracious, unifying force at the root of reality) and Eros (the fusion energy of passion) must be appropriated. It is in this spirit that Lynnie confidently refers to herself as "grace" and even "God" for Jim O'Neill/humanity who has spent most of his life in a desperate effort both to obtain and forget her/Yahweh while she/Yahweh has been patiently waiting in the wings for exactly the right opportunity to spring the trap.

In the post-classical Western religious tradition Woman

God lives in the figures of Jesus (who, despite his gender represents the feminine attitudes of accepting and unifying love) and Mary (who has not only absorbed earlier versions of the Feminine but transformed and transcended them by offering a genuinely accessible, nonjudgmental, humane presence to a suffering and sinful world). She lurks beneath unorthodox religious traditions (such as the Kabbalah with its insistence on the androgyny of God and Christian katapathic mysticism). Most importantly, however, from the perspective of a society in which Catholics represent a minority and Hasidic Jews and card-carrying mystics are rather rare, she can be found in the popular literary and artistic imagination, which has not only persisted in portraying Mary as a goddess in function if not in doctrine but has also placed the "Eternal Feminine" at the very center of the Romance from its Hellenistic beginnings to the present. As "secular scripture" the Romance offers an essential clue to the fundamentally gracious nature of ultimate reality if we grant that the intuitive insights expressed by the average person represent not naive and wrong-headed wishful thinking but are instead a valid path to God, an assumption entirely consistent with the theological position of the sacramentality of the world.

Since the feminine aspects of divine reality are most basically experienced in terms of the powers of procreation and fertility, the topic of Woman God is inextricably linked with the role of sexuality as a possible symbol for divine interaction with the world, another ancient, complex, and controversial theme which the lived actuality of the twentieth century is finally allowing out of the closet. Thus the novels of Andrew Greeley provide the perfect paradigm of an analogical universe (Catholic in its base but generally accessible) which presents both issues, that of Woman God and the sacramentality of sexuality, in popularly intelligible imagery carefully designed to explode existing preconceptions which tend to obscure and limit the ways we apprehend divine reality.

"Romance," in the context of this study should not be confused with the derogatory way the term is applied by pseudosophisticates to Harlequin-type formula writing or the afternoon soap opera, which at best represent a tame and watered-down imitation of the real thing, precisely because they refuse to enter the genuine night-world of the chaotic passions of violence and malice, and thus rarely proceed beyond the first few circles of Dante's hell. Romance, properly understood, is a major form of narrative literature, closely connected to comedy (though it may also include tragic motifs), and thematically linked to anonymous fairy tales and the ever-popular minstrel ballads of the folk tradition. Romance is deeply rooted in the collective unconscious (the source of all myths as well as "naive" literary expressions in Schiller's sense), and as such invariably shifts through levels of reality and illusion in a cosmos which is more appropriately a realm of dreams than waking. Romance might thus be considered a projection of some kind of universal or collective psyche filtered through the lens of the individual poet's private universe.

Far from constituting a misbegotten novel for intellectual lightweights and moral or aesthetic idiots, the true Romance is far older than the novel (to which it gave birth and from which it should be distinguished; though at present the two forms are generally merged). The Romance has its own unique structure which accommodates the supernatural and the numinous as well as characters who are not so much naturalistic portraits of real people as archetypal and allegorical figures. Thus Romances tend to transport us almost immediately from a specific work to the tradition out of which it grows and eventually to the mythological universe itself, which according to Frye[7] consists of two distinct, yet practically interwoven aspects—the "secular scripture" of human origin and a revelation received from a transcendent source. "One of the things that comedy and romance as a whole are about, clearly, is the unending, irrational, absurd persistence of the human impulse to struggle, survive, and where possible escape."[8] Frye fails to note that this "absurd" proclivity toward hope also lies at the basis of the religious and most specifically the Catholic imagination, which insists that in the end life and love will triumph over death (a conviction expressed, as I have shown earlier, in the structure of the annual liturgical cycle and the celebration of the Eucharist). Neither Romance nor the Christian vision deny the reality of suffering. As the Buddha recognized after his enforced isolation from the "real" world, physical and emotional torment, frustration, loss,

and eventually death are terrifying aspects of every human experience. Unlike the Buddha, however, whose pessimistic vision was limited to salvation through individual effort and renunciation, Jesus proclaimed the Good News of the maternally
tender, passionately loving divine parent who will see to it that
no torment is irrevocable, that no frustration is lasting, that no
loss is permanent, and that even death shall be overcome. Analogously, comedy as well as the Romance (particularly in its
Christianized form) generally depict the victory of the "under-
dog," the anti-hero, the human being seen not in his or her glory
but in her or his decrepitude and isolation, the movement from
alienation and fragmentation to psychic wholeness-salvation
(frequently symbolized by marriage).

The Christian transvaluation of heroism into the ultimate
triumph of the weak and suffering *qua* suffering, as exemplified
by Christ's Passion, combined with the practical skills needed to
survive under hostile domination, and resulted in the ascendancy of such traditionally "feminine" virtues as obedience and
humility (with their "shadows" of guile and deception). This
uniquely Christian perspective, according to Frye, largely accounts for the prominence of the female figure in the Romance,
where she may even take on "a redemptive role . . . like her
divine counterpart in the Christian story."[9] Frye, however, because he insists on depicting Christianity only in its official and,
one suspects, Protestant manifestation, fails to take the next
logical step of pointing to the popular feminine savior-image as
evidence for an alternate Christian God-concept lurking beneath
the doctrinal surface and emphasizing the femininity of God.
Neither does he note the correspondence of the redemptive
female of the Romance to the essential position assigned to
Mary in the Catholic tradition and beautifully elaborated in
Dante's *Divine Comedy*, the Catholic Christian Romance par
excellence (particularly noteworthy since Dante not only focuses on the redemptive Virgin but places his human, flesh and
blood, *married* beloved, Beatrice in an analogous role, allowing
her image to merge with that of Mary). Instead, Frye insists on
maintaining a radical distinction between the two traditions
based on precisely the pervasive presence of the "Eternal Feminine" in the Romance. "This means that the myth of romance,

though closely related to the myth of Christianity, and for centuries contemporary with it, should not be thought of as derived
from it. As soon as we think of redemptive female descents to a
lower world, we think of Euripides' Alcestis, who is pre-Christian."[10] By the same token, we might insist that the redemptive
male should not be thought of as originating with Christ but
with the ancient Mesopotamian god Tammuz (beloved shep-
herd son of Ianna, his mother/bride, the queen of heaven) who
had been tortured and sacrificed to the underworld and descended into hell, as two thousand years later Christ would descend
into hell. Nevertheless, Frye, determined to keep the two traditions separate, insists that while there are close connections between the imaginative universe of Romance and Christianity,
and "the myth of Christianity is also a divine comedy which
contains a tragedy as an episode within the larger comic structure, . . . they are not the same thing, and should not be confused."[11] Greeley, on the other hand, from his position within
the Catholic convention of Incarnational thinking and the sacramentality of the world does not feel the need to establish clear
lines of demarcation between the two traditions.

Toward the end of the nineteenth century, when Christianity came under attack as the "opium of the people" and responded either by withdrawing into self-righteous, rigid, and otherworldly isolation or by seeking to divest itself of irrational
elements, the "romantic" tradition (exemplified by such writers
as Victor Hugo, William Morris, Herman Melville, and Sir
Walter Scott) was unfavorably contrasted with the emerging
"realistic" narrative mode (exemplified by Honore Balzac and
Gustave Flaubert). As realism and then naturalism ascended to
literary prominence (in keeping with prevalent philosophical
scientism and positivism), even the most skillfully crafted and
symbolically pregnant Romances were generally treated with
highbrow condescension, since, being of a different form, they
obviously failed to adhere to the principles of prose narrative by
which they were evaluated. In addition, the "positive" view of
reality with its insistence on materialistic determinism either
tended optimistically to portray the solutions to the human
predicament as dependent on technological control, or pessimis-
tically engendered the modern equivalent of the Greek tragic

vision complete with the ultimate failure of the heroic to prevail against inexorable fate. Emphasis was on masculine expansion and aggression, not feminine internalization and yielding (interpreted by Nietzsche, for example, only in its negative form as the victory of envy, malice, and guile). The Romance appeared to provide an escapist alternate vision, a phony saccharin sweetness designed to help us avoid the harsh realities of a Darwinian tooth-and-claw struggle for survival, and determined to substitute for the "reality" of a meaningless cosmos the "delusion" of a world ultimately governed by a gracious and benevolent force.

This kind of reaction was anticipated by Plato's self-righteous expulsion of Hesiod and his piquant, poignant, shocking, and occasionally amusing tales concerning the "private lives" of gods and heroes, from the ideal *politeia,* which represented the first known instance in Western thought of exorcising the "lie" of preconscious and nonrational myth in favor of the "truth" of reason (or dictatorial moralism). This symbolic action established a precedent for critical outrage against all literature which required little or no literary sophistication and was apparently designed primarily or exclusively to delight. Once again we encounter the dominant Western judgmentally masculine and dualistic cosmology rooted if not in Plato (who brilliantly employed the analogical imagination to illustrate his own vision of reality and presented in the "cave myth" a pure paradigm of the Romance) then in the "popularization" throughout the Hellenic world of an overly-simplified and misunderstood Plato. Ever since and even more so once Hellenism had fused with Christianity, the elite and popular literary conventions (the former ostensively written to instruct and the latter to entertain) came to be viewed as antithetical, one moral and good, the other immoral and evil. "Popular literature," writes Northrop Frye, referring primarily to the Romance with its core elements of violence and sexuality, "has been the object of a constant bombardment of social anxieties for over two thousand years, and nearly the whole of the critical tradition has stood out against it. The greater part of the reading and listening public has ignored the critics and censors for exactly the same length of time."[12]

Frye, convinced of the intuitive wisdom of the people, insists that the much-maligned Romance represents the vital core of the literary tradition in its entirety, providing something like an eternally fruitful womb for ever new variations of literary forms. This supports my assumption of the Romance as an archetypally feminine literary form. Because of its close association with the primary processes of mythic imagination, Frye considers the Romance particularly active during transitional periods of instability when the possibilities of the elite conventions have been exhausted and new forms are about to be born. "This happens with Greek literature, when Greek romance emerged; it happened at the end of the eighteenth century in Britain, when the Gothic romances emerged, and it is happening now after the decline of realistic fiction, . . ."[13] Thus Greeley's Romances of Grace and Renewal seem to fit perfectly at this particular time and might well open up new literary (and religious) horizons.

With appalling disdain for scientific accuracy, but entirely consistent with its preconscious, primordial, and dreamlike nature, the poetic (and religious) imagination of both the Romance and Christianity views human beings as inhabiting the equivalent of a medieval pageant wagon—heaven and sky above, hell and earth below, and in between, the surface of the earth, the level of ordinary experience, the stage of our pilgrimage from birth to death. Based on this cosmology, Frye identifies four archetypal narrative movements (the path taken by the hero or heroine), two each of descent and ascent, respectively (down from "heaven" to "earth" and "earth" to "hell," and up from "hell" to "earth" and "earth" to "heaven"). "All stories in literature are complications of, or metaphorical deviations from, these four narrative radicals."[14] Combined with the Aristotelean/Ptolemaic world picture and the Christian/Augustinian view of linear time (neither of which is noticeably affected by either Galileo or Einstein, and both of which appeal to commonsense intuition), this "geography" of allegorical space and "chronology" of allegorical time frequently included four rather than three levels, since super-mundane reality was separated into two subdivisions, the sphere beyond the moon, incorruptible and uncorrupted by the Fall, and the Garden of Eden, the earthly paradise, its gates permanently sealed as the result of that first act of disobedience and thus for us unfortunate descendants of Adam and Eve a painful memory of irrevocably lost unity and perfection rather than a land (or state) to be reclaimed. This perspective is acknowledged in the Romance by occasionally identifying the supposedly paradisian with a destructive and demonic illusion. It is the tragedy of the human condition that we are forced to remember while we are powerless to renew. In keeping with its ancient roots, however, Romance tends to portray the lower level, considered exclusively demonic in the Christian vision, as the possible depository of material and spiritual-cognitive wealth (particularly wisdom having to with the enigma of death and the possibility of an afterlife).

The "allegorical space" of Christianity and Romance can, of course, also be interpreted in psychological terms. Freudians tend to consider the lower world the realm of the id while Jungians view it as the personal unconscious, that submarine portion of the psychic iceberg floating in the collective unconscious with its primordial archetypal associations. The "heavenly" segment, according to Freudians, is the rule-conscious super ego (entirely consistent with Freud's patriarchal androcentrism), while Jung would identify it with the potentially realized Self, the goal of individuation which (like the crucified Christ) represents the paradoxical intersection of uniqueness and universality, temporality and eternity, which is achieved after the essential archetypes (but most particularly the contrasexual within oneself) have been assimilated. The central region is the ego, defined by Freud as the battleground of id and superego where the subjective world of the mind is separated from the objective external world, and is defined by Jung as the organizing principle of the conscious mind, the window (more or less opaque according to one's stage of individuation) to the unconscious, the locus of personal identity and continuity. Depending on one's perspective, the analogical universe of the Romance can thus be apprehended as both contained within a microcosm "shaped" in the image of the human individual or the "macrocosm" of inner space patterned after a universal, absolute structure.

Overall, the Romance form appears to be an archetypally feminine literary mode in which the plot tends to maneuver and cluster around a central problematic situation (the alienated self or hidden God) to be resolved, and in which linear time generally yields to a synchronistic merging of past, present, and future (expressed by the use of flashbacks and analogous literary devices), most powerfully symbolized by the limit- or peak-experience (in Maslow's sense) of sexual union and mystic ecstasy. In addition, while the masculine themes of tragic violence and heroic action are sounded, the dominant motif is failure of the youthfully heroic to solve the ultimate human predicaments of alienation, separation, and death without supernatural assistance. This, of course, as the German Romantic poet Novalis pointed out in the brilliant imagery of his *Hymnen an die Nacht,* reflects the transition from the tragic Greek worldview to the comic Christian vision, which through maternally tender love achieved the metamorphosis of "Death the Terrible" into "Death, the Herald of the Wedding Feast." "A thousand hearts," writes Novalis, "raise themselves toward you, Mary, yearning for you in this shadow existence, hoping to recover from their ills. And you, oh holy being, clasp them to your faithful breast with presentient desire."[15]

seven

Descent and Ascent:
paradise lost and
paradise Regained

We had Mass as always on Saturday in my parlor. I preached about two of my favorite characters—that appear in a novel about a novel too—named Finnebar the Fair, Emperor of all the World and Everything Else besides, and his girl friend, Countess Deidre the Dark, who works after school at McDonald's selling Big Macs. Deidre was fed up with how dull the colors were in the Empire so she made Finny—who is also the greatest wizard in all the world— take her on a trip to lands which were in different colors, a red world, a green world and so forth. I was, of course, stealing from G.K. Chesterton's colored lands. Finally, they come to a world where all the colors are perfect and Deidre claps her hands for joy. Then they turn the corner and what do they see? . . . Deidre's McDonald's. The end of all our search is return to where we started and know it for the first time.[1]

If the ports that link the various cosmoi are essentially channels of love, and passionate love at that—and I think that's what it's all about to tell you the truth—then John of the Cross or Teresa of Avila might be useful guides on a pilgrimage to a cosmos which is not out there, nor in here, but "over there" or "next door" or "around the corner" or "down the street" or "across the alley" or "in the next block" or "on the other side of the park" or—at the very furthest, "over in the next neighborhood."[2]

Done. Finished. Forever. The wandering days are over, boyo.

He linked arms with his Easter/Christmas mother/child and began to walk with her to the escalator, which would lead eventually to the parking lot of O'Hare International Airport and the rest of his life.

"Tell me about it."[3]

all of Greeley's stories, even the mysteries, can ultimately be described as spiritual pilgrimages beginning with the main character's departure from a state of identity and ending by his or her return to wholeness and integration. On a literal level his heroes and heroines journey across time and space, from the fantastic future world depicted in the unpublished science fiction fantasy "The Final Planet" (Greeley's first lengthy novelette), and the bogs and mists and fairy glens of sixth-century Ireland of *The Magic Cup,* through Chicago in a bewildering variety of moods, to the sidewalk cafes of Paris, the dark corridors of the Vatican, a jungle river of Africa, Joseph Conrad's Costaguana in Latin America, and Ashford Castle, Galway City, and the Strand of Inch in contemporary Ireland. They descend into underground caves and crypts and skim the waves in sailboats. They travel by rocket ship, jet, boat, train, car, and even, occasionally, on foot. But far more important than their physical, external journey is their internal odyssey through the vast expanse of allegorical and psychological space and time. Like Jesus-Dante-Faust each one of them must empty the bitter chal-

ice and pass through darkness, sin, and death before the possibility of rebirth and salvation even arises; and like Jesus-Dante-
Faust, the mysterious, inexhaustible energy source which
sustains and inspires them, and ultimately propels them through
and beyond the realm of darkness toward the upper regions of
joyous ecstasy and realized union, is the greatest of all spiritual
forces—Love, passionate, cosmic, absolute Love "that moves
the sun in heaven and all the stars."[4]

Their world is split into two distinct realms, a region of
perfection, purity, childhood, spring and summer love, a paradise on earth, apparently untouched by the Fall, and a nether
region of humiliation, suffering, alienation, violence, and adventure, of conflict between the forces of good and evil, light
and shadow, dream and nightmare, sleep and reality. They
achieve full humanity only by temporarily forsaking the idyllic
world of vernal innocence for the dark, demonic labyrinth of
lived experience and Darwinian or Hobbesean strife, by eating
of the forbidden tree and abandoning the *civitas Dei* for the
civitas diaboli, thus coming to know themselves and others as
potentially demonic as well as sacramental. Their journey parallels that of human consciousness in Hegel's *Phenomenology* or
Goethe's *Faust* which is unable to achieve full self-actualization
and/or yield to "salvation" without first having traveled the
"path of doubt and despair"[5] and entered a "pact with the devil"
in order to comprehend the futility of all finite positions. The
process of becoming fully human according to Hegel (as well as
Goethe and Jung) inevitably involves the agonizing task of combining with and transcending one's own otherness or opposite,
"in a way that negates itself and yet passes through that negation
into a new stage, preserving its essence in a broader context, and
abandoning the one just completed like the chrysalis of a butterfly or a crustacean's outgrown shell."[6]

Yet ultimately and ironically, no matter how terrifying and
exciting the adventures, how immense the distances covered,
how apparently remote the the goal sought, and how unattainable the lover pursued, the end of the journey, the focus of all
our yearnings invariably turns out to be as commonplace and
familiar as the McDonald's golden arches of the sermon in
"Godgame," the boy or girl next door, or even our very own
spouse from whom we have drifted away in years of taking each

other for granted. Paradise Lost reveals itself as Paradise Regained, and the power of our first love carries us literally full circle to the place of our origins. The Promised Land in the West, the Many-colored Land, is both ten thousand light years away *and* in our own backyard or marriage bed.

Viewed in its archetypal significance, the image of the journey represents masculine qualities (manifested by women as well as men because of the essential androgyny of human nature) of transition, movement, activity, and desire toward a healing of the fragmented self, symbolized by union with a dimly intuited yet powerfully attractive mysterious something "located" at once in the past, present, and future, outside ourselves and within, the source and goal of all our yearnings, characterized negatively as absence of alienation, loneliness, frustration, and unfulfilled need, and positively through such metaphors as lover, spouse, the holy grail, Yahweh, Krishna, Mary, Christ. It emerges as Something, Someone Which or Who has been lurking in our neighborhood all along, incognito, but no less persistently passionate, seeking us as we seek It.

In the Christian perspective, the journey is the earthly pilgrimage, the movement of the soul toward God. It begins with an expressed or implied state of innocence and naive unity with nature, symbolized by Greeley with fictional versions of his childhood "paradise" of Twin Lakes, and is reexperienced during a hypnotic session of age regression:

> I was three years old and standing on a green, sun-drenched hill, looking at the lawns rolling down to the dull silver platter of the lake. Behind me was a big, stately Victorian mansion with turrets and porches, a magic castle perhaps. . . . EVERYTHING about Twin Lakes made me happy. The lake, the jungle-covered hill, the lawns, the boats, the "Clubhouse" (as my Magic Castle was called) with its slot machines, my friends running down the hill and jumping into the water, the lurking mystery of the pergola at night. . . . There, at Twin Lakes . . . was the matrix of my childhood and the matrix of my life.[7]

Most of his major characters have access to analogous memories of primal innocence and happiness which both sustain and drive them on in times of alienation and fragmentation. Twin Lakes seems to be the ultimate source of the summer lakes recalled by Jim O'Neill, Kevin Brennan, and Hugh Donlon, to mention only few of Greeley's protagonists, and it appears in "person" in "The Angels of September" and "Patience of a Saint." Eventually it merges with a transfigured Grand Beach, the stomping grounds of the indefatigable Ryan clan (and Greeley's own summer home). Invariably, at least for the men, those healing images of the lake blend and merge with corresponding images of sacramental, passionately pursuing and pursued femininity. As Jim O'Neill muses, "The girl is the lake is the grail is God . . ."[8]

Paradise Lost and the religious motif of the Fall appear variously in the romance (and in Greeley's stories) as lowering of social status, separation of families, loss or confusion of identity, and descent into a subconscious realm of increased erotic intensity. This subterranean libidinal world of *eros* and *thanatos*, caves and shadows, cruelty and horror, presents a nightmare scenario of ferocious beasts and demonic ordeals, terrifyingly portrayed in Anne Reilly's psychic absorption into the nether world of "Divine Justice," painted by Father Des Kenny, a lunatic latter day Hieronymus Bosch, whose artistic abomination portrays his naked victim, trapped in a swamp, a demon's claw buried in her breast "writhing in frenzied terror as the devil's pitchforks plunge toward her fresh young flesh."[9] Daniel finds himself cast into the lion's den, and Plato's prisoners inhabit an underground cave waiting to tear their returning savior limb from limb. In terms of archetypes of femininity, the hero (or heroine) must pass through the chaotic death and tomb aspects of the Great Mother. Arjuna, in the *Bhagavad Gita* encounters Her as "touching the sky, aflame, of many colors, with yawning mouths and flaming enormous eyes."[10] "As the many water-torrents of the rivers rush headlong towards the single sea, so yonder heroes of the world of men into Thy flaming mouths do enter . . . Devouring them Thou lickest up voraciously on all sides all the worlds with Thy flaming jaws."[11]

Space limitations do not permit me to discuss all or even most of Greeley's variations on the descent theme. I shall limit myself to one paradigmatic example, the "fall from grace" of Hugh Donlon in *Ascent into Hell*.

Hugh Donlon, as we have seen in previous chapters, enters the priesthood primarily (though quite unconsciously so) to please his mother and to prove to himself that he is worthy of salvation and capable of doing his best even, "indeed especially, when it is difficult."[12] Unknowingly, and ironically with the best of intentions, though rather self-righteously, he begins his descent toward hell that night at Lake Geneva when he valiantly resists the urge to take Maria into his arms and confuses the temptation to hybris and renunciation with genuine vocation, while dismissing grace in the form of Maria as insidious temptation. He continues his path toward the inferno by rejecting Maria's "half-serious dead-earnest" suggestion that he marry her as they are contentedly floating in the Chris Craft in the middle of the lake one warm night later that summer, and finally by tearing himself away from her and the very real possibility of lovemaking after a raspberry picking expedition in the woods. Three times he is given the opportunity of allowing grace to transform him, of accepting the divine invitation to be happy, and three times he denies the call to love, in a misdirected effort to preserve *his* virginity and abide by the rules of his vocation.

It should be obvious by now that Greeley uses some but not all of the standard structuring principles of the traditional Romance. Thus while the descent and ascent themes figure prominently in his stories, he replaces the inevitable preoccupation with feminine virginity and the defense thereof found in Romances from Heliodorus' *Ethiopica* to Spenser's *The Fairie Queene* with a decidedly contemporary Western or possibly ancient Celtic insistence on affirming rather than denying flesh. In addition, he seems at least partially motivated by the pastoral counselor's practical concern for providing positive role models for a healthy, fulfilled, and fulfilling sex life which he considers the most powerful hint given to humankind of how God feels about us and wants us to feel about Her, Him, and each other. Sexual attraction to the social scientist priest represents the most effective means for binding men and women to one another in permanent relationships, for inspiring them to persist in pursuing that which they already seem to possess, of starting over again, and again, and yet again. Sexual union is no longer the hidden event which happens after the story is over, but the decisive event which threatens to happen when the story begins. It is Aristotle's and St. Thomas's actuality which ontologically precedes potentiality. Maria is God for Hugh, passionately loving, implacably pursuing, ready to save him from himself long before he realizes that he might possibly be in trouble. But Hugh is determined to do the will of his kind of God, and he is perversely convinced that He could not possibly want him to do the natural and easy thing. Hugh's God is distant, stern, and demanding; Maria's God is a friend who listens (she hopes) as she discusses her plans to seduce Hugh with Him. "I hope you understand, God. I don't think you'll send me to hell. You do want me to love him, don't You?"[13] Her God is like a mother wanting above all Her children's happiness. Maria fails. Hugh's sense of sin, vocation, and rule-conscious righteousness win out. He remains technically pure and in the process condemns himself and others to needless suffering.

Nineteen years have come and gone. Hugh was ordained a priest; but as Maria had predicted the night she offered herself to him in marriage, he left the priesthood after twelve years. He impregnated and married a former nun haunted by her own demons, attained a Ph.D. in preparation for an academic career, but instead entered the business jungle of the Chicago Board of Trade, characteristically to please his father and to keep an eye on his irresponsible brother. The Romance motifs continue. Hugh Donlon is the twentieth-century equivalent of the ancient hunter stalking wild and dangerous beasts, most specifically Ben Fowler, a fellow trader, who betrayed him during his tenure as priest. Like those lower-world sojourners of old, Hugh takes on the characteristics of his prey. The hunter metamorphoses into the animal. Lucius in *The Golden Ass* turns into a donkey, and Adam and Eve are provided fur "coats" after the Fall. Hugh is desperately unhappy and drugs his sense of futility, self-loathing, and horror in fleeting, painfully intense adulterous relationships with both Ben Fowler's daughter and wife. Maria, his guardian angel (appropriately named Maria *Angelica*), his good spirit, seems gone, but for occasional happy dreams of sailing on the *Pegeen,* making love with a deliciously naked blond Sicilian imp with her face smeared with raspberry juice. . . . And so, one Christmas Eve Hugh finds himself alone in the house with Helen Fowler:

"You're a disease, Hugh," she said. His hands slipped underneath her shirt, touching her breasts lightly. She winced with pleasure. "I don't ever want to be cured. . . . Not here: Ben or Lisa might come. There's a room in the basement." . . .

Soon both their bodies were covered with sweat. . . . Their slippery bodies combined easily and naturally and remained joined, as though glued long after their passions were spent.

"Ben will be home soon," he said wearily. . . .

She screamed as if she'd been stabbed.

Ben Fowler stood next to the Christmas tree, cigar in hand, his face a purple mask of triumph. He raised the cigar hand to identify the adulterers to the world, his lips moving as the accusing words jammed his mouth.

But not a word came out. . . . The mask on his face turned dull white and then darker purple.

He stumbled forward, swayed to regain his balance, then toppled sideways to the floor, knocking down the Christmas tree as he fell.

Hugh pushed around him. Fowler's body was spread-eagled under the tree and surrounded by Christmas gifts. His face was decorated with evergreen and tinsel and his accusing right hand, still brandishing the cigar, had shattered the pieces of the Christmas creche and smashed to bits the manger and the little figure within it. . . .

". . . In the next phase, I think you are going to cut yourself off from everyone, man, woman, child—everyone."

"Why would I do that?" Hugh felt his stomach lurch.

"Because you're still running," Cleary said, shaking his head. "Down the nights and down the years."[14]

Hugh has demolished his enemy, and in the process almost succeeded in destroying himself. In a perfect inversion of images, Christmas, the celebration of the Incarnation, turns into his Golgotha, his spiritual death, preceding his descent into the very pit of hell. The symbols are overpowering: demonic sex (dimly intuited as a loathsome disease, a fatal addiction) in the basement room; Fowler's stroke and collapse into the Christmas tree; the smashed creche and figure of the Christ Child.

As Pat Cleary, Hugh's wise priest friend, recognizes, Hugh is still running, still falling into the void. His external circumstances appear to improve. Ben's stroke has saved him from exposure, business goes well, he finds himself ambassador to an unstable African republic. In typical romance manner he appears to be super human, but the brilliant facade conceals the emptiness within. He is brutalized by native soldiers. His wife and a female Peace Corps volunteer are tortured, humiliated, and almost raped in a nightmarish jungle scene. His brother betrays him in a silver market scheme, selling him for the contemporary equivalent of thirty pieces of silver. "Poor Hugh, Tim thought. He would get one with a poker up his ass."[15] The bitter cup must be emptied to the last drop. True to the Romance motif of the hero falsely accused of a major crime and separated from the heroine and his friends, Hugh Donlon is convicted of stealing five million dollars worth of his clients' money, and he ends up in federal prison. He has reached bottom and entered his dark night of the soul. In a gracious universe any further spiritual development and narrative movement must and will be an ascent.

Hugh's eventual escape from hell (with Maria's determined and far from subtle assistance) and his Easter night "homecoming" to the "Bethlehem" and "Lake Geneva" of her warmly lit house, have been discussed previously. Thus I will explore the Romance theme of ascent by referring to *Virgin and Martyr,* which in many ways is a companion piece to *Ascent into Hell* and may structurally be the purest Romance Greeley has written since *The Magic Cup.* Inasmuch as men and women can be alike, Hugh Donlon, the priest who gives up the active priesthood, and Cathy Collins, the nun who leaves the convent, are almost exact counterparts. Both are compulsive perfectionists desperately trying to earn salvation while simultaneously searching for a maternally loving, passionately tender God who does not demand that sanctity by purchased at the expense of their personal integrity. Both of them decide on clerical and religious life for the wrong reasons. Both are brutalized by psychopathic, authoritarian, and incompetent religious superiors. Both eventually leave their respective communities and marry immature, self-centered, and sexually inadequate partners. Both are betrayed by persons they love and trust, Hugh by his brother for silver, and Cathy by Father Ed, a revolutionary priest, with a kiss, for money and "the Cause." Both are imprisoned. Hugh's torment at Lexington (which compares favorably with conditions at his old seminary) consists of self-imposed isolation and profound depression. Cathy, on the other hand, is raped, sodomized, shocked with electricity, burnt with cigarettes, suspended from the ceiling, whipped, and thrown into a filthy cell. On the way to the commandant's seaside villa, Garcia and Lopez, two sergeants, rape her in the back of the car with her arms extended in the form of a cross. "Just like Jesus," grins Lopez.[16] A few hours later she has managed to break her straps and is free, with her rosary blessed by Pope John wrapped around a loaded forty-five in her purse. She is in control of her own fate for the first time in weeks, possibly for the first time ever.

Her shot was off target. It tore into his chest, which exploded in a gush of blood. . . .

In the slowest of slow motion, she saw Garcia leap for the gun. She fired again, blowing away his shoulder. Then, as he screamed in pain, she calmly and deliberately pulled the trigger a third time, sending a bullet crashing into his skull. . . .

She rubbed as much of the bloodstain off the ground as she could, reloaded the ammunition clip in her own automatic and, without looking back at the corpses she had made, began walking away from the mountains toward the sea.

The sun was high in the sky and the Sierra hidden in the mists the next morning when she staggered across the railroad tracks and collapsed on the beach of the Golfo Placido in the shade of a huge rock some giant must have thrown there a long time ago. . . .

Now she must plan, a shrewd, deadly beast on the run. First she must swim in the gulf. . . . She would be clean and refreshed. Then she must hide till night and follow the railroad track to the nearest *barrio*. . . . If there was a station, she would wait till dawn and buy a ticket. . . . She would find Angela in the crypt in the basement of the old church and then ride the bus with her to Santa Maria. . . .

So she stripped off her clothes and plunged into the gulf. The water was warm and soothing, stinging her wounds only slightly. She floated for a few minutes, absorbing strength and healing from this primal source of life. . . .

Before she fell asleep, she opened the notebook they had left in her purse and . . . made a quick sketch of the scene, ocean, beach, rock and railroad track. If she survived, she would paint it someday.

A train rumbled by on the track. . . . Tomorrow with any luck she would be on the train, headed for home.

Wherever home was.

She finished the sketch.

It was the first time in years that she had drawn even a sketch. She then ate another stolen orange and slept till late afternoon.[17]

In the middle of the fifth decade of the rosary, the murmured words slowed down and stopped, like a car running out of gas. She had asked for nothing, wanted nothing from whatever might lurk in the church—save for blessing for a generous woman. But that which was in the church intruded all the same, assuring her that she was loved, deeply, powerfully, passionately loved. . . .

Then there was no more time and space, only a vast and reassuring peace.

Although the worst was over and she was now Angela, complete with her long blond hair, blue eyes and thick glasses . . . she teetered on the edge of panic on the bumpy ride down to Santa Maria. For the first time escape seemed a real possibility and not a dream.[18]

The themes of healing, reintegration, and ascent are sounded. First Cathy kills her tormentors and metaphorically crushes the demons which have been haunting her, literally (though without her conscious awareness), since she was touched by Evil during an uncanny vision at the home of Little Angelica who had died of bone cancer at age seven. In Lopez and Garcia she figuratively annihilates everyone who has ever savaged her. She exorcises not only Mother David Mark, her sadistic director of novices, Father Tierney who tried to rape her, Leo Touhy, the homosexual ex-priest pop-guru who made her his wife and slave; but in a sense she shatters two thousand years of institutionalized spiritual, emotional, and physical battering of women. Evil must be destroyed. The forty-five, an instrument of death, has been symbolically sanctified by its association with her rosary, the last of three blessed by Pope John who once, an eternity ago, suggested that she try to be a "good teacher" rather than a frustrated saint and ever since has been a quiet but persistent voice for sanity in her life. She leaves behind the mountains of death and walks across the wilderness toward the cleansing waters of the sea. She rests in the shadow of a rock. We are reminded of the "spiritual rock" which relentlessly pursued the Hebrews through the desert, the rock from which the water flowed "for the people to drink," the rock which "was Christ,"[19] the Nursing Mother sharing Her liquid of life with Her children, the rock which is the Church. She swims in the clear waters of the gulf, submerges herself in the natural sacrament, allows herself to be cradled and healed. Once again she touches the primal roots of her inviolate self, that fragile core which somehow, mysteriously, has remained intact through all those years of ever-increasing disintegration. It is as though the weeks of imprisonment, starvation, torture, and sexual abuse have activated or tapped a reservoir of inner strength almost submerged and shut off after years of psychological brutalization and mental and spiritual rape mostly perpetrated by representatives of the Church. The hidden artist reasserts herself. Cathy is truly on her way home.

Her mode of escape, the allusion to being a "shrewd, deadly beast on the run" particularly connected with the Angela identity, her alter ego hidden in the Rio Secco crypt, reflects the comic theme of the triumph of cunning, the primary weapon of the disenfranchised, the weak, the woman. The goddess of wisdom is also the goddess of guile, as Athena admits (with considerable pride) as she compliments Odysseus on his brilliant strategy of concealing the Achaean troops within the wooden belly of the Trojan horse.[20] It is with the aid of lies and deceit, secrecy and disguise that the weak triumph over the mighty in New Comedy. Heroines, such as Terence's Andria, do their work under cover until the time is right for their identity to be revealed. The Narcissus, mirror, twin, or *Doppelgänger* theme of double identity or the double heroine (or hero) is another common romantic escape device used by Shakespeare, Richardson, and Jane Austen, among others, and immortalized (in its male variation) by Charles Dickens in the *Tale of two Cities*. The "double heroine" motif traditionally involves two women (preferably virgins and frequently portrayed as "dark" and "light"), one of whom is often killed to save the other, like Thisbe in Heliodorus' *Ethiopica*.

The motif of feminine cunning as a means of salvation is even associated with the character of the Virgin Mary in popular imagination. Medieval legends portray her as resuscitating sinners to allow them to confess and repent before dying, and as keeping the dying alive until they have done so. She is forever plotting to outwit the devil, who occasionally complains to the Lord concerning her flagrant subversion of justice. This is also one of the roles she plays in Goethe's *Faust* where she appears as as *Mater Gloriosa* leading the way to heaven, the Eternal Feminine who is not only the transforming inspiration for the human spirit but as Mother of Mercy also manages to dupe Mephistopheles and rob him of his victim.

Cathy's alternate identity buried in the crypt at Rio Secco sounds a universal, archetypal motif of death and rebirth, of the nightmare-illusion of the tomb revealing itself in waking reality as the fecund womb engendering new life. Cathy's experiences in her dual identity echo the adventures of Anatheia in Xenophon's *Ephesiaca*. After narrowly escaping crucifixion, Anatheia is thrown into an underground den with two vicious mastiffs, drugged with a death-like sleep-producing potion, buried alive, and finally liberated by grave robbers. The theme of the apparently dead and buried heroine also figures prominently in Shakespeare's *Cymbeline*, and appears in the ancient Sanskrit drama *The Clay Cart* in which the lovely and virtuous Vasantasena, protected by the righteous and undeservedly impoverished Charu-datra against the king's evil brother, ends up being choked and buried alive. Charu is accused and convicted of the crime. At the last moment she shows up in court and clears him, in a typically romantic "courtroom recognition scene" of the type also found in *Virgin and Martyr*. The theme of the apparently dead and buried virgin is very ancient and can be traced to the Mesopotamian myth of the moon goddess Ishtar who periodically descends into the underworld to "raise the dead," an admittedly ambivalent effort which might result in an upper world populated by zombies, since she also threatens to devour the living to make room for her partially reconstituted dead. "Keeping in mind the Christian parallel, it is as though there were two aspects to the sacrificial victim, one in which she is a hostage for death, and so exposed to death herself, and another in which she is what has come instead of death. In the latter aspect she is, potentially, the conqueror of death and the redeemer of its captives."[21] Thus she appears in a contemporary incarnation as Bob Fosse's Angelique, the terrifying, captivating, inescapably tender, passionately loving, and supremely beautiful angel of death Woman God played by Jessica Lange in *All That Jazz*. In one sense Cathy has died during her imprisonment, torture, and rape, a death symbolized by the her alter ego's "burial" in the Rio Secco crypt. In a second sense, that death constitutes, through the process of double negation, the death of someone already killed, the death of Cathy, the empty human shell left after her novitiate, and thus actually represents a new birth, the leaving behind of the chrysalis as the butterfly emerges. In a third sense, Cathy herself, having passed through death and rebirth, reveals herself as sacrament of redemption, a living conduit of love and grace.

Cathy finally recognizes that she is loved, "deeply, powerfully, passionately loved." That love is called Nick Curran, who has been pursuing her, faithfully if ineptly, since she was a teenager, torn between following her instincts which told her to love Nick, make babies, and pursue a career as an artist, and her "vocation" which insisted that she must strive for sainthood and perfection by triumphing over her natural inclinations. That love is called Blackie, cousin, friend, and priest, who has tried in vain to keep her from destroying herself. That love is called Mary Kate, Blackie's indefatigable sister, a psychologist aware of Cathy's deep-seated feelings of inadequacy. That love is called Pope John who once winked at her during an audience and blessed her rosaries. That love is called Mary who hears her unspoken plea in that silent church, and half way through the fifth decade of the rosary spreads Her blue mantle around her and engulfs her in a Mother's "vast and reassuring peace." That love is called grace, in the immortal words of Blackie Ryan, "a combination of mist and quicksilver" which "sneaks in through the cracks and crannies, fills up the interstices that our plans and programs and personalities leave empty, takes possession of the random openings we give it and then, when we least expect it, BANG! there's the big surprise."[22] Cathy Collins is ready to go home.

eight

EROS transfigured

Blackie shrugged. "You're probably the only person in Grand Beach who read Alfred North Whitehead. If you want, I'll be simple: God is engaged in the business of creating beauty by drawing us forth in hope and love. Sexual attraction is but one dimension of hope, the trickiest of the games that God plays with us. It's Her best technique yet to lure us into generosity and risk-taking which are the raw materials of beauty. Bluntly, your attraction to Ciara Kelly is a trick God has played on you. 'Love Ciara Kelly, love Me' is what She is saying to you. 'Pursue Ciara Kelly, the will-of-the-wisp, the Holy Grail, and you pursue Me, the divine will-of-the-wisp . . ."[1]

God who is a romantic, on the basis of the evidence, and indeed a passionate one, almost certainly will settle for nothing less than romantic passion between the once and future lovers.[2]

When he awoke, lying on her bed, Hugh saw Maria standing above him, hands on her hips, golden and glowing in the late afternoon sun, wearing only her glasses and the plain gold cross at her throat.

"I must seek forgiveness."

"That's nonsense. Remember your sermon at Marge's wedding? Forgiveness is there to begin with. It's given, just as it was given to that poor woman in the Bible they were going to stone to death."

"A naked woman quoting scripture?"

"Why not? It gets attention. Titian—"

"What does he have to do with it?"

"His painting of sacred and profane love. Profane is a stodgy old prude with all her clothes on and Sacred is like me." She raised her arms. "Except she's not wearing glasses."

He circled her waist with his fingers and drew her close. She put her hands on his head, Sacred love offering her benediction. His fingers moved up to her breasts. Holding one in each hand, he kissed them, first one, then the other, with infinite delicacy. She sighed and her eyes dilated with pleasure.

God in heaven, how he loved her. The only one he'd ever loved.

Then he drew back once more.

"Maria . . . I must climb out of hell . . . I can't. . . ."

"No, you don't. You can't escape that way. You should stretch up your hands to God." She recaptured his hands. "And let Him pull you out." She pulled him back to her. "This way."

He wrapped his arms around her.

"Why do you bother with me?" he asked.

Her eyes filled with tears. She leaned her head against his shoulder. "Because I love you, you crazy so and so. I've always loved you and always will, no matter how much you hide from me."

For the first time in four decades, tears spilled out of Hugh Donlon's eyes, tears of agony and pain, of frustration and disappointment, of failure and despair. Maria's arms enveloped him. He buried his head against her chest, his tears washing her breasts, a child in his mother's arms sobbing as though his body would tear itself apart. . . .

And so it was that, close to a monastery named after a garden in which Jesus wept, but not in it, Hugh Donlon forgot about his glacier and experienced peace and happiness.[3]

She was wearing a rosary around her neck, the crucifix hanging between lace-covered breasts. The rosary from her escape, of course.

I drew her head against my chest and unfastened her bra, kissing her back and pathetically thin shoulder blades. I chose a small area on one of the shoulder blades and caressed it with my index finger, carefully and slowly, as if I were healing all of her through that one spot. She sighed peacefully.

"The pleasure is mine," I said as I began to kiss and nibble at my twin captives, feeling confident that the Person watching me from her rosary did not mind sharing her and indeed had always intended to share her with me.

I'm doing all right, I told Him, but don't desert me now.[4]

Red caught sight of Eileen's profile across the room. How could you lust for a woman as much as he did and still have a religious experience. . . .

"God kind of slides into bed with you?" He caught Eileen's eye over the Cardinal's shoulder and winked. She blushed and turned away. He thought he would explode with love for her. . . .

". . . Lust, love, affection, tenderness, guilt, desire, need, adoration—how did you separate them? The presence in the green glass tower, the Cheshire Smile, the complacent woman soon to be enjoyed on his bed, how did you unmix them? God and Eileen, how untangle them?"[5]

a s I have pointed out in previous chapters, despite the Incarnation with its life- and world-affirming message of the potential goodness of organismic reality, traditional Christian views tended to see human nature in one-dimensional, sharply etched black and white terms. Human beings were considered uneasy fusions of the sexual (earthly) and spiritual (heavenly) aspects, baptized Platonic rational souls trapped in the cage of the body, and the word- and life-negating ideal of renunciation of physical desires as method to *achieve* salvation emerged as *the* Christian ideal in a manner reminiscent of Theravada Buddhism or even Jainism. Since Patristic times Eros has been identified with "human" (i.e. animal) lust, and as such potentially demonic, since passion was suspect *qua* passion. In one of the ironic twists of the history of thought, Hellenistic dualism masquerading as Christianity split the Platonic Eros into its "earthly" and "heavenly" parts, and then adopted that aspect of the Platonic Eros which yearned for spiritual perfection, baptized it in the name of Agape, and pitted it against its own earthly twin, which was envisioned as proceeding from the powers of generation and the sensual-aesthetic love of physical beauty. Soon all passionate desire came to be viewed as sexual desire and as such dangerous and potentially evil. Demonic Eros was contrasted with angelic Agape, the positive and virtuous form of love, divine charity (*caritas*), undefiled by incontinence, desire, and passion. The former was described as selfish, the latter as self-less. Paradoxically, in another one of those convolutions of thought (which, as Hegel reminds us, invariably gives rise to its own opposite), the Protestant Reformation, despite its insistence on the futility of human effort and the gratuity of grace, only succeeded in intensifying the split between the human being *qua* nature and the human being *qua* spirit. As the Cross emerged as the central, indeed the exclusive Sacrament, it obscured the cautiously optimistic Catholic vision of nature, human and otherwise, as more good than evil, pervaded by sacramental potential, and permanently hallowed by the mystery of the Incarnation. Those who insisted that salvation could not be earned through strenuous effort developed a theology which in practice demanded that its adherents ideally divest themselves of every last bit of natural dignity, that they literally sacrifice their human identity, their freedom, their organismic and instinctual selfhood upon the altar of a radically other, absolutely righteous, and essentially "inhuman" deity. Thus theologians such as Anders Nygren envisioned grace not as the perfection of all that is specifically human but as its utter destruction; and they insisted not only on exorcising "vulgar" or sensuous Eros (whose essential defect was taken for granted), but also the far more insidious "heavenly" Eros, marked as demonic by its egotistical, acquisitive desire to possess that which is judged good and true and beautiful, in order to gain *happiness*[6] for the individual self. There is, obviously, a distinction between genuine love which accepts the other and seeks the other's good, and pseudo-love which seeks to possess the other as a means of self-gratification. It is inappropriate, however, to identify those two versions of what is commonly called "love" with Agape and Eros. Jesus in no way encourages this distinction, and he disparages neither sexual passion nor love of self and the human desire for happiness unless these become ends in themselves. "In the elimination of Eros man has been eliminated," notes Martin D'Arcy, and nothing could be more contrary to the spirit of the Incarnation, to the reality of a God who took on flesh.

Greeley's message concerning erotic love, while entirely consistent with incarnational thinking, may nevertheless strike many people as revolutionary, blasphemous, and even heretical. Most of us might have some difficulty accepting God as the Grand Voyeur watching, and not merely watching, but doing so with delight and approval, as Hugh and Maria, Nick and Cathy, Red and Eileen are, to put it bluntly, having SEX, particularly if we remember that by traditional standards only Red and Eileen are not committing the sin of fornication. Ironically, it is much easier for us to imagine God observing erotic activity with stern disapproval, ready to zap those involved for any number of possible violations of the divine sexual code, than it is to envision God as either a loving and proud parent delighted to see Her children experience supreme pleasure, or as a passionate spouse vicariously and enthusiastically participating in the occasion. The image of splendidly naked Maria as sacred love conferring the benediction of her unbridled passion upon Hugh, the idea of a human-divine ménage à trois, of Jesus watching from

Cathy's rosary while Nick is nibbling at her nipples, is profoundly shocking, sufficiently so to shake a few of our cherished preconceptions.

Erotic love, insists Greeley, which has long been regarded at best as frivolous and at worst as demonic by most (male and generally celibate) representatives of the official Church, actually constitutes *the* symbol of divine passion par excellence. Greeley's insight, anticipated in part by Martin D'Arcy in his comprehensive study *The Mind and Heart of Love*, which neatly transcends the love dualism presented by Anders Nygren and Denis de Rougemont, consists in his insistence that *agape* and *eros* need not be viewed as mutually exclusive, and must, indeed, be allowed to join in our imagination and comprehension as they are already inextricably intertwined in our lived experience and by analogy, if we are indeed formed in the divine image, in God. If we are to experience the true force of divine passion, we must allow it to be *passion*, not in the sense of suffering and denial, but in the sense of supreme affirmation and transforming, liberating, glorious divine fire which draws us relentlessly toward fusion with another, and through that temporal union on towards ultimate cosmic communion.

Eros is of such central importance to this study that I shall attempt to retrace the motif in its historic evolution. After an initial discussion of the Platonic Eros as "he" appears in the *Phaidros* and the *Symposion*, I am going to base my analysis of the medieval and modern Eros in part, though not exclusively so, on the ideas of Martin D'Arcy as expressed in *The Mind and Heart of Love,* which in turn presents a critique of the conflicting hypotheses offered by Denis de Rougemont and Anders Nygren. I shall then explore the topic of God as Love and some of the mystical implications of that vision in the context of comparative religion. I shall finally offer evidence from contemporary theology and psychology for the image of a transfigured, "baptized" (but not domesticated or dispassionate) Eros as appropriate analogue for divine love.

Any serious discussion of Eros must begin with the consideration of "his" Platonic origins. In Plato, specifically in the *Phaidros* and the *Symposion*, Eros is the mediator who seeks to reconcile the contingent and finite to the eternal and infinite.

Depicted as the offspring of poverty and plenty, forever yearning and forever unfulfilled, mean and lowly in appearance, yet possessed of inner beauty, he takes on human form in the figure of Socrates.

Significantly, Socrates' own discussion of Eros is based on a tale told him by the priestess Diotima (the *only* woman to appear in the Platonic dialogues) who describes love as being neither (or both) mortal and immortal, a messenger "between gods and men, conveying and taking across to the gods the prayers and sacrifices of men, and to men the commands and replies of the gods; . . . For God mingles not with man; but through Love all the intercourse of God with man . . . is carried out." She continues on with her story of the origin of Eros as the son of *poros* (Plenty) and *penia* (Poverty) conceived the night of Aphrodite's birthday in the garden of Zeus. She describes love as desire for "the everlasting possession of the good." "There is a certain age at which human nature is desirous of procreation—procreation which must be in beauty and not in deformity; and this procreation is the union of man and woman, and is a divine thing; for conception and generation are an immortal principle in the mortal creature, . . ." This passage is essential. It presents proof that Plato was not himself the kind of dualist who utterly and completely rejected the world of the senses and physical pleasure. Ultimately, Diotima describes love as "the love of generation and birth in beauty" arguing that "to the mortal creature, generation is a sort of eternity and immortality, . . . and if, . . . love is of the everlasting possession of the good, all men will necessarily desire immortality together with the good: Wherefore love is of immortality."[7]

According to the first Socratic speech in the *Phaidros*, Eros yearns for harmony, beauty, and union both on the physical and metaphysical level. *Together* both levels form a dialectical unity of complementary poles; vitality apart from a spiritual guiding principle is chaotic and blind, spiritual love without vitality is hollow and barren. Aesthetic love, the delight in beauty, mediates between those two forms of love. Physical love, while not as noble and conducive to the attainment of ultimate beauty as spiritual love, can nevertheless serve to launch us in the right direction. Vital functions are neither denied nor condemned *unless* they are absolutized and isolated from the whole. Sensual, sexual love is analogical to spiritual love if it is guided and directed by the latter. Both envy (the egotistical manifestation of selfishness) and jealousy (the lustful manifestation of selfishness) are absent in genuine love which delights in discovering common, shared values in the other. Eros is that driving force which makes us rejoice in discovering in others talents, aspirations, and immortal values which we also treasure or "worship." Eros seeks to transcend the poverty and limitation of life in the symbolic languages of the arts and religion and the reflective language of philosophic speculation.

If we wish to do justice to Greeley's vision of Eros, it will first be necessary to divest ourselves of the associations conjured up by those who insist that Eros and Agape are mortal enemies and mutually exclusive. Denis de Rougemont, in particular, must be confronted since his analysis includes not only the themes of Eros and Agape but also bears on such additional topics central to this study (and the understanding of Greeley's, that is, the Catholic, mythological universe) as the Celtic influence on medieval culture, the worship of femininity, and the Romance.

In *Love in the Western World* de Rougemont begins his argument by insisting on the radical difference between the passion that is expressed in the troubador tradition, exemplified by Chretien de Troyes' *Tristan,* and the Christian notion of love. Courtly love, he claims, can be traced to the reemergence of pagan Eros, disguised under poetic symbol and myth. Thus passionate love entered literally through a back door. Having once been readmitted, it began to be accepted as an appropriate emotion; and it infiltrated Christian culture, masquerading as a positive contribution to Christianity, until it literally pervaded the analogical universes of mystics, saints, and poets. Neither Francis of Assisi nor St. Teresa nor Dante were immune to its insidious poison. According to de Rougemont, Eros as portrayed in the Romance associates the two themes of love and death. This kind of fatal linkage results from connecting *passion* with suffering, which is in turn the mark of an essentially pagan and Oriental dualism propagated throughout Europe by the Celts with their belief in a melancholy, fatal kind of immortality, symbolized by a woman who is at once the manifestation of eternal desire and the dark lady whose beguiling charms spell death.

He considers this demonic Celtic female to be simultaneously the vanishing vision which calls us toward spiritual heights, and the unholy eternal courtesan who leads her followers to damnation. "Eros has taken on the guise of Woman, and symbolizes both the other world and the nostalgia which makes us despise earthly joy. But the symbol is ambiguous, since it tends to mingle sexual attraction with *eternal* desire."[6] Celtic dualism merged with Manichaean thought to produce the Cathar heresy which condemned the Flesh and worshiped Woman, going so far as to substitute the Mother of God, the feminine source of love, for the Holy Spirit, the Third Person of the Trinity. The Cathars also considered marriage to be essentially demonic and in its association with physical pleasure and procreation inextricably tied to the evil material world. On the one hand, de Rougemont accurately identifies dualism as the fatal flaw of Western thought, on the other hand he inaccurately insists that this flesh-hating dualism also constituted an essential aspect of the Celtic tradition. While the ancient Celts were profoundly aware of the dialectical nature of reality, their mythology affirmed rather than denied flesh and was deeply rooted in the appreciation and worship of the creative fertility of divine femininity. It seems more likely that the Crusades may have opened up certain "subterranean" currents, probably emanating from the Orient, which encouraged the reemergence in Southern France of Gnosticism, not only in its Christian form as Catharism, but also in its medieval Jewish form as Kabbalism. There is something fundamentally inconsistent about de Rougemont's argument. He attacks *both* the denial of sexuality *and* its fulfillment unless the fulfillment takes place within the institution of marriage in an essentially domesticated and dispassionately tamed and desiccated form. He criticizes the troubadors for encouraging adultery *and* for presenting Eros in its spiritualized form as an eternally unconsummated yearning for the unattainable lady of the knight's aspirations. Ultimately, his attack on Eros focuses on the one central issue: his absolute opposition to even the remote possibility of Woman-God.

In addition, his wholesale condemnation of Catharism reflects little understanding of the heresy which actually is no more than a category for a multitude of diverse sects which share a common status of having been pronounced unorthodox. In addition to their radical dualism, which posited a cosmic battle between the God of Goodness and the evil Lord of the World (*Rex Mundi*), most Cathars or Albigensians apparently insisted on the importance of direct, personal revelation, accepted a form of reincarnation, and recognized the feminine principle in ultimate reality as well as in the preaching and teaching ministry of their faith. Unlike many representatives of orthodox Catholicism, they did not identify evil with femininity. Since they distinguished between a good world of spirit and an evil world of matter, they obviously rejected both the Incarnation and the significance of the crucifixion. Jesus was either a divine phantasm or a human prophet. While they discouraged procreation as serving the aims of the World God, they accepted sexuality as an expression of human love, combining it with abortion and birth control. They appear to have had strict rules against homosexuality. Cathar beliefs, insofar as they can be identified, thus appear to have presented a serious challenge not only to the central Catholic theological doctrine of the Incarnation, but also to misogynist theories and practices as well as to the power and authority of the Roman Church.

De Rougemont explains that the Church, aware of the immense peril presented by the Cathar heresy, responded to it by ruthlessly ferreting out and punishing its followers, by insisting on the sacramentality of marriage, and by seeking "with eminent wisdom . . . to satisfy by 'orthodox' means the human craving that had produced the symbolical cult of Woman. From the middle of the twelfth century onwards, there was a succession of attempts to promote a cult of the Virgin."[9] De Rougemont continues, with undisguised disdain for the ascendancy of Mary, a pragmatic if unfortunate compromise, that "the cult of the Virgin filled what the Church felt, in face of the danger threatening it, to be a vital necessity. Several centuries later the Papacy could do no more than sanction the recognition of a sentiment which had not waited until dogma to triumph throughout the arts."[10]

De Rougemont contrasts this fatal, irrational, pagan, adulterous Eros with the Christian Agape of insoluble marriage and structured family life. "The symbol of Love is no longer the infinite *passion* of a soul in quest of light, but the *marriage* of Christ and the Church."[11] Agape originates in the Incarnation which reconciles the finite and the infinite and subsumes the tragedy of death into the comedy of eternal life, turning defeat into victory. Agape approves of marriage since it accepts the other and finds fulfillment by seeking the other's good. De Rougemont assumes that the Church was opposed to the gnostic and Manichaean distrust of marriage. In this he is both right and wrong; for while the sacramentality of the world has been a persistent theme in Catholic thought since the beginnings of Christianity (and clearly informed Thomism), it has also been under constant attack by the dualists, who tended to oppose genuine sexual fulfillment within marriage. Even the sacramentality of marriage ultimately came to mean not so much the acknowledgment of the sacramentality of sexuality as a barbed wire fence surrounding human desire with a rigid and inhumane code of "thou shalt nots." For most of its two thousand years the Church herself has been caught in the web of the very heresy she sought to exorcise. Nuptial (sexual) love is a sacrament, marriage is a sacrament, once there is genuine intimacy and a lasting commitment. In the final analysis, the sacrament of marriage is not bestowed by the Church; it is bestowed by the partners upon each other. Not all sexual acts are sacramental, but they have the potential to be so if they occur within the context of genuine interpersonal caring. It is this aspect of the sacramentality of marriage which has implicitly at least been recognized by the Second Vatican Council. A young priest explains this development to Anne Reilly in "The Angels of September":

"A sacrament, Mrs. Reilly, or should I say Dr. Reilly"— the young priest tried again—"is a revelation of the power of God's love in the world. Marriage is a sacrament because the permanence of the union between a man and a woman reveals the permanence of God's commitment to us. . . ."

"Yet the Vatican Council said with great wisdom that sacramental marriage is not merely the handing over of the rights to one's body but a gift of the total person. If there is no interpersonal communication possible, if man and woman do not achieve a certain bare minimum of sharing their personhoods with each other, then there is no communication or sacrament."[12]

With cavalier disregard for historical accuracy, de Rougemont insists that courtly poetry and the medieval Romance in particular, originated during a time when the Christian ethos and the sacrament of marriage had been universally accepted within Western culture. He considers it quite paradoxical that precisely at this point in history a poetic tradition should develop which celebrated love outside of marriage. As a matter of fact, marriage was not officially recognized as one of the seven sacraments until the Council of Trent (1545 - 1563), four centuries *after* the emergence of courtly love. Medieval marriages were considered matters of private contract, routinely entered without benefit of clergy, frequently in the process of consummation, and generally but not universally blessed by Church officials on the church steps or porch, as Chaucer's oft-wed Wife of Bath tells us. In addition, medieval marriage was considered to be an economic association designed to produce legitimate offspring (hence, the insistence on feminine fidelity) and to provide a way to keep property in the family. This kind of pragmatic association between men and women only accidentally allowed for the luxury of love. Thus one might speculate that it was precisely the growing emphasis on combining love and marriage which led to the nuptial Sacrament (the cynic might, of course, accuse the Church of harboring the ulterior motive of seeking to strengthen her hold on the private lives and alliances of the increasingly more powerful and independent secular rulers of post-Reformation Europe).

De Rougemont identifies Eros with the irrational desire for ultimate, perfect unity which carries the lover beyond sexual desire, beyond the fetters of the world. No one who dedicated his life to the service of Eros can possibly agree to the sacramentality of the world. Eros is inextricably intertwined with Thanatos. He quotes from Novalis' *Hymnen an die Nacht* which he considers a modern paradigm of the "romantic," anti-Christian poetic spirit which allows death to blend with love. It is precisely this point which Greeley addresses in most of his novels. Thus Monique offers the following comment concerning Jim O'Neill in *Death in April,*

Women are his problem. He hates us and fears us, but also charms us and flatters us. Death and women—he flirts with both, risks himself with both, and then runs. They are the same for him, poor man. To be possessed by a woman is to die. Classic syndrome. The last of the knights of the round table, a red-haired Lancelot forever seeking his grail, his sacred vessel.[13]

"Making up your mind whether I'm life or death?"[14] Lynnie, the teenager asks him. And again, a quarter of a century later, "Still trying to figure out whether I am death?" she murmurs sleepily after an afternoon of lovemaking.[15] Greeley recognizes the essential connection between sexuality, femininity, and death. He also recognizes the association between God and death, writing "The most striking image of the womanliness of God in recent years was presented in Bob Fosse's film *All that Jazz*."

Demanding, sexy, a bit sinister, inescapable, tender, and passionately loving—that's what the angel of death is like, Fosse tells us. The angel may also be God. Fosse is not sure, yet twice in the movie he brackets scenes with Ms. Lange in references to God; and at the end he gives us a choice: either life ends with a lifeless corpse being zipped up in a plastic bag or in the consummation of a love affair with a beautiful spouse.[16]

Despite de Rougemont, the association of love and death is inevitable and need not lead to pessimism or rejection of the world. Infinity, for the finite creature, *is* death. But at the same time, it is precisely in and through love that death can be overcome. Love, as the young couple in the Song of Solomon recognized, is stronger than death, and in taking on flesh and accepting mortality Jesus transcended the tomb. Thus Kevin in *The Cardinal Sins* can assure Ellen, "If my faith means anything to me, it means the electricity between us survives death, just as the sun survives the night."[17] Greeley's Eros is not the one of the Cathar heresy and the Manichaeans; it is in a sense the child of the fruitful encounter of Eros and Agape—a new-old kind of loving passion joined to light rather than darkness, of death confronted, vanquished, and transcended rather than death triumphant.

D'Arcy's critique of de Rougemont focuses on his failure to allow for any kind of transformation of passionate Eros into Christian Agape and, more importantly, the fact that his model does not include the possibility of love *between* Eros and Agape. This is partially due to de Rougemont's insistence on considering courtly and romantic love simply a medieval incarnation of the Orphic-Neoplatonic-Gnostic Eros. While D'Arcy does not discuss the problem in those terms, it seems to me that de Rougemont succumbs to the very temptation he seeks to exorcise: radical dualism which insists that one point of view is absolutely correct while the other one is absolutely false. D'Arcy posits his ideal of love as friendship, which he considers the fundamental paradigm for all love relationships.

> The perfection of love, as we shall argue, is to be found in personal friendship whether between a man and a woman, between man and man, or between man and God. When God revealed himself as love, the last fear was removed from man's heart. Neither God nor nature nor other human beings were enemies and a menace. They could all be looked at with interest and love, and in the case of persons love could be mutual. Even Eros, if it knows its own nature, can go with Agape.[18]

This, I argue, is Greeley's Eros: the passionate intimacy (genital or nongenital) of friendship. In *The Friendship Game* he writes:

> Love and friendship are the same thing—the open, trusting commitment of oneself to another human being. Since one always gives the whole of oneself in such a gift, including one's body, all friendship is sexual. The special kind of sexuality in a marriage relationship (which is the model and the root of all human friendship) can only be fully human and fully pleasurable when it exists in a context of friendship. Marriage does not destroy love; it requires it and becomes meaningless in its absence. If romantic love

declines as the marriage years lengthen, it is because friendship has not developed, . . . it is because the married lovers do not have the courage and the playfulness to be passionate friends.[19]

Like de Rougemont, Anders Nygren in his *Agape and Eros* focuses on the opposition of his versions of the two modes of love. However, instead of identifying Eros with de Rougemont's dark, lawless, destructive, and utterly irrational passion, he considers Eros an essentially intellectual and rational passion. The archaic Dionysian frenzy of *The Bacchae* has been transformed, after Plato, into the Apollonian yearning for clarity and order, the striving for the Good, the True, the Beautiful. The pagans, he insists, sought happiness; the Christians sought God. The pagans were egocentric; the Christians were altruistic. The pagans knew Eros; the Christians discovered Agape. Based on Paul's definition of love, Nygren discusses this revolutionary new kind of love which is a stumbling block to the Jews and folly to the Gentiles, a love which refuses to distinguish between the deserving and the undeserving. Unfortunately, pagan Eros proved strong and persistent, infiltrating Christian thought in such major theologians as Augustine, whose noble *caritas* is no more than the Platonic Eros directed toward God, identical, apart from its object, to base *cupiditas* which is the Platonic Eros directed toward the material world. Good human beings come to the enjoyment of God through the world; bad human beings want to use God to enjoy the world. Charity is an ordered love; cupidity a disordered one. Nygren insists on a sharp distinction between selfish and theocentric love. Eros is egocentric, desires the good for self, is a form of self-assertion, primarily human, and is determined by the quality of the object. It is the will to have and possess. This obviously contrasts with unselfish love. But Nygren expressly identifies it with a noble kind of love found among mystics and poets. He thinks that all traces of self must be removed, and he curtly dismisses medieval philosophy as partially founded on Platonic and Aristotelean thought, representing a synthesis of Eros and Agape. He specifically criticizes St. Thomas for basing his concept of *caritas* on the "friendship" of Aristotle, thus presenting us with yet another form of self-love.

Nygren takes as his starting point the absolutely sovereign goodness of God as the sole source of the finite actions of human beings. Everything depends on God and nothing on us. Agape is entirely due to divine initiative. We can do no more than passively respond. The way we love God can neither be rooted in desire (*amor concupiscentiae*) nor friendship (*amor amicitiae*), both of which originate within us. God cannot be the means to satisfying human desire. Neither can He be our friend since He and we are not equals.[20] There is no room whatsoever in Christianity for any kind of self-love. In 1 Cor 13 Paul takes up arms against the Gnostics, distinguishing Christian love from Eros-Gnosis. Gnosis is egocentric; Agape is theocentric. The opposition is absolute. That which is true of one cannot be true of the other. In the Gospel of John Agape is finally fully stated as identical with God. God's love is the cause of both our love for him and our love for our neighbors. All Agape is merely the overflow of divine love. Alas, even John was already infected with the evil of Eros.

Nygren misinterprets the Latin Fathers and the scholastic writers because he neglects to note (or point out) that *caritas* is a grace of supernatural origin. The Catholic universe posits a hierarchical progression from the animal world to the spiritual world. As human beings we are denizens of the border region. It is in us that matter and spirit meet. We constitute the apex of the animal world and the nadir of the spiritual world. We are related to God, and through that kinship an exchange of love between God and us is possible. On the other hand, we are so weak in comparison to God's infinite perfection that this friendship cannot be egalitarian except for God's love or grace. God himself infuses us with the potential for loving him on equal terms, thus elevating us above and beyond our natural limitations. This love is utterly and completely gratuitous, a divine gift freely bestowed upon us. We need and indeed can do nothing to deserve it.

The Fathers and the scholastics thus would agree with Nygren's insistence on the gratuity of God's gift of grace and charity. They would differ with him concerning the lack of weight he gives to the appropriate human response, thus limiting human freedom. Friendship always involves two individuals. Although our capacity to share friendship with God is of partially supernatural origin and transcends our innate capacities, we nevertheless are not robots. We have the right to accept or refuse, and merit does exist in the form of cooperation with divine love. Greeley consistently and vigorously addresses this point. Invariably his characters are offered the opportunity for grace (often in the form of human love), and just as invariably they refuse the invitation, at least initially, and often repeatedly, generally out of a sense of unworthiness or in order to live up to some kind of twisted personal ideal of self-sufficient renunciation. Saint Thomas distinguishes between natural and supernatural love: everyone loves God insofar as He is the good upon which all natural good depends; insofar as He makes all people happy in supernatural bliss, He is loved with supernatural love.[21] D'Arcy emphasizes that the duality set up between love of self and love of God is false. In loving ourselves we love God, for we know ourselves as cherished by God. Cupidity means loving oneself exclusively; altruism means thinking primarily of the whole (God) before thinking of oneself.

> But in the Christian Revelation we learn a new lesson about God; we are given the power to understand that God is Our Father, that His nature is love, and that He intends to share His love with us and give us a vision of His essential loveliness. The act in which we respond to this invitation is supernatural charity.[22]

It is this kind of universe which Greeley presents in his stories. His characters move against the backdrop of the supernatural. Men and women sin and suffer, they love and hate and grow estranged, evil seems to prevail, but all of that sinning and suffering takes place under the living Presence of the relentlessly pursuing, boundlessly caring God who lurks beneath and beyond Her crooked lines and redeems the ravages of time in the mystery of love.

> The reader should . . . bear in mind that no sharp divisions can be made at any moment in their history between the two loves. It is always, we must remember, a full human person who is loving, and in that love there are sure to be many different strands. Thought will be there

and emotion, joy and sorrow, self-regarding and self-for-
getting desires, the longing for fusion as well as for beatitude.[23]

The Christian always knows that God is not the kind of
being who destroys what He has created out of love. Quite
the opposite! He is the archetype of love who always wishes well to His beloved. The consequences of uprooting
what Nygren calls egocentric love would be, if only we
were to follow out the logic of his thought, to extinguish
human love altogether. . . . As I say, to rule out all the self
entirely is to make an abstraction of love which has no
life.[24]

D'Arcy reminds us that the most basic cosmic law is that of
give and take, gain and loss, ebb and flow manifested in the
fluctuations and oscillations of change and growth. Nothing can
come into being without something ceasing to be, the joy of
possession is forever pitted against the ecstasy of surrender. It is
this primal rhythm of the universe which the Taoists call the *wu
wei*, often falsely interpreted as passivity. *Wu wei* is far from
passive; it is the supreme activity of acting without exertion by
allowing oneself to be immersed within and penetrated by the
underlying energy pattern which drives the universe. In other
words, it involves responding with love to Love. Yielding to
Reality in this manner constitutes an act of worship rooted in
our respect for the sanctity of nature, writes Thomas Merton,
continuing that "The world is a sacred vessel which must not be
tampered with or grabbed after."[25] In his discussion of love and
the *Tao*, Merton quotes part of the sixty-seventh chapter of Lao
Tze's *Tao te Ching*, the last seventeen lines of which I shall cite in
Wing-Tsit Chan's translation.

I have three treasures. Guard and keep them:
    The first is deep love,
    The second is frugality,
    The third is not to dare to be ahead of the world.
Because of deep love, one is courageous.
Because of frugality, one is generous.

Because of not daring to be ahead of the world, one
    becomes the leader of the world.
Now to be courageous by forsaking deep love,
To be generous by forsaking frugality,
And to be ahead of the world by forsaking following
    behind—
This is fatal.
For deep love helps one to win in case of attack,
    And to be firm in the case of defense.
When Heaven is to save a person,
    Heaven will protect him through deep love.[26]

    Merton points out that the term translated as *love* is rendered as *mercy* by John C.H. Wu, allowing us to grasp the concept in its root meaning as the compassionate love a mother feels for her child. If we connect Lao Tzu's maternal love with Chuang Tzu's "description" of the Tao as the eternal interpenetration of the primal feminine and masculine forces, the *yin* and the *yang* which out of their fusion generate all of "reality," and then associate this image of cosmic intercourse with the Christian vision of the Trinity as personhood perfected rather than obliterated in the process of radical merging, we might be able to approach an understanding of divine love as it can and should be reflected and experienced on the human level.

    Human love, D'Arcy reminds us, is distinguished from animal lust by respect for the individuality and dignity of others as persons which keeps us from either totally and brutally possessing and utterly and completely yielding. Lower passions are sublimated and spiritualized. God's love does not consume us like fire, there is communion rather than extinction. "Finally, this law of the two in one, of giving and taking, is to be found in its primordial and perfect expression in God himself, where in the mutual love of the Trinity all is given without loss, and all is taken without change, save that a new Person is revealed in this wondrous intercommunication Who is Love itself."[27]

    The mystical concept of Zen *satori* is another manifestation of this love. It involves breaking through egotism and merging with ultimate reality in a feeling of absolute dependence which is simultaneously and paradoxically experienced as supreme liberation. The process is described as actively-passive or passively-active, a delicate balancing act between self-maintenance and self-abandonment, a mystical union which does *not* constitute a complete loss of self in the One, but rather the supreme realization of the individual self in the Other. It is, in the words of Thomas Merton,

> a recognition that the whole world is aware of itself in me, and that "I" am no longer my individual and limited self, still less a disembodied soul, but that my "identity" is to be sought not in that *separation* from all that is, but in oneness (indeed "convergence"?) with all that is. This identity is not the denial of my own personal reality but its highest confirmation. It is a discovery of *genuine identity* in and within the One, . . .[28]

Bernard Lonergan acknowledges that the traditional dictum *Nihil amatum nisi praecognitum* (nothing is loved unless it is first known) is valid under some conditions but cannot be reconciled with the empirical datum of the persistent human habit of falling madly, helplessly, and often foolishly in love, thus allowing for the radical breakthrough of a new beginning, and the exercise of what he calls vertical liberty in which one's world is literally turned inside out and upside down. Even more importantly, the Latin truism in no way accounts for the gratuitous gift of God's love which pours itself out over us and floods our souls and hearts, tearing us beyond our limited, obstinate, static selves and allowing us to become that dynamic process of being-in-love, which seems to have a great deal in common with Plato's intoxication with Eros. Particularly since the object of our passion, and passion it is rather than desiccated properly sanctified and domesticated "charity," is neither given nor even understood. Yet, paradoxically, this dynamic "state" of being-in-love fulfills our essential need for moral self-transcendence, thus offering us the deepest of joys coupled with the most profound peace.

It is in and through love that we come to appreciate certain values we have not previously understood, such as the values of prayer, repentance, worship, and belief. Lonergan insists that in religious matters love precedes knowledge and, as God's gift and identical with grace, constitutes the very condition and beginning of faith. When a man and a woman love each other, he writes, without acknowledging or avowing their love, they are not yet in love. "Their very silence means that their love has not reached the point of self-surrender and self-donation. It is the love that each freely and fully reveals to the other that brings about the radically new situation of being in love and that begins the unfolding of its life-long implications."[29]

He moves from earthly and presumably also erotic passion to the relationship of God with His/Her creatures. "What holds for the love of a man and a woman, also holds in its own way for the love of God and man. Ordinarily the experience of the mystery of love and awe is not objectified. It remains within subjectivity as a vector, an undertow, a fateful call to a dreaded holiness."[30]

Authentic love, both erotic and agapeic, puts us in touch with a reality whose power we cannot deny.[31] We do not work ourselves into a state of love, as we might into a habit of justice. We "fall," we "are" in love. While its power lasts, we experience the rest of our lives as somehow shadowy. The "real world" no longer seems real. We find ourselves affirming the reality of ecstatic experience, but not as something merely decided upon by us. In all such authentic moments of ecstasy, we experience a reality simply given, gifted, happened.[32] It is through love that God works within us because at the depth of our hearts all of us respond to the same mystery of love and awe, and we find being in love with God the ultimate fulfillment of our capacity for self-transcendence.

Carl Gustav Jung considers Eros a *daimon* whose powers range across the heavens and into the very depths of hell, the father/mother of all higher consciousness and possibly the quintessence of divinity itself.[33] He also refuses to accept the common distinction between Eros and Agape, and instead presents a portrait of Love which fuses the Platonic and the Christian. He writes:

> Eros is a *cosmogonos*, a creator and father-mother of all higher consciousness. I sometimes feel that Paul's words— "Though I speak with the tongues of men and angels, and have not love"—might well be the first condition of all cognition and the quintessence of divinity itself. Whatever the learned interpretation may be of the sentence "God is

love," the words affirm the *complexio oppositorum* of the Godhead. . . . Here is the greatest and the smallest, the remotest and the nearest, the highest and the lowest, and we cannot discuss one side of it without also discussing the other. No language is adequate to this paradox. Whatever one can say, no words express the whole. To speak of partial aspects is always too much or too little, for only the whole is meaningful. Love "bears all things" and "endures all things" (1 Cor 13:7). These words say all there is to be said; nothing can be added to them. For we are all in the deepest sense the victims and instruments of cosmogonic "love." . . . Being a part, man cannot grasp the whole. He is at its mercy. He may assent to it, or rebel against it; but he is always caught up by it and enclosed within it. He is dependent upon it and is sustained by it."[34]

The folly of distinguishing between Eros and Agape according to the simplistic and superficial categories of "selfish love" and "true love" respectively, is powerfully demonstrated by Hans Küng who points to Yahweh's "jealously" passionate love for His faithless spouse, Israel, a love which is symbolized by the prophets and the composers of the Song of Songs as Eros, and which emerges in the New Testament in the Greek *agape* for one's spouse, friends, children, and even enemies, an Agape which in no way precludes or denigrates earthly, passionate, and sexual love. "Why should loving desire and loving service," asks Küng, "the game of love and fidelity be mutually exclusive?"[35]

When *eros* is depreciated, however, *agape* is overvalued and dehumanized. It is desensualized and spiritualized (then falsely called "Platonic love"). Vitality, emotion, affection are forcibly excluded, leaving a love that is totally unattractive. When love is merely a decision of the will and not also a venture of the heart, it lacks genuine humanity. It lacks depth, warmth, intimacy, cordiality. Christian charity often made little impression because it had so little humanity.
Should not all that is human be echoed in all love of man, love of neighbor and even love of enemies? This sort

of love does not become selfish, seeking only its own, but strong, truly human, seeking with body and soul, word and deed, what is for the good of the other. In true love all desire turns, not to possession, but to giving.[36]

It is this kind of divinely human, humanely divine love, a true and boundlessly fruitful marriage of *eros* and *agape*, the passionate Spirit of the Incarnation, which is the most powerfully grace-conferring sacrament in Greeley's novels, a love which not only inspires hope, rebirth, and renewal, but which ultimately assures the continuance of the Church (physically, in the form of children, as well as spiritually) as the first fruits in the marriage between Christ and His people, who are baptized in the waters into which the candle has been thrust.

part three

the goal

nine

holy grail and magic princess

Later, when they were preparing to ride to Agadhoe, Brigid searched among the rubble. . . . After a few moments she found it. Her hair hanging limp, clutching her borrowed blue cloak with one hand, she held aloft in triumph for all to see a badly dented silver chalice with glittering jewels. "We must not forget the magic cup!"

Cormac did not know whether to laugh or cry, so he took the cup from her hands, and despite the Kerrymen, kissed her.[1]

The last of the knights of the round table, a red-haired Lancelot forever seeking his grail, his sacred vessel.[2]

Lynnie and the lake. The girl is the lake is the Grail is God. . . .[3]

On the rock, after we had worn each other out with swimming, we began to touch each other's bodies, as though we were touching the sacred vessels in an ancient sanctuary.[4]

Then the strange light came, a soft bowl of light, rising up from the waters of the lake, floating slowly down the beach. It circled around him, then enveloped him. Time stood still. Peace, joy, forgiveness, love, flooded into the depths of his being. The light warmed him. It cleansed and renewed him. Ellen was in the light; the woman on the boat; Maureen, too. All the women in the world were there with him, nursing, healing, loving him.

Then they merged into a woman in a white and gold gown. She told him what to do if he were to be free of the damnation that was fighting for his soul.[5]

Was it really fornication, this sin he had not confessed? It had not seemed to be. . . . Sacred Love she called herself . . . the first step in a lifelong union? He hardly knew her—two weeks at Lake Geneva, a few encounters scattered over a quarter century, a weekend fling. . . . Yet he loved her with the certain knowledge that she was the love of his life. How could he give her up again?[6]

No way. I had other things in my life now. Like Ciara Kelly. My holy grail.[7]

I was pursuing my holy grail, seeking not only love but happiness, my elixir of youth, my leprechaun's gold, at the end of the rainbow or wherever else this woman leprechaun had hid it. . . .

I wanted to fill her, impregnate her, fertilize her, bring my child to life inside her—even as I knew even before we had made love that she was already carrying my child. . . .

. . . I wanted a woman and a child, a family, a community.[8]

O f all the symbols and archetypes of Woman God which appear in Greeley's novels, none is more pervasive than that of the Holy Grail which or Who is also the Magic Princess, the primal inspiration and ultimate goal of the human pilgrimage and quest. In the fall of 1984 I conducted the first phase of a study investigating the attitudes of American parish priests toward Andrew Greeley and his novels. One of my Indiana respondents who knows Greeley personally insisted that he was motivated by two fierce loves—that of the Catholic Church and that of his Irish heritage, in that order. No one who examines Greeley's scholarly work or his novels and stories can argue with this observation, and nowhere do those two loves coincide more forcefully than in the mysterious ambi- and multi-valent ancient symbol of the Holy Grail, which also provides Greeley with a ready-made archetype for his theological preoccupations with the sacramentality of sexuality and the womanliness of God.

Almost nothing can be said about the Grail with even marginal certainty apart from the fact that it originated in the mists of ancient Ireland, in that pregnant transitional era when ancient myths of the eternal battle of Light and Darkness and powerful female deities such as the triple goddess Brigid merged with the new faith of Christianity to give birth to symbols, stories, and rituals which synthesized the two traditions. In a poem at the beginning of *The Mary Myth: On the Femininity of God,* Greeley paints a subtly haunting panorama of that seminal period in the development of the Christian West.

> At morning's first misty light
> They came out of the primal bogs
> And worshiped in the holy woods.
> They tended the sacred fire
> And sang of the land of promise
> > Beyond the sea in the fabled west.
>
> They told tales of heroines and gods
> Sad Deidre, mighty Finn
> Noble Dermot frenzied Maeve.
> Then Podraig—
> And soft as summer rain
> A new and loving god
> > Came gently to their dreams.[9]

In order to capture at least some of the complex symbolic wealth of the Grail/Magic Princess Quest theme as it appears in Greeley's novels, I am going to relate several tales and episodes which pertain both to the Celtic association of powerful and sexually active Femininity with immortality (i.e. salvation) and to the motifs commonly connected with the Grail Quest.

A pre-Christian story tells how Connla, the son of Conn is visited by a ravishingly beautiful young woman who tells him of her love for him and begs him to follow her to the Land of the Living, a joyous region of immortality and perpetual feasting. She is invisible to all but him, though others can hear her; and his father, concerned that his son might forsake his responsibilities, commands his Druid to banish her with a mighty spell. Connla lingers, sick with love and longing, until one day she returns in a boat made of glass and repeats her invitation. He leaps into the boat which sets sail toward the land of joy inhabited only by women. He disappears into the unknown never to return.[10]

That Land of the Ever-Living Women is also visited by Maelduin who has been sailing the oceans to avenge his father's murder. Like Odysseus, he and his companions find themselves on an island of perpetual youth and immortality, inhabited by a gorgeous and passionate widowed queen (who initially appears in full armor) and her seventeen nubile daughters. She makes Maelduin her consort and offers her daughters to his crew. After three months all but Maelduin grow homesick and decide to leave. A faithful leader, he consents to accompany them despite his love for her, but as the boat is about to cast off, the queen appears and throws a rope which he catches, allowing himself and the boat to be pulled back to shore. After another three months they escape once more, as the queen weeps bitterly at their departure.[11]

This story, presumably under Christian influence, already includes the motif of the beguiling *femme fatal*, not originally part of the Celtic heritage.

Jean Markale in *Women of the Celts* relates an earlier version of Maelduin's journey involving Bran, the Son of Febal, who ends up spending eternity upon the marvelous Island of Women. In this pre-Christian legend women's charms are still considered entirely beneficent. A later, fully Christianized variation introduces St. Brendan on his ultimately futile voyage "in search of *paradise*, showing that the Land of Women is the Celtic conception of heaven."[12]

A handsome young man from the Land of Happiness holding a magical branch with nine golden apples appears to King Cormac, Son of Art. Cormac agrees to give the stranger his son, his daughter, and even his wife in exchange for the branch. Ireland grieves, but Cormac shakes the branch and happiness returns. After a year he decides to set out to find his family. In the midst of a luscious plain he is welcomed and lavishly entertained at the house of a handsome, tall couple. There he discovers to his amazement that his gracious hosts not only own seven cows which give enough milk to supply the whole world, but also seven pigs which, after having been killed, roasted, and eaten, will spring back to life from their bones and fully regenerate every night. The host reveals himself as God Manannan and tells Cormac that he brought the branch to him because he wished to be joined to him in friendship. A table is set with a tablecloth which instantly produces any food demanded. The god opens a door and calls for Cormac's wife and children. He then places a magic cup on the table. The cup will break if a lie is spoken and restore itself if the truth is said. The cup attests to the fact that Cormac's wife has not been touched by a man since their parting. After the feast Cormac and his wife go to sleep and find themselves, the following morning, back at Tara with the god's gifts, the magic cup, the magic branch, and the magic tablecloth.[13]

Markale tells the story of "The Adventures of Art, Son of Conn," which in pre-Christian form contains most of the major themes of the Grail quest as recorded by Chretien de Troyes, Wolfram von Eschenbach, and countless others. It is this version of the Grail story which Greeley cites in *The Magic Cup* as the basis for his own retelling of the legend.

Because King Conn of the Hundred Battles had taken as a concubine Becuma Cneisgel, a woman of the Tuatha De Danann, exiled from the Land of Promise for some mysterious crime, Ireland was struck by infertility. The people tried sacrificing a child, for which a cow was substituted. But because the king could not send away his concubine, for he was bound to her by a *geis*, he still lacked a third of Ireland's harvest. One day, Becuna Cneisgel won a game of chess against Conn's son Art and forced him with another *geis* to bring back and marry a mysterious Delbchaen, the daughter of Morgan, who was on a distant island. Art left and had to overcome fantastic trials in his search for the fortress in which Delbchaen had taken refuge. He was received by her mother, who made him drink the contents of a cup; he had to choose between the two, one full of poison, the other of wine, each held by a woman. Forewarned by a fairy queen, Art chose the right cup, and then all he had to do was cut the head off his lady lover's mother, seize all her treasure in the castle, and take Delbchaen back to Ireland. Then Becuna Cneisgel gave up and left Ireland, which immediately returned to its former prosperity.[14]

Numerous versions of the Quest for the Holy Grail exist. In outline form it relates the story of an innocent young knight, brought up by his widowed mother in isolation, setting out to make his fortune in the world. On his travels he encounters numerous adventures, most notably a lovely maiden in distress whom he saves from a bothersome suitor and whom he either leaves or marries and then leaves in order, significantly, to seek his mother. He arrives at a fabulous castle owned by a languishing fisher king where a magnificent banquet is served from a luminous magic bowl, platter, cup, chalice, or even stone which is carried by another beautiful young woman. Out of naive courtesy (he has been advised to stop asking so many questions) he fails to inquire either about his host's mysterious illness or about the purpose of the Grail. The following morning he discovers the castle deserted and hears a disembodied voice chiding him for failing to ask the question which could have lifted the enchantment from the castle and the malady from the king. Then the castle literally vanishes from his sight. He spends years in a futile quest to reclaim it, and finally after numerous further adventures, purified by suffering and healed of doubt, he discovers that he is the fisher king's nephew, and he is allowed to return and assume his fated position as the new Grail King.

One of the major puzzles concerning the Grail story involves the motif of the unasked question, the "unspelling quest" which, according to Roger Loomis, can only be found in Irish mythology.[15] He refers to the Reverend Caesar Otway who in 1841 reported a tale from County Mayo (the home of Greeley's grandparents[16]). The tale concerns a certain local drunk by the name of Watty O'Kelly who has the chance to win a fortune in gold if by asking the right question he should succeed in lifting the spell from an enchanted island and castle, which is visible only once every seven years. He asks the wrong question and is dismissed in shame. The magic castle vanishes.[17]

In Chretien's version of the story, Perceval, shortly before he visits the Grail castle for the first time, finds himself at the castle of Blancheflor, a lovely young woman who is literally under siege by an unwelcome suitor. That night he discovers her kneeling next to his bed wearing nothing but a robe over her night shift. "Perceval comforted her, kissed her, and drew her into bed with him. That night they slept together mouth to mouth."[18] Most interpreters, however, assume that he leaves her a virgin. Blancheflor is considered a version of the Celtic Morgan (called Morgain la Fé in the Breton tradition) who is also associated with the Sorcerer Queen of the Shining or Transparent Castle, the Irish goddess Morrigan, and the Welsh goddess Modron, who has a habit of propositioning earthly males only to be rejected.[19] Morgain possesses a horn of magic power which can test truthfulness and heal the sick and wounded. She also appears in a sinister role as a relentless revealer of the truth. In both *Perlesvaus* and *La Queste del Saint Graal,* Perceval is depicted as chastely refraining from intercourse in order to pursue his quest in perfect purity. In Chretien's version he leaves the young woman after killing her enemy and receiving her offer of marriage. Wolfram, on the other hand, implies that the union was consummated the third night (thus sealing the marriage, in typically early medieval manner *without* benefit of clergy). Parzival sets out in search of his mother and (unknowingly) the Grail, leaving his young wife pregnant with his twin sons Kardeis and Lohengrin. Apparently the Irish story of Cuchulainn and Fand blended with that of Modron to produce the Blancheflor-Condwiramurs episode. Cuchulainn is portrayed as being warmly welcomed by the beautiful Fand who sings a

song in his praise and spends the night with him. Untouched by
the Cathar scruples of Southern France, they take full advantage
of the situation. In another version of the tale, the passionately
pursuing maiden is called Blathnat (which means Little Flower),
the fairy mistress of an enchanted and mysteriously revolving
fortress.

Robert de Boron, in his *Roman de l'Estoire dou Graal*, de-
scribes God commanding Joseph of Arimathea to arrange a table
for thirteen people, leaving one seat empty, to seat Bron, the
Rich Fisher, by his side, and place the Grail on the board. In
Perlesvaus, Gauvain is seated next to the mysteriously ill Fisher
King at a table set for thirteen. A beautiful young woman brings
in the Grail. Gauvain sees the image of a child in the center of the
Grail. In the *La Queste del Saint Graal*, twelve knights, including
Galaad are entertained at the castle of the Maimed King and
behold the vision of a child descending into the eucharistic wafer
contained in the Grail.[20] It takes little imagination to see the
archetypal connection between the Grail as vessel/womb being
fertilized (medieval medical theory assumed that during intercourse a fully formed miniature human was inserted by the
father into the mother's nurturing uterus) and the Christian
story of the Annunciation/Incarnation. The motif is then spun
out to include the image of the Eucharistic Cup, which both
represents Christ and provides nourishment of a spiritual kind.
In the Vulgate cycle the Grail is portrayed as a holy vessel which
mysteriously supplies all manner of good food (*viands*), and is
identified with the horn of plenty. It is also connected with the
Dysgl of Rhydderch, the Welsh platter of plenty of the god Bran
the Blessed, and the motif of the chalice or drinking cup which
Erin fills for Conn.

Basic motifs seem to include a magic castle, inhabited by
the languishing Maimed Fisher King and a beautiful maiden
(sometimes introduced as his daughter) who serves as the Grail-
Bearer. The Fisher King was portrayed as wounded through or
between the thighs with a javelin, a euphemism for emascula-
tion. The barren King is associated with the barren land. Wolfram specifically describes the injury as being genital.[21] In the
Didot Perceval the languishing king is called Bron. All of these
stories seem to be variations on the Welsh motif of Bran (Bron)
the Blessed whose foot had been wounded and who, with his

companions, lived for eighty years without aging perceptibly and held miraculous banquets for thirteen.[22]

The Maimed King is also associated with tales concerning a fiery lance which injures a hero; or else a lance, dripping with blood, which is mournfully carried through the Grail Castle. The fiery or bleeding lance has in turn been connected with Lug's spear. In a continuation of Chretien's romance, Gauvain sees a lance bleeding copiously into a silver cup.[23] Celtic mythology tells of the Luin of Cetchar, a fiery spear, which was periodically plunged into a caldron filled with blood, and which was also identified with the weapon originally owned by King Pisear, but used by god Lug at the battle of Moytura. Lug was a sun and sky god, and as such was associated with lightning. The bleeding lance may thus have originated from the flashing weapon of the sky-god and been associated with the spear which pierced Jesus' side.[24] Perceval's visit to the Grail castle shows a number of parallels to King Conn's visit to the palace of god Lug where a magic cup held by a beautiful girl figures prominently. The cup is eventually presented to Conn by the god.[25] The Grail-Bearer has also been identified with Eiru (Ireland) who passes through periods of barren ugliness and fertile beauty.

Loomis draws the following inferences:

Firstly, that the Grail tradition is Celtic in origin, and secondly, that it "violates the most elementary proprieties of Christian ethics and ritual" and thus could "not have originated in a pious fabrication."[26]

> Perceval came from his amorous, if not immoral, affair with Blancheflor directly to the Grail castle; he saw a beautiful damsel pass repeatedly through the hall from one chamber to another, bearing a jewel-decked vessel; obedient to Gornemant's warning against talkativeness, he failed to ask the question, "Whom does one serve with the Grail?"; for this reason the Fisher King remained unhealed of his wound and great calamity lay in store for Perceval and the others. Does this sound like a work of pious edification? Would a holy relic or even a common paten or ciborium been placed in charge of a lovely damsel, not of a priest or a sacristan? . . . No wonder the Church has never

recognized the Grail romances as authentic and has displayed a shrewd suspicion about their unorthodox background.[27]

Loomis is correct from the perspective of official dualistic doctrine of Christianity interpreted solely in androcentric and flesh-denying terms. The Grail story is obviously at variance with a theology which insists on the masculinity of God, the inferiority of women, and an ethos of negative sexual asceticism. In his pre-Vatican Two days (Loomis's study was first published in 1948), the image of a ciborium placed in the care of a *woman* must have appeared both blasphemous and heretical. The Catholic tradition, however, also contains a popular strain which emphasizes the role of Mary as the Mother of God, the *theotokos* or God-bearer, and, in function if not in doctrine, the manifestation of the nurturing, healing, maternal, passionately and tenderly loving aspects of divinity. Seen in this perspective, the Grail emerges as an extraordinarily powerful symbol for divine femininity in all its aspects, and it is rendered particularly important through its association with Christ. The fact that the Grail is a "baptized" pagan symbol takes on additional significance if the Incarnation is properly understood as sanctifying all of creation. It is in this perspective that Greeley's Quest for the Grail must be understood. Rather than simply assuming that the Grail story is non-Christian, we might more properly inquire what it can teach us about the fullness of God and the true meaning of the Christian message. Seen in this light, the Grail might be interpreted as the womanly counterpart to the masculine cross, signifying the intersection of the infinite and the finite, Spirit and Nature, the Incarnation with its promise of the Resurrection and Life Eternal. In the archetypal code of mythos and the collective unconscious, the cross can be interpreted as representing the (masculine) tree of life and the grail the (feminine) lake of life. While the grail was (understandably, though unfortunately) never given magisterial approval as an official Christian symbol, it nevertheless has haunted the popular religious imagination for more than eight-hundred years, making its appearance in countless Romances and innumerable legends. The Grail, we are told, is the cup from which Jesus and the disciples drank during the Last Supper. Or else it is the bowl which Joseph of Arimathea used to catch the blood of Jesus after his side was pierced. It was brought to France by Mary of Magdala. It was even identified with the Philosopher's Stone, symbol of alchemical transformation and *coniunctio oppositorum,* which in turn shows common characteristics with the mysterious Tao. Wolfram describes it as a luminous, sacred object of infinite bounty, producing food for the hungry and permanent health for the faithful. Most significantly, as I have stated above, the Grail represents the fertile maternal cosmic womb which in turn is associated with the vessel of life-giving liquid and the principle of nourishment as such.

It seems more than coincidental that the Grail story began to captivate the medieval popular imagination at precisely the time that dualistic Manichaeanism reemerged in the form of the Cathar heresy in the south of France. In the Celtic tradition and among many of the early troubadors, most specifically Wolfram von Eschenbach, human love and the yearning for sexual fulfillment were portrayed as positive values. Parzival attains both the spiritual Grail and his beloved, Condwiramurs. Ultimately they merge into one, and together they reveal the nature of God. In Wolfram's tale, the love of woman and sexuality (if connected with fidelity) are portrayed as a mysterious and immensely powerful secular sacrament. Around that same time, Elizabeth of Hungary, one of the few married saints of the Church, loved both her young husband and Christ with consuming, tender passion. The sacramentality of sexuality, far from being Greeley's invention or a cheap sell-out to the contemporary preoccupation with sex in all its forms, reveals itself instead as a major religious theme, an aspect of Christianity as founded by God-become-Flesh, thus sanctifying for all time the material world. Chretien's version of the story, however, was influenced by Cathar dualism, which ironically survived the bloody mayhem of the Albigensian crusade and infected the already partially Neo-Platonic Catholic tradition with a new dose of life- and world-negation. During the waning Middle Ages this would lead to an almost total polarization of heaven and earth, spirit and flesh. Thus it can be argued, as Etienne Gilson has done, that the Quest for the Holy Grail is closely linked to Cistercian ecstasy, God's love manifested as grace (symbolized by the Grail), the divine gift for humanity, eliciting the human response of pure and spontaneous love leading to the *unio mystica*, entirely purged of all carnal dimensions. In a perversion of the early troubador ideal, the earthly goal of yearning must now always remain beyond reach. Love of God and the God of Love, chaste Agape and passionate Eros were at war; and the latter was temporarily defeated. Under Dominican auspices lyric poetry became exclusively devotional, yearning and desire were transferred to the Virgin, and by the fourteenth century the knights of the round table were chaste and celibate.

All of Greeley's protagonists must go through a symbolic reenactment of the passion, death, and resurrection of Christ. None of them are alone on their odyssey, their personal quest for the Grail. The Grail turns out to be an actively pursuing force, drawing them on toward the fulfillment of their yearning. Like Goethe's archetypal hero, Faust, or Dante in the *Divine Comedy*, they are supported, urged on, and ultimately saved through divine caring, tenderness, and affection, qualities traditionally connected with the womanly aspects of an androgynous deity and symbolized in the novels by a flesh-and-blood lover. This lover generally turns out to be the original girl (or boy, in the case of *Virgin and Martyr*) next door, their first and long-forsaken/betrayed love. The end of our explorations, as T.S. Eliot put it, is to return whence we started and recognize it for the first time. The God whom we seek also seeks us and turns out to have been living in our neighborhood all along.

Greeley's first published novel, *The Magic Cup*, based on the legend of Art the Son of Conn, already sounds the basic theme which is going to be replayed with variations in all the subsequent stories. Cormac MacDermot, son of a king and a Christian in still largely-pagan Ireland, accompanied (much against his better judgement) by the little slave-imp Brigid-Biddy and his faithful wolfhound Podraig (a large-pawed, affectionately slobbering canine version of the saint with a weakness for good-looking women) sets out on his quest to find the Magic Cup and the Magic Princess, in a setting reminiscent of the journey of Tobias who travels with the angel Raphael and a dog. (The animal companion is also a common Romance motif.) As the story progresses, the identity of Brigid becomes more and more mysterious, merging at once with the triple goddess of Kildare and the Virgin Mary. On the pagan harvest-fertility feast of Lugnasa—traditionally celebrated on August 1, only two weeks before the Catholic feast of the Assumption—Brigid has her first vision of an incredibly beautiful, dark-skinned, gentle woman, who will appear to her periodically throughout the story.

> She felt herself melting into the warm sun and blue sky. The hard green turf beneath her was becoming soft, the harsh festival music turned into gentle strings. Someone was humming. She was dressed in the richest of saffron tunics, laden with gold jewelry. She was a bride on a wedding bed. The beautiful woman was standing over her smiling complacently. "Did I tell you that you would be Queen of Ireland? Will you take care of him for me?" Was it Queen Ethne? No, it was someone else, someone even more beautiful.[28]

The associations of Mary and the still pagan Brigid, the slave girl and the queen, the bride and the protectress, are sounded while the harsh tones and rhythms of the old gods and rituals are resolved into the gentle strains of the new faith. As about-to-be-converted pagan femininity, Brigid is a perfect human manifestation of the Grail. Eventually, after many adventures and numerous attempts on his part to escape his destiny, even Cormac realizes that she may be the Magic Princess of his dreams. They are separated, he almost perishes, but in the end they are reunited and he is saved through her love and cunning. They even manage to return to Tara with a badly dented but no less splendid magic cup.

The major characters in *The Magic Cup* are reborn in the subsequent novels. Cormac MacDermot and Brigid appear in *Death in April* as Jim O'Neill and Lynnie Conroy. "Lynnie and the lake. The girl is the lake is the grail is God, . . ."[29] Jim muses early on in the story, preconsciously aware of the path prepared for him, the invitation extended. His Parisian psychiatrist friend Monique puts its succinctly:

> Women are his problem. He hates us and fears us, but also charms us and flatters us. Death and women—he flirts

with both, risks himself with both, and then runs. They are the same for him, poor man. To be possessed by a woman is to die. Classic syndrome. The last of the knights of the round table, a red-haired Lancelot forever seeking his grail, his sacred vessel.[30]

Woman God, the Grail, is both the ultimate goal of all our longings (particularly if we are male), and precisely because of Her immense power and fascination, a source of deep existential terror, inspiring awe as well as love. She represents a simultaneously attractive and dread-full invitation to radical intimacy, an intimacy frightening in purely human relationships but absolutely terrifying in its transcendent implications, as mystics pervaded by the fire of love can testify. The possibility of becoming most fully ourselves is often experienced as a fate worse than death.

He brushed her lips with his knuckles. "We can't stop each other from growing old," he said, trying to feel tragic.

"We can help each other grow old gracefully, she insisted.

More religion. "Are you grace for me too?" he asked skeptically.

Her eyes widened in surprise. She patted his hand like an affectionate parent. "Of course, dear," she said as though she were expecting the obvious. "I'm God for you." . . .

Back in his room, with the windows open to catch the soft lake breezes, he sat down to work. He hesitated as he put a new sheet of paper in the typewriter. His fantasy was the knight saving a magic princess. Once the magic princess was saved the knight might not want her. The fantasy was only a temporary energy source. Her fantasy involved grace; she took it seriously. It was a dangerous comic fantasy. He began to type, then paused and rubbed his chin thoughtfully. A *Comedy of Grace*: a title like that deserved a story.[31]

In real-life situations, the Grail attained, God encountered, the boy or girl next door captured, the summer-love transformed to lasting union, do not represent the conventional "they lived happily ever after" romance/fairy tale ending. The questing knight may liberate his magic princess, they may each find their Grail in the other, and consummate their relationship in ecstatic lovemaking; but life goes on, spring and summer evolve into autumn and winter, and their commitment will have to be renewed a thousand times. The Grail will continue to be a taunting and haunting horizon, more or less within reach, but ultimately the best we can hope for. And it really is a lot, to "help each other grow old gracefully," by being God for one another, not in the sense of idolatry, but in the sense of allowing divine grace, experienced in and through our friend-spouse-lover, to transform and guide us. This, after all, is the meaning of the sacramentality of the world.

Greeley's God, like that of Ignatius Loyola and Karl Rahner, operates in and through the demands of daily life. Dedication to one's work, acceptance of oneself and others, and love for one's mate are sacraments. Greeley balances the need for human effort with emphasis on the absolute gratuity of grace, and he proposes that human fragmentation be healed through a positive asceticism (learning to be an empathetic, tender, caring lover in our personal relationships), and this will facilitate renewed psychic integration and the attainment of full personhood.

This purifying, illuminating, transforming, unifying Love is the source of joy and peace. Grounded in God, experiencing reflections of divine passion in each other, lovers are mysteriously connected with all of humanity. This kind of love seems to be a Christian version of the Vedantic insight expressed in the *Brihadaranyaka Upanishad*, "Lo, verily, not for the love of the husband is the husband dear, but for the love of the Self [*atman/ brahman*, i.e. ultimate reality, "God"] a husband is dear. Lo verily, not for the love of the wife is a wife dear, but for the love of the Self is a wife dear."[32] Being God for others, allowing others to be God for us, permits each one of us to write and star in our own personal "comedy of grace."

Cormac and Brigid become Kevin Brennan and Ellen Foley of *The Cardinal Sins*. While their love remains unconsummated, it allows Kevin to mature into a compassionate and caring priest, precisely because the love is both passionate and erotic. "If my faith means anything to me, it means that the electricity between us survives death, just as the sun survives the night,"[33] he is finally able to admit, thus accepting his own sexual nature. He thus achieves the psychic *coniunctio*, appropriation of the *anima* in Jungian terms, essential for self-actualization. It is only after this vital step has been taken that his choice of celibacy becomes truly meaningful, since it now involves a transformation/transcendence of lust into spiritual passion.

> In her joyous laughter we were both young again; our lives were beginning; they stretched out ahead of us like the mysterious forest beyond the pond.
>
> "Laughter, like love," she said, as if reading my mind, "is stronger than death. You know that, Kevin. You preach it. Why don't you practice it? Why don't you let all of us love you?" . . .
>
> Part of me had died with Maureen in that room in the Gemmi Clinic. Another part was being born here by my spirit-haunted pond.
>
> Pain . . . chaos . . . rebirth . . . death . . . laughter . . . resurrection. Love stronger than death. A woman wrote that line at the end of the Song of Solomon.
>
> Maureen, Patsy, Mom, the Colonel, Cardinal Meyer, . . . all stronger than death. Ellen, who would go into the valley of darkness laughing.
>
> "You *will* let me love you?" A hint of anxiety in the grin.
>
> "Do I have any choice?"
>
> "None whatever. You never did.[34]

The Grail, even in Kevin's case, is attained through sexual love. There is no such thing, to paraphrase Paul Tillich, as love entirely stripped of all erotic vibrations. Humans are first and foremost sexual beings, and celibacy is simply one alternate form (a charism if you will) of being sexual. It does not demand that the quest for the Grail be abandoned, nor (despite St. Bernard whose use of blatantly erotic imagery belies his protestations) that those engaged in the quest cut themselves off from potentially sexually significant relationships. Kevin may be a priest, but it is through his relationship with Ellen that he touches the God of Love.

Cormac and Brigid are Sean Cronin and Nora Riley in *Thy Brother's Wife* (which shows intriguing parallels to the medieval Persian *Wis and Ramin*, an early alternate version of *Tristan and Isolde* with its sacramental-though-illicit lovemaking scene). Sean breaks his vows and in the process, accidentally by design, allows himself and Nora to be saved. "The rest of the world gradually faded back in, creating a halo around Nora's strong facial bones and radiant auburn hair. . . . Sean felt the muddy waters of damnation swirl around him."[35] He has spent his entire life struggling to be a saint by denying much of his essential humanity. Like Parzival on Good Friday he feels distant, alienated from God. He is alone, going through the routine motions of being a good priest, but zeal and passion are lacking.

With Nora he dares to accept the divine invitation to radical intimacy, he dares take the ultimate risk, a leap of faith into the unknown. For a long time he fails to grasp the true significance of this *felix culpa*. He is haunted by guilt, torment, self-contempt, until eleven years later he finally comprehends the pattern. "You damn fool," he writes into his spiritual journal, "You missed God's sign for thirty years." He finally realizes that "because he had lost his mother, God had sent him Nora, the best sign of God's love he would ever have. . . . Talk about the twisted lines of God."[36]

Cormac and Brigid are Hugh Donlon and Maria Manfredy in *Ascent into Hell*. As we have seen, Hugh's quest has taken him from the active priesthood to the heights and depths of worldly involvement. A man on the run from himself, life, fate, and God, he is drained and hollow, the ghost of who he might have been. He is in hell. Then, after his release from prison, Maria (like Lynnie of *Death in April* of Irish/Sicilian ancestry), possibly Greeley's most spectacular Magic Princess/Holy Grail, literally kidnaps him for a weekend of loving and healing. "I love you," she says, "I have always loved you and always will, no matter how much you hide from me."[37] But Hugh is not convinced yet, not until the infinitely resourceful Lady God arranges one more sign. Right in front of Maria's house, he finds himself called upon to absolve and anoint a dying woman, appropriately and providentially called Grace. "As dusk spread, Hugh felt a burst of light and warmth engulf him, drawing him toward the same Love who had crept out of the hedge in front of Maria's house to take Grace Monaghan home."[38] Hugh's dark night of the soul is yielding to perfect peace and joy. He has to die before he can live. And so he enters Maria's house, God's mansion, "a pleasant house, inviting, reassuring, comforting. And once you went into its light you never left."[39] He has come full circle, through Gethsemane to Bethlehem.

Cormac and Brigid are, to a lesser extent, Danny Farrell, and most definitely Noele Farrell in *Lord of the Dance*. Like his predecessors, Danny wants to escape his daughter Noele, *Virgo Grail* instead of Madonna Grail. He is at O'Hare, ready to board a jet, determined to evade his child, his wife, his destiny. "And then, suddenly there she was, striding purposefully down the length of the ticket line with the Holy Saturday sunlight burning bright in her long red hair, piled high on her head like a flaming strawberry ice cream cone."[40] God's love cannot, will not be denied. His Grail had come to claim him. "He linked arms with his Easter/Christmas mother/child and began to walk with her to the escalator, which would lead eventually to the parking lot of O'Hare International Airport and the rest of his life."[41] It is in scenes such as this that Greeley pursues his early vision of sanctifying technology and the city, literally creating new symbols, appropriate to the twentieth century.

Cormac and Brigid are, in an intriguing reversal of gender roles (entirely consistent with Greeley's view of the essential androgyny of God/humanity), Cathy Collins and Nick Curran in *Virgin and Martyr*. Cathy seems to be questing both for a pseudo-grail of artificial personal sanctity, and (unconsciously) for the real Grail of a maternally tender God who does not demand that grace be earned by strenuous efforts designed to destroy her already fragile self. She finds a sacrament of such a caring God in Nick. "He thinks I am his virgin bride, she thought, and maybe I am. . . . Then she considered that Nick might be Christ for her—might always have been, the only hint she had of God's love."[42] Nick, of course, finds in her *his* Grail. At the end of the book Father Blackie Ryan, Greeley's fictional alter ego, is mentally planning his friends' Christmas wedding, only a week away, "for Cathy would want him in her marriage bed as quickly as possible."[43] With his usual slightly cynical pragmatism he observes:

Nicholas and Catherine, Nick and Cathy, would live happily ever after. That is to say, they would have only three or four serious fights each week. . . . At least one day a week they would not speak to each other— . . . And on five days their life would be ordinary and routine.

But on the remaining day . . . ah, perhaps on that day they would know the love which is reputed to reflect the Love that launched the universe in a vast BANG.

Maybe even a day and a half some weeks.

Not much, perhaps. Only a little bit—a little bit of light in the gloom, a little bit of life in the entropy, a little bit of love in the indifference.

Maybe that is enough. Maybe, even, it is everything.[44]

Cormac and Brigid are Red and Eileen Kane in "The Patience of a Saint," that Christmas-Pentecost story of a man reborn and a marriage renewed, or possibly truly, sacramentally consummated for the first time. Red has lived with his Grail for twenty years, that teenage "witch with the green eyes"[45] whom he finally married, almost despite himself. For most of those twenty years he has failed to realize consciously just what she means to him, until he narrowly escapes being hit by a car and calls—her name. The Spirit, ever on the lookout for an opening, intervenes, and as we have seen, a passionate though complicated marital love-affair ensues. "I might lose Eileen,"[46] Red worries, concerned that his mysterious passionate wife with her ice green eyes and her legal mind might reject the new Red Kane. "I'd bet on her," says Blackie. Still, he cautions, "the grail is never fully possessed, but must always be pursued—that's the agony, the joy, and, to be candid, the fun."[47]

Cormac and Brigid are, most definitely, Brendan Ryan and Ciara Kelly in "Rite of Spring," which in many ways recaptures the fairy world of the *Magic Cup* in a contemporary setting, complete with numerous allusions to pagan fertility rites and a climactic conclusion right "on location" on the Strand of Inch. Like Jim O'Neill, Brendan is aware of his love for the elusive and mysterious Ciara as a quest for the Grail, a magnificent obsession which takes him from his sedate and celibate existence as a Chicago attorney (with a strange penchant for mystical experiences) all the way into the very eye of the Irish civil war. His Grail inspires him, revitalizes him, literally gives him the spine to refuse a supposed "friend's" demand that he put his career on the line to protect another "friend" who has betrayed him. "No way," he says. He has other things in his life now. "Like Ciara Kelly. My holy grail."[48]

> I was pursuing my holy grail, seeking not only love but happiness, my elixir of youth, my leprechaun's gold, at the end of the rainbow or wherever else this woman leprechaun had hid it. . .
>
> I wanted to fill her, impregnate her, fertilize her, bring my child to life inside her—even as I knew even before we had made love that she was already carrying my child. . . .
>
> . . . I wanted a woman and a child, a family, a community.[49]

> Finally, as the orchestra's music swelled to the mad crescendo of the sacrificial dance, I lost the remnants of my self-control and claimed her completely. My brain was clogged with insane images of her body swelling with the shape of my child within. Spring, fertility, love, life all rushing together to create unbearable pleasure. Ciara by then was able to reply, an aroused, passionate woman as out of control as I. Our own rite of spring was accomplished. We drained the holy grail together.[50]

More powerfully than in any other story, Brendan Ryan's Grail represents the symbol in its archetypal womb-fertility aspect, including the strange vision of the child already contained within the vessel. It is in and through Ciara that Brendan, once married to the aloof and tormented Madonna (the Virgin goddess in her barren manifestation) experiences not only the primal, powerful, life-giving femininity of Woman God but, for the first time ever fully, his own sexuality and thus—himself. In and through Ciara he is reborn and emerges a different man, confident and strangely young again. Unlike Greeley's other Magic Princess Grail characters, Ciara is not the girl next door,

nor is she Brendan's long-lost first love. She doesn't even come
from Chicago. There is something about her and their relationship, though, which suggests the possibility of a bond which
transcends space, time, and possibly even death. The ancient
Celtic motif of reincarnation is sounded ever so subtly. Brendan
experiences her as though she were his first love, as though he
had always known her, as though they had already spent a life-
time together. *Per saecula saeculorum.* In a sense she is his Irish
ancestry calling, alluring, enticing. She represents everything he
has ever wanted and never dared hope to attain. In his imagination he and Ciara are ancient mythological figures. He identifies
himself with the Celtic hero Finn (Fionn) McCool, who along
with the above-mentioned Cuchulainn, supplies one of the major sources for Parzival's childhood.[51]

In "Godgame" Rau dreams of a wonderful colorful magic
land of light and peace and love. In that land there dwells a
woman whose face he cannot see. He looks at his bride,
B'Mella. "I have wondered for years who she is," he finally
says, "and now I know that she is you."[52] He, too, has been
searching for and has finally found his Grail.

Greeley's Grail is certainly no "coy mistress." In the honored Celtic tradition She is an enthusiastic and active participant, weaving her "spells" with wisdom and vigor. She is the
Light which pierces our darkness when least expected, touching
sinners and saints alike. It is She whom Patrick experiences in
his mystic encounter with the luminous Grail rising from the
dark waters of the lake after his abortive attempt to rape Ellen.
She engulfs him with her gracious presence. "The light warmed
him. It cleansed and renewed him. Ellen was in the light; the
woman on the boat; Maureen, too. All the women in the world
were there with him, nursing, healing, loving him."[53] She
catches up with Hugh in front of Maria's house; and She turns
herself into a sunbeam moving lazily down Jefferson Avenue for
Noele, a laughing sunbeam, the manifestation of a dancing
God. She is Grace, totally gratuitous and given, described by
Blackie in *Virgin and Martyr* as a "combination of mist and
quicksilver,"[54] *a la* William James. Ultimately, She is the source
and object of dozens of big and little "epiphanies" scattered
throughout Greeley's novels, moments of divine self-revelation

and human response, of vocation, conversion, and marriage celebration.

There is at least one major epiphany in every novel. In the *Magic Cup,* Brigid experiences her moment of renewal in a vision of Mary and Jesus as she contemplates suicide standing on the cliffs above the churning sea. Suddenly she finds herself in the company of two gentle and oddly familiar strangers. She rails against them. She wants to die. Hope is a lie, an illusion. "I don't believe in hope. I don't believe in the two of you," she screams defiantly. "Do you think, child, that matters to us?"[55] replies the woman. In those simple, loving words God and World are reconciled, and Brigid experiences the healing power of the Madonna/Christ, as her bonds of despair and despondency are mysteriously untied.

For Jim O'Neill in *Death in April,* for Annie Reilly in *Angels of September,* and for Diana Lyons in "An Injudicious Affair," the epiphany takes the form of receiving and accepting forgiveness. Jim has viciously assaulted Lynnie and knows himself beyond redemption. "You love me and you're too goddamn much of a coward to take a chance on me," Lynnie has taunted him. "Mama's little boy is still afraid that Mama is going to come back and take away his balls again."[56] Her words have struck to the quick. She is right, and he cannot admit it. So he hits her, hard, twice, sending her sprawling across the bed. Soon, but not soon enough rage gives way to shame and repentance. What he has done is beyond forgiveness. Or is it? Two days later he finds out: "'Will you listen to him?' She took off her sunglasses—no black eye. 'He loses his temper once in his life and he thinks he is a jet-set caveman.' Her voice was unsteady, her eyes anxious. A curious kind of absolution. Without confession or contrition."[57] Jim accepts the offer.

Annie confesses that almost fifty years before she had started a fire at Mother of Angels elementary school. "I killed my two sisters and ninety other children and nuns."[58] Her friends refuse to condemn her. "Why don't you hate me?" she asks Blackie, Mary Kate, and Mike the Cop. Mike puts his arms around her, drawing her close. "Because we love you, that's why, goofy!"[59] Half a century of guilt and torment are lifted. Annie is forgiven by her friends who symbolize the Church which symbolizes God.

Diana has taken Conor Clarke's love and defiled it in an act of deliberate, malicious, Judas-like betrayal. She considers herself beyond hope, and yet, inexplicably, she finds herself asking for his forgiveness. "Her doom absorbed her, overwhelmed her with a torrent of protection that was both sweet and paralyzing, possessed her so totally that she had nothing left to distinguish her self from his."[60] Primal terror and psychic exposure give way to—laughter. Like Jim and Annie she learns to yield to grace.

Kevin's epiphany in *The Cardinal Sins* takes the form of Maureen's death. Part of him has died with his childhood friend, and precisely out of that death he is ready to be reborn, he is ready to let go of his armor of self-righteous pride and accept the sacrament of God's love in and through Ellen. "You *will* let me love you?" she says. "Do I have any choice?" he wonders. "None whatever. You never did."[61]

Both Nora in *Thy Brother's Wife* and Noele in *Lord of the Dance* experience their epiphanies in the form of a gently laughing, maternally tender divine presence.[62]

Hugh's epiphany in *Ascent into Hell* is Maria, the naked woman quoting Scripture, Sacred Love stretching out her hands toward him to show him the way out of hell. "You should stretch your hands to God. . . . "And let Him pull you out. . . . This way."[63]

Unlike most of Greeley's epiphanies which tend to occur toward the end of the books, Red Kane in "Rite of Spring" experiences his epiphany at the beginning. In the form of that "cosmic baseball bat" which assaults him at the corner of Wacker and Wacker, this most spectacular of all the epiphanies, constitutes the occasion and major motif of the story inextricably linked to Red's radical transformation and the subsequent renewal of his and Eileen's marriage, a relationship which symbolizes the passionate love affair of Yahweh/Christ with Israel/humanity, as "the daughter of Jerusalem turns into a Mother from Sligo."[64]

For Sue in *Happy are the Meek* the epiphany occurs as she is pursued by "a wolfpack of fire" and manages to save her daughter and escape from the hell and literal inferno of a Satanic ritual. "She pulls Laurel to her feet and with one final burst of energy and hope stumbles onto the little porch and topples toward the two stairs to the sidewalk. Firemen in black and yellow suits drench them instantly with water. It feels cold and clean and good."[65]

For Lisa in "The Clean of Heart" epiphany comes on the eve of the Feast of All Saints as a reawakening, a physical resurrection, after weeks in a coma which was precipitated by a murderous attacker driven by deadly envy.[66]

In "Godgame," a story about a story about a story, and possibly Greeley's most literary effort thus far, the science fiction medium allows him to give his imagination free reign while he explores the relationship of God and the world as analogous to the relationship of an author to his narrator and other characters. The epiphany motif in its association with Woman God emerges here in countless variations, affecting every one of the major characters and generally linked to the presence of the mysterious woman-child, Ranora, "a mixture of Tinker Bell and Ariel, a sprite, an imp, a pixie, . . . a female leprechaun, a trickster, a wise woman, a conscience, a sister, a daughter, a mother, and a haughty archangel."[67]

Early on in "Godgame," Greeley, author as well as narrator, sets the theme of the story by telling yet another story, that of a young woman's renewal of hope. "The struggle between light and darkness and the triumph, contested but indomitable of light over darkness, . . . , has become the critical symbol (the 'privileged symbol' Paul Ricoeur calls it) of what her life means, the core of her religion, the cosmos-making story in her existence."[68] It is in the resolution of this struggle, not only in "Nathan's God Game" but in *all* of Greeley's stories that the Grail reveals Herself as the *epiphaneia*, the glorious manifestation of Christ as the light of the world. *Surge, illuminare, Jerusalem: quia venit lumen tuum, et gloria Dei super te orta est* (Isaiah 60:1).

ten

a church to come home to

Gulls screeched over her head like the lost souls who were freed from hell Samaintide. Far beneath the foaming white waves smashed against the base of the cliffs. The sky was angry, the sea morose. How long . . . would it take to fall? How long would the pain last? . . . .

There were two people with her, a man and a woman—both smiling and gentle. Who were they? Where had they come from? Why had she not heard them?

"Peace be to you, princess," they said, so softly she could just hear them above the howling wind.

"Lug and Erihu be with you," she said in return, making clear that she was still a pagan.

They laughed.

She knew who they were. "You cannot stop me," she told them fiercely, drawing the purple mantle even tighter.

"Yes, we can," said the woman with a most attractive smile. "We won't let you do it."

"I'm free to do what I want," the princess shouted defiantly.

"Most certainly," said the man in a resonant, tender

voice. But, gentle princess, you don't really want to jump. Just this minute you were thinking about hope." He was even more charming and persuasive than—

"I don't believe in hope. I don't believe in the two of you."

"Do you think, child, that matters to us?" said the woman affectionately.

She wore a shining white cloak. The princess wondered where she got it.

"The Expected One will come," said the man. "You must wait for him. He needs your help. You must be here." He extended his hands as though he, too, were seeking her help.

"I am tired of waiting. He will never come." She was less certain now. Maybe these visitors *knew*.

"Waiting is praying, dear one," said the woman, "and praying will bring him." . . .[1]

"I am still waiting for the real sin, the only sin," I said.

She tilted her head. "I've told everything."

"You haven't told the one important thing. You were mad at God and mad at the Church and pretended for a long time you could get away from both."

"That's the only one that does matter, isn't it?" she said. All right, Kevin, I'll say it and you'll have to mop up the tears on this hard floor of yours. I blamed the Church and God for things that were inside me and my family. I focused on all the ugly things and forgot about Father Conroy and Sister Caroline and First Communion and May crownings and High Club dances and midnight mass and all those wonderful things that I love so much. I gave them all up because I was angry. I blamed the Church for Tim's death. I loved him so much. I couldn't save him, and I thought the Church should have saved him. Even when I was doing it, I knew I was wrong and that someday I'd be kneeling on the floor before you and pleading to be let back in."

"And now you have done it," I said, feeling a huge burden lift away and go spiraling off into space. "And the damn-fool Church says, 'Ellen Foley Curran Strauss, we really didn't notice you were gone, because we never let you go.'"

She put her head against my knee and wept. Then she gathered herself together and said, "So Ellen's worst sin was against Ellen. . . . For these and all the sins of my life I am heartily sorry and ask pardon of God and penance and absolution from you, Father. Is that the way to say it, Kevin. I feel so dreadfully out of it."

"It will do," I said, relaxing.[2]

t he Grail/Magic Princess represents both Woman God and the Church. Thus Noele in *Lord of the Dance*, conceived at Easter and born at Christmas, is a symbol both for the relentlessly pursuing deity and the Church as the best she can be. Brigid, on the other hand, might be interpreted as the Church in her harlot incarnation, corrupt, manipulative, envious, willing to sell herself for profit and power, and yet spectacular and redeemable, for "Brigid," after all, is linked to "Bride." Nora, in *Thy Brother's Wife* who supports and "mothers" all those she touches is another obvious Church analogue,[3] as is Eileen in "The Patience of a Saint." The Grail/Communal Womb aspect of the Church as source, nourisher, and goal of the faithful appears in the indefatigable Ryan clan with its Madonna penchant for not only cherishing and protecting each and every member of the family but also for adopting an assortment of needy strays, deserving or otherwise.

According the Catholic doctrine as restated in *Lumen Gentium* of Vatican Two, "The origin and growth of the Church are symbolized by the blood and the water which flowed from the open side of the crucified Jesus (cf. Jn 19:34),"[4] a symbol which is also connected with the Grail. The Church is the sheepfold "to which the sole and necessary gateway is Christ (Jn 10:1-10); the Church is a cultivated field, a City."[5] To reinforce these archetypes of femininity, the Church is called "a bride adorned for her husband (Rv 21:2ff) . . . the spotless spouse of the spotless lamb, and our mother."[6] In her identity as exile, "while on earth she journeys in a foreign land away from the Lord (cf. 2 Cor 5:6),"[7] and as such she also represents the pilgrim on his or her way home. She "encompasses with her love all those who are afflicted by human misery, . . . [and], clasping sinners to her bosom, at once holy and always in need of purification, follows constantly the path of penance and renewal."[8] She is compared to "the mystery of the incarnate Word."[9] By being identified both with the Mystical Body of Christ, "a single mystical person,"[10] and His Bride, she is envisioned primarily in terms of sexual imagery, called to "reveal in the world, faithfully, however darkly, the mystery of her Lord until, in the *consummation*, it shall be manifested in full light."[11]

In *The New Agenda*, Greeley includes a chapter on the Church entitled "From Ecclesiastical Structure to Community of the Faithful." This "headline" captures Greeley's vision for the Church in a brief, poignant, and pregnant form. The hoped-for movement of the Church from a rigid, authoritarian, and hierarchical bureaucratic institution shaped in the image of a judgmental father and tyrant toward the Church as a democratic fellowship of human beings engaged in a common dialogue with God, a Church shaped in the image of a loving Mother and Spouse, an implacably resourceful and supportive family, is a common and major theme in all of Greeley's novels. Hardly a newcomer, her spirit pervades the parables of Jesus whose radical message of genuine love may finally elicit a truly responsive chord in the democratic, pluralistic, and humanistic ideologies of the twentieth century. It is a Church which has remained alive, despite all official attempts to compromise and destroy it, in celebrations of Christmas and Easter, in stained glass windows, and in popular tales of Mother Mary and a host of caring saints. This Church lives on in the anonymous multitude of sensitive, reasonable, committed, parish priests who have for nearly two millennia, against all odds and largely eclipsed by their vociferous dogmatic brothers, foolishly persisted in their quiet labor of love. This ideal potential Church exists as a backdrop and horizon against which the shortcomings of both the Garrison Church of the early twentieth century and those of the post-Vatican Two Church appear in sharply etched relief. It is the *telos*, the actuality drawing the potentiality toward its fulfillment.

It is this kind of Church which is seen as emerging in the conversation of pagan Brigid with Jesus and Mary. Brigid finds herself in an unredeemed world, a world of barren cliffs rearing up from a melancholy, churning sea toward an angry sky, a world of emptiness and howling winds, a world without hope in which the ultimate defiant challenge of human dignity in the face of cosmic futility consists in suicide. "Their" laughter transforms the tragedy into comedy. "They" have arrived bringing joy and hope. Brigid's proudly desperate "I don't believe in hope, the fatal leap from the rearing cliffs into the yawning void, yields to the Christian "leap of faith" into the embrace of God represented on earth by the supportive community of the faithful. "I don't believe in the two of you," Brigid/humanity screams defiantly. "Do you think, child, that matters to us?" is the gentle reply. At the core of Christianity there lies a spirit of loving acceptance. The ancient gods have served their purpose; their season has passed; they are preserved and fulfilled, not annihilated. "The Expected One will come," refers on the literal level to Cormac. On the metaphorical level it characterizes the fundamental attitude of the Church preparing for the *eschaton*.

It is this kind of Church which is manifested in Kevin in his crucial conversation with Ellen (frequently noted by readers but totally disregarded by critics). The real Church emerges as a medley of warm images of communal life and shared humanity, as "Father Conroy and Sister Caroline and First Communion and May crownings and High Club dances and midnight mass and all those wonderful things that I love so much." The real Church (like Jesus and Mary) wraps us all up in her blue cloak of hope and love. "And the damn-fool Church says," in Kevin's words, "'Ellen Foley Curran Strauss, we really didn't notice you were gone, because we never let you go.'"[12]

A church created primarily in the image of a stern and patriarchal God, a Despot rather than a Friend, a Judge rather than a Lover, a traditional Father rather than a Mother, is bound to view itself as unyielding guardian and enforcer of *the Law*. Feminine nature (subtly or not so subtly inferior and evil) is subjugated to masculine (definitely superior) spirit. In Skinnerian terms, emphasis is on prohibition and punishment, aversive control, rather than positive reinforcement. Applying Maslow's theory, one might say that individual autonomy and self-actualization are discouraged in favor of safe and humble conformity to the *status quo.* Power is the name of the game. The hierarchical structure has become an end in itself, an idol, as Paul Tillich might note. The clergy is caught up in an untenable position. On the one hand, priests are considered elevated members of society, men apart, whose (inevitable) human weaknesses must be carefully concealed from the laity, lest the "ordinary faithful" lose respect for the Church. On the other hand, priests and/or religious are themselves no more than anonymous cogs in a vast bureaucracy.

Consequently individual excellence is suspect, as Greeley argues in the three novels of the *Passover Trilogy* in which his major competent priest characters all find themselves harassed and persecuted by fellow clergy and superiors for no other reason than their insistence on going beyond the call of duty, for daring to distinguish themselves as exceptionally dedicated and professionally responsible, rational individuals. Monsignor John Farrell in *Lord of the Dance,* slightly phony, vain, venal, self-righteous, but on balance a good priest, has committed the unpardonable sin of being a huge success hosting a Sunday night television show, which "earned for its host the criticism and the envy of many of his fellow priests and the animosity of the cardinal archbishop."[13] In lines which ring of personal experience and pain, Greeley describes John's reaction to Dads Fogarty's (a "brother" priest) attempt at humor in the diocesan newsletter:

> He reread the Fogarty article. It was not funny. . . . It did not even begin to measure up as satire. It was simply nasty, vicious, heavy-handed ridicule. . . . The "guys" were closing in. Again John Farrell felt sick to his stomach. . . .
>
> Which was the greater sin, vanity or envy?
>
> He would either cave in to the pressures of the clerical culture—far more of a threat than the cardinal's psychopathic rage—or become a permanent outcast among the men who were the most important people in his life outside of his own family.[14]

Greeley uses the expression "clerical culture" to indicate a particular kind of passively aggressive, authoritarian, rigid, resentful, and essentially inauthentic mode of relating to others characteristic of a certain segment of the "Catholic Establishment" (priests and religious) dedicated to the cult of humble mediocrity. The most noxious symptom of this collective neurosis consists in corrosive envy, most generally turned against those who are perceived as having strayed from the reservation. "Unable to fight their psychopathic leader," ruminates John Farrell, "the clergy of Chicago stayed alive by eating their own."[15]

This kind of Church rewards docile, noncontroversial mediocrity appropriate to a smoothly running mechanism with interchangeable elements. In addition to individual excellence, mystical experiences and private revelations are considered threats, since they bypass the ordinary chain of command. Even the traditional concept of the *ecclesia semper reformanda* is confined to the straight jacket of officially sanctioned pronouncements. Precisely because of this rigidity, this kind of Church, supported by an exoskeleton rather than a spine, is extremely vulnerable to attacks of manic irrationality once any of the rules are relaxed (as some of the recent developments in Holland might indicate).

It is this demonic potential within the Church which Greeley assaults with such vigor and determination in his fiction (and nonfiction). "Without Andrew Greeley, the American Church would be even more dishonest, boring, and irrelevant than it is," wrote one of the respondents in my "Clergy on Greeley" survey. He continued, "He loves his ecclesial family so deeply that he is willing to serve her with courageous independence and fierce love." Greeley's role might be considered analogous to that of a surgeon struggling to cut out a spreading cancer about to cripple a beloved patient to whom he is irrevocably tied, though he himself, I am sure, would much prefer to be remembered as a bard poking fun, a Peter Pan, a leprechaun.

While constructive criticism of the institutional Church constitutes a major thematic strand in *The Cardinal Sins*, *Thy Brother's Wife*, and *Ascent into Hell*, it takes on even greater significance in *Virgin and Martyr* which deals not so much with weaknesses in the Church as manifested by individuals, as it constitutes an analogical assessment of basic institutional policies of the contemporary global Church. Greeley's position throughout is one of loyal dissent. Blackie Ryan, at that time still in the seminary, makes the point in the course of discussing the 1960's clerical tendency to marry without proper dispensation. "To refuse even to attempt to obtain a dispensation seems to me deliberately and self-consciously contemptuous of the church. I am no defender of the abuses of power of those in church authority. I reserve the right to criticize as Paul criticized Peter, 'to his face.' But I can't be contemptuous of the church. It may not be much of a church now, but it's the only one I have."[16]

John Blackwood Ryan, eventually Ph.D., monsignor and rector of the Cathedral of the Holy Name, a specialist on Whitehead and James, and a seminary instructor in Greek and philosophy, is the latest and most appealing in a series of rational, sensitive, humane, paradigmatic priest-characters presented in Greeley's novels. In addition to being a genuinely caring human being, Blackie is a competent professional. He is a capable administrator, a shrewd and empathetic counselor, and a trained philosopher who continues to publish despite his far-ranging responsibilities. We first encounter him in *The Magic Cup* as both Abbot Colum, the holy man of Celtic pride and temper, and Bishop Enda, the wise and gentle mediator, passionately committed to the new faith (and his wife, Lady Ann) while remaining tolerant of the pagan gods and customs still present during this transitional era. He also appears in two incarnations in *Death in April*. He is the anonymous bearded priest whose sermon about the sexual symbolism implicit in the blessing of the Easter waters by plunging the lighted candle into their depths, sounds the perennial theme of God's passionate love affair with His people. This also introduces the central image explored in *Lord of the Dance*). He is also "Uncle Mike" described (like his literary descendant Blackie) as a "wee leprechaun priest . . . short, bouncy, green eyes sparkling with merriment."[17] He is what is good in Kevin and Patrick in *The Cardinal Sins*. He is Jimmy McGuire in *Thy Brother's Wife* who consistently tries to protect Sean from his destructive tendencies towards arrogant perfectionism and self-laceration. He understands the saving significance of Sean's "sin," despite the latter's horrified protestations to the contrary. He is Xav Martin in *Ascent into Hell*, a wise and sensible scholar at Hugh's seminary, and Dick McNamara "Ace" in *Lord of the Dance.*

Enter Blackie, whose veneer of cynical objectivity merely serves to accentuate his passionate dedication to the Church and those he loves with implacable fidelity, taking it upon himself to pursue truth and justice at any cost to himself. "As my friend Father Bill Grogan points out to me," writes Greeley in his memoir, "God is represented in my books by two kinds of characters, the implacable, generously loving Maria and the ingenious determined mystery solver Blackie."[18] God on earth, God Incarnate, the Mystical Body of Christ, becomes the Church; and as such the Maria/Blackie syzygy symbolizes not only the androgynous God but also the ideal Church, at once, to use a Hegelian image, combatants, battle, and battleground, the process of her own genesis. Blackie makes his first major appearance in *Virgin and Martyr* (after being introduced in the seasonal story "A Star for Christmas,"[19] which in turn evolves into the second chapter of "Happy are the Clean of Heart," the second of a series of Blackie Ryan mysteries based on the Beatitudes). In the Ryan clan Greeley presents an analogue for the Church at her best, utterly loyal to each and every family member, always ready to adopt "strays," engaged in an affectionate communal conspiracy designed to rescue whoever needs rescuing at the time. Ned Ryan, naval hero of the Battle of Leyte Gulf, a paradoxical mixture of tenderness and strength, makes a loving patriarch and "pope," particularly in conjunction with passionate, mercurial Kate Collins Ryan, his first wife and mother to John Blackwood (Blackie) and his sister, Mary Kate Murphy, a Freudian analyst happily married to a Jungian colleague. In the Ryans, Greeley's preconscious has crystallized the perfect image for his ideal Church, something sought after but never quite achieved in the earlier novels. He writes:

> The Ryans and their relatives are a kind of symbol for the Church, loyal, faithful, zany, tender, resolute. When they decide that they are going to adopt someone who needs their help, they do not even bother to ask. Their niece Catherine, their distant cousin Brendan, Mike Casey, Nick

Curran, Lisa Malone, are gathered into the clan with affection, persistence, and ingenuity. The Church has a long
way to go before it comes close to that model.[20]

In some ways *Virgin and Martyr* seems to be a literary
version of *How to Save the Catholic Church* by Greeley and his
sister, the theologian Mary G. Durkin. Many of the same problems are identified and parallel solutions are suggested. Neither
the reactionary Counter-Reformation immigrant Church of the
first half of the twentieth century nor the post-Vatican Two
Church of the past two decades is immune to scathing criticism.
There is something in *Virgin and Martyr* to offend virtually
everybody. Everybody, that is, who resents having pet causes
and pseudo-theological security blankets scrutinized and shred-
ded. The message is clear: the American Catholic Church is in
trouble. The global Church is in trouble. The twentieth century
in the form of a post-Vatican Two hurricane (or appropriately
Italian scirocco) has invaded her hallowed halls with a vengeance. The forces of change must be harnessed and controlled
lest they sweep away the structure. Still, and this essential point
must not be forgotten, *Virgin and Martyr*, in keeping with Greeley's faith in a loving and gracious God, is a work filled with
hope. The end of Catholicism and the Church is never a real
possibility. The Church will survive. In an altered form, and yet
mysteriously, eternally the same. Many of the birth pangs of
transition, however, could be alleviated, the period of readjust-
ment could be shortened if certain problems were identified and
solutions put into effect. A head-in-the-sand ostrich policy will
only prolong the agony.

On the institutional level, the major problem the Church
faces consists in a combination of Curial intransigence and Papal
isolation, which resulted, for example, in the "disastrous" birth
control encyclical *Humanae Vitae*, destined to be largely disregarded by the lower clergy and laity alike. This has lead to a
general decline in the power of ecclesiastical authority and an
increasing tendency of the laity to affiliate with the Church on
its own terms. In other words, the Church is plagued by a
scarcity of competent and genuinely educated leaders drawn
from the ranks of a relatively poorly prepared clergy.

Reflecting on this sad state of affairs, Blackie notes, "Most priests and nuns are not very well educated. They are not trained in disciplined intelligence, careful reflection, precise expression and respect for the grey, complex nature of reality. Indeed, such qualities are thought to be unnecessary for virtue if not a serious obstacle to it."[21] In all fairness, this statement should probably be amended by adding that this cult of mediocrity is certainly not limited to the preparation of clergy, and that, relatively speaking, priests and religious might well be somewhat better educated than the average college graduate. But this, unfortunately, means no more than being at best the proverbial one-eyed king in the land of the blind.

In the wake of the Second Vatican Council, this mixture of enthusiasm and incompetence leads to a "humid jungle of (half-assed) ideas and schemes,"[22] Blackie observes with his usual tact.

> The quick answers, the simple theories, the ready-made programs of the Counter-Reformation and the Immigrant Church had been swept away, leaving room for new answers, new theories, and new programs. But it was necessary that all of these be pre-packaged, clear and easy to apply. There was no time to inquire too deeply, no time to contemplate complexity, no room for hesitation and doubt.[23]

Manic social and political zeal took the place of careful, dispassionate reflection. *Virgin and Martyr* constitutes a full-scale assault on banners raised in the name of flash-in-the-pan relevance. Popular versions of liberation theology (adapted from Marx), charismatic renewal (borrowed from Pentecostal Protestantism), self-actualization (stolen from Maslow, albeit misunderstood), Third World rhetoric, encounter groups, women-priests, married priests, gay liberation, hastily deposed saints, . . . The list seems endless.

Greeley does not imply that these causes should not be legitimate concerns of the Church. No one has argued more consistently and forcefully than he for the utter absurdity of excluding women from the priesthood or the need for the Church to come to terms with her mystical tradition. Neither does he oppose civil rights, social justice, nuclear responsibility, and self-actualization. He simply argues that it is counterproductive to disconnect the reins of rationality and professional competence, and to put the cart of social and political action before the horses of faith, hope, and love. In a world permeated by rational reflection and transfigured by the all-embracing Love Greeley champions, the kind symbolized by the Madonna/Christ spreading Her mantle, no one would be left out in the cold.

Virgin and Martyr is an indictment not of issues but rather of the inept and amateurish manner in which these issues have been approached. Why is it, Greeley wonders, that so many theologians insist on seeking solutions to very real and urgent problems in alien traditions, while they neglect to look for answers in a rich and promising heritage? What makes Marx so much more appealing than Pope Leo XIII? Why does it occasionally appear that there is so little middle ground between the extremes of rigid fundamentalism and wholesale rejection of the past? "I think it's too much too soon," Blackie comments concerning the manic frenzy of the sixties. "We can't replace a culture that's at least five hundred years old in a few months. We have to proceed slowly, give it time, resist the temptation for the quick fix, the overnight update, the easy solution."[24]

Thus, ultimately, *Virgin and Martyr* is a passionate plea for quality, honesty, and sanity. Cathy, the female protagonist, a would-be saint who spends most of her life running away from herself by embracing "big causes," and who spouts traditional "sweet bridegroom Jesus" pieties as convincingly as she spouts "male-pig" feminist and "American Imperialist" revolutionary rhetoric, finally comes face-to-face with Reality in the form of a young woman, one of those she and her group have supposedly come to save. "Why cannot you North Americans leave us alone? Why must we be exploited by both your capitalists and your Marxists? Why do you impose on us your religion?"[25] It is obvious that she despises the corrupt right-wing military dictatorship running her country (Costaguana, taken from Joseph Conrad). Still, she insists, "Who asked you to be our advocates? . . . Who voted for you?"[26] Interesting question.

Blackie's observations about the plight of religious orders can be applied to the Church as a whole. "They had a wonderful ideal," he muses, "which toward the end they imposed mostly through power and envy. When the big changes came in the church and power and envy were turned into different forms, they found that they no longer understood what the ideal was." The orders and the Church, however, will survive, "in new forms. In communities that support instead of control, that fight envy instead of institutionalizing it, communities in which power is in the service of love."[27] This is a Church, to return to my earlier analogy, shaped in the image of a maternally tender God, a Friend rather than a Despot, a Lover rather than a Judge, a Spouse rather than a Master, a Mother rather than a traditional Father.

Not only *Virgin and Martyr* but almost all of Greeley's novels have their share of inept priests whose insensitive bumbling traumatizes innocent lay members of the community. Ellen Foley, Anne Reilly, Red Kane, Brendan Ryan, and Suzie Quinlan (of *Happy are the Meek*) have all been cruelly mistreated by official representatives of the Church. Anne Reilly, in particular, is almost destroyed by a priest's arrogant inhumanity:

"The Church is not interested in compassion, Mrs. Reilly," he said superciliously. "Our presumption is in favor of the sacramental bond. We must protect the sanctity of the bond, even if the cost is human suffering. People are not important, sacraments are." . . .

"Are you contemplating remarriage, Mrs. Reilly?" he asked bluntly.

"I must solemnly remind you that you put his and your immortal souls in grave jeopardy if you attempt such a marriage."

"I know that, Father. I won't marry him."

He didn't believe me. "Should you do so, you will cut yourself off from the Church's sacraments and from God's love for the rest of your life."[28]

This entirely uncaring and inhumane attitude on the part of "Step-Mother" Church is contrasted with Blackie's gentle and healing presence as he tries to explain to an exasperated and furious Anne that her sacrifice of a potentially loving marriage to the idol of *nomos* was entirely unnecessary.

"Yet the Vatican Council said with great wisdom that sacramental marriage is not merely the handing over of the rights to one's body but a gift of the total person. If there is no interpersonal communication possible, if man and woman do not achieve a certain bare minimum of sharing of their personhoods with each other, then there is no communication and no sacrament." . . .

He sighed and said, "Yes, indeed, Dr. Reilly. I will say it for you. Because you were a good Catholic laywoman and did what the Church told you to do, you've been abused, cheated, treated unjustly, unfairly. I wouldn't blame you if you walked out of this office and out of the Catholic Church and never had anything to do with us again."[29]

Greeley clearly recognizes the awesome responsibility born by representatives of the Church for the lives of individuals. As Blackie, the Punk, comments toward the end of *Angels of September,*

"And if you ask me, the only diabolism in this whole story is the diabolism of the ecclesiastical institution which was obsessed with sexual sins to the exclusion of all else, which emphasized guilt and punishment to the exclusion of all else, and was staffed by clergy, many if not most of whom hated and feared women. Blame the church for Anne Marie O'Brien Reilly's sufferings, not just after the fire, but for all her life."[30]

It is up to Mick, the Cop, Annie's Grail, lover, and future husband to put the pieces together and reflect on the Church as "Fair Bride/Loving Mother" and Whore:

"You know, Blackie," he went on, "it's the same church that's tormented her that's also helped her become who she is."
"I never said we were consistent, did I?" Blackie replied.[31]

Greeley never tires of contrasting the Church in her two

destructive manifestations, as authoritarian, reactionary, rule-ridden fossil and as manic incarnation of sloppy social activism dedicated to change for the sake of change with the *Real* Church of Christian Love. It is to this Church that Red Kane turns in his hour of need. "Where do I go for help? he asked himself again. The answer was still obvious. The only institution in the world that could help him now was the Roman Catholic Church—the *real* Catholic Church. . . . 'Holy Name Cathedral,' he told the driver."[32] One might even argue that by installing Monsignor Ryan as the rector of the cathedral, the parish church of the entire city, the bishop's own church, Greeley implicitly affirms his support of the institutional Church. He is not waging war against the hierarchy as such, merely against excessive authoritarianism, mediocrity and incompetence in leadership. More than eight centuries ago, Bernard of Clairvaux suggested that those in ecclesiastical power might be well advised to act more like mothers and less like masters. "Grow gentle," he wrote, "divest yourselves of ferocity, spare the rod and offer your breasts—breasts filled with milk not swelled with pride."[33]

Ultimately Greeley, like his protagonist Sean Cronin of *Thy Brother's Wife*, continuously reaffirms his commitment to the Church symbolized by the medieval hymn *Ubi Caritas et Amor*, Agape and Eros. She is his Magic Princess and his Holy Grail.

> Where charity and love prevail
> There God is ever found;
> Brought here together by Christ's love
> By love are we thus bound.
>
> With grateful joy and holy fear
> His charity we learn;
> Let us with heart and mind and soul
> Now love him in return.
>
> Forgive we now each other's faults
> As we our faults confess;
> And let us love each other well
> In Christian holiness.

Let strife among us be unknown,
Let all contention cease;
Be his the glory that we seek,
Be ours his holy peace.

Let us recall that in our midst
Dwells God's begotten Son;
As members of his body joined
We are in him made one.

No race nor creed can love exclude
If honored by God's Name;
Our brotherhood embraces all
Whose Father is the same.[34]

eleven

fIRE and WATER:
mysterium coniunctionis

"It is not so much the resurrection of Jesus we celebrate during this season, nor even the hope of our own resurrection, which is much harder to believe in. We celebrate, rather, something even more incredible—the mystery of God's passionate love for us, a passion revealed in the blessing of the Easter waters in which the lighted candle is plunged three times. This ancient symbol of intercourse tells us that we are thrust into life at the beginning of a passionate love affair to which we are invited to respond. God loves us with a passion that makes human love look weak by comparison. The resurrection of Jesus and the promise of our resurrection are the signs of this dazzling and terrifying love. To believe in the resurrection is to believe in such love and to believe that in the comforting embrace of God's love our own love becomes not only possible but necessary. So we celebrate always, but especially at this time of the year, the possibility of love and the conviction that love is stronger than death."[1]

This dazzling young woman was, unaccountably, the fruit of his loins, a child of fire and water. As Irene would say, a red and green Christmas child. Part giggly teenager, part sophisticated woman of the world, part ancient Irish witch. And each of her parts was almost impossible to resist. Noele, his ravaged daughter, now superbly triumphant. Wounded and invulnerable. Battered and resilient, indestructible.[2]

That's when the Lord God intervened.

Later Red would insist to his priests and his psychiatrist that he heard a "whooshing" sound in the air behind him, like someone swinging a mighty two-by-four. Or an outsize baseball bat. . . . There was a transient instant when he knew something was going to happen, that he might be well advised to duck, and that it wouldn't do him much good to try.

Then time stood still, the whole of eternity filling a single second and a single second filling the whole of eternity. He was opened up like a lock on the Chicago River and everything flowed into him, the 333 Wacker Building, the City, the blue sky, the world, the cosmos. With them came a love so enormous that his own puny identity was submerged in it like a piece of driftwood in the ocean. The invading love was searing, dazzling, overwhelming. It filled him with heat and light, fire that tore at his existence and seemed about to destroy him with pleasure and joy.

Later his psychiatrist would ask him contemptuously whether it was more like sex with his wife or his lover. He could only shake his head in dismay at the question. What happened on Wacker Drive was to the best sex what sex was to a bite of Hershey bar. The flaming, cosmic passion which had invaded him both threatened to deprive him of life and bathed him in extraordinary peace. Redmont Peter George Kane SAW.

What did he see, they would ask him when they wanted later to institutionalize him.

He SAW.

What?

The unity of everything in the universe and his own place in that unity, the certainty that everything would be all right. . . .

Time and space dissolved at the corner of Wacker and Wacker. The man who was Red Kane dissolved with them. A creature who used to be Red Kane was now dancing merrily on a flaming sea of ecstatic love. That creature was part of the sea on which it danced and had only a body and a three-piece, slightly frayed and more than slightly unpressed gray suit in common with what was once Red Kane.

Then the sea calmed down and the flames died out. Eternity slipped out of time. The cosmos retired to its proper place. The veils fell back into place.[3]

For the moment, it was sufficient to know that the Lord God had entered his life like a barrage of skyrockets exploding over Grant Park on the Fourth of July and that the first order of business was to once again envelop his wife in the fire of love which had, in some as yet inexplicable way because of her, taken possession of him on the banks of the Chicago River. . . .

Their love became an unrestrained eruption of two fire storms compelled to merge forever. . . . Finally there was satiety and peace. The naked female animal who had raced wildly down the mountainside with him was now a peaceful little girl, asleep in his arms.[4]

One of Greeley's favorite symbols to express the erotic dimensions of divine love is the Easter Vigil ritual of blessing the Baptismal waters by plunging the lighted Easter candle into its depths. This rite constitutes a "converted" version of an ancient pagan fertility rite, which in turn represents in Jungian terms the *mysterium coniunctionis* described as "the collision of the masculine, spiritual father-world ruled over by King Sol with the feminine, chthonic mother-world symbolized by the *aqua permanence* or by chaos."[5] The flame is extinguished as the celebrant lowers it into the font, three times according to the Tridentine liturgy, immersing it each time more deeply, in an obvious reenactment of intercourse. The old formula is clear. The power of the Holy Spirit descends into the water "Totamque huius aquae substantiam regenerandi *fecundet* effectu,"[6] and *fructifies* (impregnates, fertilizes) all the water in order to have it effect the new birth. The death of the cross has been overcome in the life of resurrection. Once again the archetypal motif linking death, marriage, sexuality, and rebirth is sounded. Greeley comments on our culturally conditioned inability to see the relationship between sexuality, the cross, and resurrection:

> The Christians of early Rome, who transferred the pagan spring fertility rite of plunging a candle into water, had no such difficulties. They knew that the lighted candle represented the penis and the water represented the vagina and a womb; and they knew, too, that their pagan friends and neighbors performed this rite in order to guard the fertility of their fields, their animals, and their wives. The early Christians thought that when Christ rose from the dead, he consummated his union with his bride, the church. If the resurrection looked like a sexual symbol then and does not look like one to us, the reason, perhaps, is that they had a much clearer realization than we do that life presumes fertility.

In *Memories, Dreams, Reflections,* Carl Gustav Jung describes a period in his life when in 1944 after fracturing his foot and suffering a serious heart attack he hovered for weeks at the brink of death. During that time he experienced a number of incredibly beautiful and significant visions which involved a series of mystical marriages. First came the kabbalistic union of Malchuth and Tifereth in the garden of pomegranates. He writes "At bottom I was myself: I was the marriage. And my beatitude was that of a blissful wedding."[8] He continues that next he experienced the Nuptials of the Lamb. "These were ineffable stages of joy. Angels were present, and light. I myself was the "Marriage of the Lamb."[9] Finally, in a classical amphitheater, he participated, as among dancers "upon a flower-decked couch All-father Zeus and Hera consummated the mystic marriage, as it is described in the *Iliad*."[10]

Summing up the experiences he writes:

> There is something I quite clearly remember. At the beginning, when I was having the vision of the garden of pomegranates, I asked the nurse to forgive me if she were harmed. There was such sanctity in the room, I said, that it might be harmful to her. Of course she did not understand me. For me the presence of sanctity had a magical atmosphere; I feared it might be unendurable to to others. I understood then why one speaks of the odor of sanctity, of the "sweet smell" of the Holy Ghost. This was it. There was a *pneuma* of inexpressible sanctity in the room, whose manifestation was the *mysterium coniunctionis*.
>
> I would never have experienced that any such experience was possible. It was not a product of imagination. The visions and experiences were utterly real; there was nothing subjective about them; they all had a quality of absolute objectivity."[11]

Ecstasy is ambiguous, supreme pain turning into supreme pleasure, supreme pleasure turning into supreme pain, a logical surd, a paradox akin to Cusanus' coincidence of the maximum and the minimum. It is something we both fear and seek, something utterly terrifying and, once achieved, a hint of perfection that we do not wish *ever* to end. It represents the edge, the horizon of finitude, and that which both brings and transcends death, the promise of psychic wholeness beyond the puny box of space and time. The link between sexual union, ecstasy, birth, death, and the transcendence of temporality is a primal intuition of the human soul.

The mystery of human sexuality and most particularly the uniquely human association of genital union not only with a permanent commitment to another (which might be reduced to the expediency of child raising and property management) but far more significantly, with the powerful emotions of love and friendship, inextricably links Eros (sexual *love*) with our perception of ultimate Reality (God). If the divine is envisioned as gracious, and if the cosmos emerges as essentially benign, we will be far more likely to take the risk of radically disclosing ourselves to another person, not only or even primarily by allowing him or her to see us in our physical nakedness but also by daring to expose the most tender and vulnerable inner core of our selves, than if we conceive of Reality as evil, capricious, or indifferent. We will dare surrender, precisely because the risk is not quite as great, and because we somehow expect that the Really Real will protect us from being totally destroyed. The very fact that Eros exists attests to the human propensity toward hope. It seems highly significant that romantic love made its first major appearance (though most generally in a non-genital, sublimated form) in human history in Christian medieval Europe, within the context of the hopeful Catholic analogical universe and at a time when popular piety focused most emphatically on Woman God in the form of the Virgin Mary. It may be equally significant that the twentieth century is finally allowing a further addition to the erotic spectrum: the realization that marriage, friendship, and genital fulfillment can and should be combined, and that the figures of spouse and playmate, of cherishing parent, lover, and best friend can all merge in that multifaceted creature called Wife or Husband. The master–slave relationship has evolved into the possibility of genuine equality, allowing for a conscious appropriation of the sexual dimension as communion par excellence and *the* symbol of the divine/human relationship. In her various incarnations, the slave girl from Jerusalem is at once the "Mother from Sligo" and Red Kane's best friend and passionate lover.

There are two ways of channeling and containing the raw energy of sexuality. The first (grounded in fear) surrounds it with the fences and dams of social and religious taboos and proscriptions; the second (grounded in acceptance) links it to tender, caring love which finds personal joy and satisfaction in making the other happy. The Greeks certainly envisioned their gods as sexual beings who expended a great deal of energy on their various *amours*. While most of them occasionally descended from Mount Olympus to pursue a particularly luscious maiden or handsome young warrior, this association generally had disastrous effects for the human "victim" thus honored, particularly if it was female, as Mary R. Lefkowitz points out in *Heroines and Hysterics*.[12] After Zeus impregnates Io he transforms his human lover into a perfectly formed heifer who naturally incurs the jealous wrath of Hera who relentlessly persecutes her bovine rival. Eventually, before delivering her son, Io is returned to human form. After the birth she conveniently disappears from the mythological stage. Yahweh, on the other hand, is envisioned as both passionate and faithful. This archetypal association of passion and love, anticipated in the Old Testament (albeit compromised by patriarchal misogynism) and consummated in the New Testament, provides the metaphysical foundation for an entirely different attitude both toward sexuality and toward women.

Ultimately, our yearning for sexual union cannot be separated from the uniquely human struggle to wrest meaning from a reluctant cosmos, to break out of isolation and alienation, and to merge with the the universal forces of life. This is clearly expressed in the symbolic code of the Jewish and Christian Scriptures which insists on portraying Yahweh as bound in a unique and passionate love relationship with his bride Israel and eventually with all of humanity. Judaism and Christianity have their beginning in the Sinai experience. For on that mountain El Shaddai, the God of the Fruitful Mountain, became Yahweh, the One Who causes things to be, the passionately pursuing, implacably loving, faithful and demanding Spouse who liberated His bride from bondage in Egypt, provided her with sustenance in the desert, and led her to the Promised Land "flowing with milk and honey." Even Yahweh's unbridled anger at His wayward bride takes on added significance if interpreted in terms of a passionate lover rejected and denied. The devastation of the flood yields to the renewed commitment of the rainbow. Yahweh's love affair with His people follows the familiar pattern of rhythmic cycles of alternately "falling in love, settling down, bottoming out and beginning again."[13] Comparative primatology and human brain physiology have demonstrated that violence and sexuality are closely linked, and it seems only logical that if we are formed in God's image, the divine original will display or be portrayed as displaying the same kind of passion/wrath association, only far more powerfully. Cosmic passion gives rise to cosmic fury. I am tempted to change the familiar quotation to "Heaven knows no fury like that of a (Woman?) God scorned."

Furthermore, while orthodox Judaism, in keeping with patriarchal and androcentric attitudes, tends to consider Yahweh exclusively in masculine terms, Greeley observes that "there is some evidence to support the notion that the writer of the book

[Genesis] considered God to be androgynous. God is not to be thought of as a 'He,' but rather as a 'He-She.' He continues that "when a husband and wife, then, seek unity with one another, they are attempting to achieve in their union a perfection which exists permanently in God."[14] This insight is strongly supported by the heterodox mystical tradition of the Kabbalah. According to Gershom G. Scholem, "at the heart of the Kabbalah we have a myth of the one God as a conjunction of all the primordial powers of being and a myth of the Torah as an infinite symbol, in which all images and all names point to a process in which God communicates Himself."[15] Kabbalistic mysticism interpreted the Scriptures to reflect an ultimate reality which creates by depositing the "world sperm" into the primordial womb yielding the additional seven archetypal potencies, and which eventually in the form of male potency (*yesod*) consummates the *hieros gamos* with the *Shekhinah* or female potency, seen at once as mother, wife, and daughter. Scholem continues that despite objections by strictly rabbinical, non-Kabbalistic Jews, this mystical conception of the feminine principle of the *Shekinah* as providential guide of Creation achieved enormous popularity among the masses of Jewish people. In a process analogous to the Catholic popular affection for the Virgin Mary, and the development of the Grail symbol, Jewish popular piety found ways to resist and subvert the orthodox insistence on the radical gulf between the Creator and creation with its rejection of the analogical imagination. Medieval rabbinical Judaism was distinguished by extreme rationalism, and in an almost Calvinistic manner it sacrificed God's living reality to His absolute purity. Undaunted by philosophical speculation, the people expressed their intuition that the true life of God consists in being experienced as part of the living world, and that living world most definitely included sexuality.

Eventually the *Shekinah* came to be identified not only with the mystical *Ecclesia* of Israel but also with the human soul, which is thus envisioned as originating within the feminine principle of God. Sin forces the *Shekinah* into exile causing the separation of the Tree of Life from the Tree of Knowledge, life from death. Scholem writes:

"The reunion of God and His *Shekinah* constitutes the meaning of redemption. In this state . . . the masculine and feminine are carried back to their original unity, and in this uninterrupted union of the two the powers of generation will once again flow unimpeded through all the worlds."[16]

Luria's hymn for the Sabbath meal captures much of the ritual connected with the sexual imagery. The ninth *sefirah*, *yesod*, "the foundation," is correlated with the male and female sex organs, and fish is an ancient symbol of fertility. Thus Catholics eating fish on Fridays are unknowingly reenacting a Jewish ritual designed to render the weekly intercourse on Friday night fruitful. The three branches are grace, judgment, and appeasing love; they are the three pillars of the world of the *sefiroth* from which all souls emanate.

> I sing in hymns
> to enter the gates,
> of the field of apples
> of holy ones.
>
> Between right and left
> the Bride approaches
> in holy jewels
> and festive garments.
>
> Her husband embraces her
> in her foundation,
> gives her fulfillment,
> squeezes out his strength.
>
> Bridesmen go forth
> and prepare for the bride,
> victuals of many kinds
> and all manner of fish.
>
> To beget souls
> and new spirits
> on the thirty-two paths
> and three branches.

> All worlds are formed
> and sealed within her,
> but all shine forth
> from the 'Old of Days.'

Sexual desire among humans thus reveals itself as far more than mere procreative instinct, it seeks to reenact the primal, divine drama of Yahweh's union with His bride. Greeley writes:

> In such a perspective, it becomes possible to say that when a husband and a wife who are deeply in love with each other reach the climax of their sexual orgasm, they have achieved something that is in the strict sense of the word, "godlike," because they have temporarily fused the Male and the Female. The *coincidentia oppositorum* has taken place, however briefly in them, and the primal fracture has been temporarily fused.[17]

Making love as reenactment of the cosmic process involves developing the kind of capacity for surprise which is characteristic of the Judeo-Christian worldview. As Jung implies, and Blackie Ryan insists on reminding us, God's quicksiver grace invariably appears at the most unlikely and inconvenient moments in the form of "BANG! there's the big surprise." Greeley quotes Richard Rolle:

> "I cannot tell you how surprised I was the first time I felt my heart begin to warm. It was real warmth too, not imaginary, and it felt as if it were actually on fire. I was astonished at the way the heat surged up, and how this new sensation brought great and unexpected comfort. I had to keep feeling my breast to make sure that there was no physical reason for it. . . . Once I realized that it was from within, I knew that this fire of love had no cause material or sinful but was the gift of my Maker."[18]

In the case of Red Kane, the original divine "surprise" takes the form of a "cosmic baseball bat"[19] which strikes him precisely at the corner of Wacker and Wacker when he notices in passing "the similarity between the color of a new glass skyscraper and his wife's ice green eyes,"[20] thus establishing for the reader an immediate association of God, the City, 333 Wacker, a coolly aloof, mysteriously self-contained, elegantly carved, curvaceously feminine building, and Eileen, his attorney wife of twenty years. When Red moves instinctively, to his own utter amazement, from this merry dance "on a flaming sea of ecstatic love," this self-shattering and self-reconstituting mystical experience, toward a renewed zest for life and most particularly toward the pursuit of his wife whom he had neglected for years, he actualizes in his life the tremendous power of the Holy Spirit, the divine fire of passionate zeal and dedication. Like the apostles, Red Kane has literally been raped by that searing, dazzling cosmic passion which breaks into his spatio-temporal chrysalis and allows his true self to emerge for an eternal instant in an indescribable experience of terrifyingly joyous transformation and radical union with the Really Real which nevertheless preserved his selfhood intact. Like those occasionally cowardly and usually pedestrian, average disciples of Jesus, like Paul on the road to Damascus, Red Kane will emerge from that encounter as the man he is meant to be, his life's purpose for once sharply in focus. Gone are the self-protective walls of pessimistic, jaded cynicism and self-pity. Dead is the Old Adam, the former Red Kane with his persona of the hard-boiled journalist obsessively dedicated to destroying foolish romantic notions of hope and happiness, the husband and father who needs neither his wife nor his children and considers love a childish illusion. The banked fires of passionate love at the innermost core of his being have been set ablaze, reinforced by a generous dose of divine lighter fluid. Red Kane has made contact with Reality, and Reality is Love. Reality is Grace. The cosmos is ultimately good. Red Kane has ceased to be afraid.

Once that fear is gone, that natural instinct to protect ourselves from the pain of rejection, we are free to act out our wildest fantasies. We are free to pursue potential lovers the way we wish to be pursued, to give fully and freely, and to receive greedily and joyfully. Filled with the Spirit of Love and Surprise, we too can dare to be unabashedly loving and surprising, thus personifying the theological insight that . . .

. . . the capacity to cause surprise and delight in others by erotic self-display is a continuation of Yahweh's work. It is not merely that by creating wonder in others our faith is manifested in the basic wonderfulness of the universe—the great surprise that Yahweh began on Sinai is continued and expanded.[22]

And so, dimly intuiting that he and Eileen have been given a second chance, realizing like Jim O'Neill and Hugh Donlon and all the others that his woman is God for him, Red Kane envelops "his wife in the fire of love."[23] They consummate their *hieros gamos* to the tune of the Song of Songs suggested to him by that lurking Cheshire Smile manifestation of the cosmic baseball bat called Spirit. Instead of falling on her like a savage bent on sating his lust, he roams her body "like a gazelle or young stag roams the mountain,"[24] delaying immediate, crude satisfaction for the joy of making his wife come alive and alight with every cell of her body, in every hidden recess of her soul, preparing her with his teasing fingers, setting her on fire with need, translating for her, on the earthly plane, the mystic ecstasy which has ravaged and transformed him at the corner of Wacker and Wacker. He takes away "her sanity, her separateness as a person, her boundaries of self-protection,"[25] while in a remote part of his brain he asks the question, eternally addressed by humans to their God, "What does she [She] see in me?"[26] He yields to passionate grace, allowing her lips and fingers, "the little foxes of her amusement"[27] to do their potent magic, submerging him into the very cauldron of primal creativity and supreme delight, until their passion becomes "an unrestrained eruption of two fire storms compelled to merge forever."[28]

Like Brendan and Ciara, together they have drained their Holy Grail, consummated their *hieros gamos*, their *mysterium coniunctionis*, their Nuptials of the Lamb. Once achieved, the sexual ritual will have to be reenacted again and again in order to build on the promise of their new beginning and keep the demons of routine boredom and creeping alienation at bay. But at least now, thanks to the Spirit's surprise appearance, they have a chance at a life together. "It is a mistake," writes Greeley, to think that God's love for us is the mild, circumspect *agape*, a bloodless, "nice" affection from which all passion has been drained. The God of the Testaments, New and Old, is not a "nice" God at all but a lover consumed with *eros*. It is disgraceful for his followers to mate with each other in any but the most fervent, erotic way. The greater the pleasure that man and woman give to each other—in bed and in every dimension of their relationship—the more is God present with them.[29]

One question remains. What might it be like for the physical, mortal human being to experience fully the passion of God? Would we, like that shrub in the desert be set ablaze without being consumed? It is in the science fiction story "Amazing," about Sean Seamus Desmond, Nobel Prize winning physicist, protected and pursued by his stunningly sensuous and utterly feminine guardian angel, that Greeley most specifically (and at times humorously) addresses this topic. Gaby, as Sean affectionately calls her, is at once a vision of "incredibly lovely patterns of color and light, dancing and spinning, weaving textured images that suggested the sounds of a symphony orchestra whose melodies would fill the Cosmos"[30] and a stunning, mature woman with "silver hair, smooth girlish face, full voluptuous figure, neatly encased in sweater and skirt, smooth skin, flawless facial bones, elegant and slender legs, soft brown eyes with long lashes,"[31] capable of reducing matter (such as enemy agents) to nuclear plasma like a fusion generator.

In their dark maroon suite, her gentle hands made the hurt go away, mother again curing her injured little boy. . . .

His lips moved to her breasts, her fingers tightened their grip on his head.

She was skilled in tender and prolonged foreplay. It probably takes them a couple of hundred years, Sean thought, as waves of sweetness rolled over him, like the peaceful waves of a caressing ocean.

Then, when it was time that he must enter her, their love changed. It became a fire rushing through a forest, a river plunging over a waterfall and dashing to the sea, a hurricane battering against the coast, molten lava running down a mountainside.

The sweetness, the pleasure, the joy were intolerable. Sean was drawn into a raging blast furnace, an out of control inferno which would devour and destroy.

Again he knew that he was going to die, ecstasy would tear him apart. He did not want to die, but he did not want to give up the ecstasy. Soon his heart would explode through his ribs and his body would tear itself into tiny pieces. It did not matter. Everyone must die. What better way than to be consumed by an overwhelming love.

Then it stopped. Abruptly and decisively the passionate embrace ended. Sean lay on his bed, spent and exhausted. Sexual fulfillment had not occurred and was both irrelevant and impossible. He had been pulled back from or perhaps thrown out of the blast furnace a second before his life would have been sacrificed.[32]

Gabriella, of course, is not God. She, like Sean, is one of God's creatures, but as an angel far closer to the primal force of pure energy than her human lover. One might speculate that divine passion is as far removed from her "blast furnace" as finite human passion is removed from hers. God loves us the way we love one another, only infinitely more so. No wonder mystics so often resort to erotic imagery to describe their experiences of divinity. Again the link between sexual orgasm and death appears. For the human organism to touch the Ark of Covenant means death, a death which reveals itself as eternal life. To be reborn, we must first die. Mass must be fully converted into energy. Space and time must be transcended. Death, as Jung realized in his visions, is the consummation of life, that ultimate union which can only be described in nuptial imagery. At the end of all our yearnings we shall be united in the Nuptials of the Lamb.

conclusion

"I'll always love you, Peter. Always."

"Oh?" I said intelligently—for lack of something else to say. "Why?"

Her turn. "Count the ways." More tears. "And if God choose, I shall but love thee better after death."

Then something happened—hormones in youthful animals, I suppose. Our arms encircled each other, our bodies pressed desperately together. If you are going to have only one skyrocket passionate kiss in your life, it might as well be with someone like Laura. She was as ethereal as the first shaft of light after a summer thunderstorm, as magical as the aurora on an August night, as solid and substantial as the noonday sun in the sky above us.

I was immersed, submerged, drowned in a soothing gentle cauldron of grace. Whatever the resident angels and saints might think, I resolved I would remain there always, even if she did taste strongly of lemonade and faintly of a post tooth brush cup of coffee.[1]

. . . "A proper portrait of God's justice would picture him dragging all of us into heaven by the skin of our teeth."

"Or other available parts of our anatomy," Blackie added, continuing his attempts at helpfulness. "By Her own admission God is horny."[2]

"'Adeste Fideles'," the priest went on, "is the oldest of Christmas carols, and one of the oldest hymns the Church has. . . ."

The carol was indeed light and delicate. The procession down the aisle seemed to be on tiptoe. Next to him Eileen was singing softly in her sweet, clear voice. Amazingly, Red was singing too.

Chaos swept through St. Clement's, blurring the whole church and the whole world. The cosmos once again dissolving. He reached for Eileen's hand, to protect her, no, to seek her protection.

Unaccountably her arm was already around him. She never made the same mistake twice. Exit mother from Sligo, enter daughter of Jerusalem.

There was another sound, overpowering the carol music, like hurricane surf at Grand Cayman, perhaps.

No, it wasn't surf. Not yet. It was a sound which was not a sound, a swooshing noise behind his head. Some warm breasted, bright winged character swinging a cosmic baseball bat.

Again.[3]

This book, as I indicated in the introduction, is about the God-Who-Is-Love, as mysteriously alluring as Juliet and as passionately pursuing as Romeo—only infinitely more so; a God who is at once the Holy Grail and the Questing Knight, the Magic Maiden and her Prince, the *Shekinah* and Yahweh, Mother Earth and Father Sky. A God, in short, like ours. A God who (through the dynamics of evolution) created us female as well as male according to the divine original, a God who equipped each individual with a lateralized, "androgynous" brain, and the overpowering urge to reverse the birth process by merging with another of (usually) the opposite gender.

If this God is to be approached in His/Her fullness, and the radical implications of the Incarnation are to be comprehended and allowed to permeate and transform the world, if the world is to be "consecrated," if Christianity is to be the living religion for today and tomorrow rather than the embalmed fossil of the past (enshrined in the idolized unchanging "Church" for Catholics, and the equally idolized unchanging Word for Protestants), then Woman God (the loving, gracious, unifying force at the root of reality) must be appropriated.

Since the feminine (*and* masculine) aspects of natural and/or divine reality are most fundamentally experienced in terms of the powers of procreation and fertility, the topic of Woman God is inextricably linked with the role of sexual attraction, (which, as a comparative study of myth and ritual shows, was intuitively recognized in early religions), and the topic of Eros emerges as a possible symbol for divine interaction with the world.

In the Judeo-Christian tradition, both Woman God and the sacramental potential of passionate love have been deliberately buried and distorted by official doctrine, which is contaminated at its root with a combination of Greek dualism and Hebrew as well as Greek androcentrism. In the Western context, dualism and androcentric patriarchalism have reinforced one another, constituting in their interaction a vicious circle of ideological "harmonic vibrations" combining to produce ever more powerful and destructive "waves."

For the first time in two thousand years social and ideological conditions are such that the feminine aspects of divinity and the sacramental potential of sexuality can be explored openly and the divisive forces of dualism can be overcome. Even contemporary science has discovered the ultimate folly of radically separating subject and object, matter and energy. Teilhard's noosphere is emerging whether we want to admit its Presence or not.

In the Judeo-Christian imagination Woman God lives in the figures of Jesus (who, despite his gender, represents the feminine attitudes of accepting and unifying love) and Mary (who has not only absorbed earlier versions of the Feminine but transformed and transcended them by offering a genuinely accessible, nonjudgmental, humane presence to a suffering and sinful world). She has also remained alive in unorthodox religious traditions (such as the Kabbalah with its insistence on the androgyny of God and the Christian katapathic mystic tradition) and the popular literary and artistic imagination which persisted not only in portraying Mary as a goddess in function if not in doctrine but also put the "External Feminine" at the very center of the Romance. As "secular scripture" the Romance offers an essential clue to the fundamentally gracious nature of ultimate reality if we grant that the intuitive insights expressed by the average person represent not naive and wrongheaded wishful thinking but are instead a valid path to God, an assumption entirely consistent with the theological position of the sacramentality of the world.

The novels of Andrew Greeley, whose "priesting" takes the form of sociological scholarship and the writing of popular fiction, provide the perfect paradigm of a (Catholic) Christian analogical universe by presenting both issues, that of Woman God and the sacramentality of sexuality, in popularly accessible imagery carefully designed to explode existing preconceptions which tend to obscure and limit the ways in which we apprehend divine reality.

Thus, ellipse-like, the reflections presented in this study revolve around two symbolic foci: Eros, the divine passion eternally seeking to unite the primal polarities of masculinity and femininity, and God in His womanly manifestation as the eternal Mother/Seductress forever plotting to attract and cherish Her children and lovers (analogous to Her masculine manifestation, Yahweh/Faust as power of relentless pursuit). Ultimately, the ellipse turns into a circle as both foci collapse into the single center which in the context of this study unites both Eros and Woman God: the analogical universe of Andrew Greeley's fiction. Greeley's "Romances of Renewal" are interpreted as a contemporary prophet's attempt to capture the essence of God as androgynous deity relating to us and expecting us to relate to Her/Him with the kind of passionate intensity appropriate to a world sanctified by the Incarnation and tending, according to Teilhard de Chardin, towards convergence and union in the Omega Point.

As Northrop Frye observed, ours is a transitional era characterized by "an energy common to subject and object which
can be expressed verbally only through some form of metaphor," a new-old "hieroglyphic," "kerygmatic," or "proclamatory" use of limit-language designed to release God from a
linguistic cenotaph, a language which can be "uncoded" by exploring the polysemous meaning (archetypal, metaphorical, and
allegorical levels) of the stories told.[4]

It is this kind of language of the analogical imagination
(identified by David Tracy as the way to dissolve the Gordian
knot of dualism) which Greeley uses in his stories, as shocking
to us as Jesus' parables of the employer who refuses to adjust his
pay to merit and the father who welcomes back his runaway son
with a party must have been to His Torah-steeped contemporar-
ies. "Surely our God who has promised to reward us according
to merit cannot be this *unfair*," one imagines the disciples grumbling, particularly when their foolish Rabbi insists on sending
the woman taken in sin on her way without demanding that she
be stoned or even express regret. "Surely it is blasphemous to
think of God as a physical lover, as enthusiastic voyeur, and as
participant in a ménage à trois," mutter and scream contemporary clerical critics of Greeley's novels. "God as a naked woman
chewing a cross, how disgusting!" The point in all those images
is the same. God loves us so much that Her/His passion explodes
all the commonsense categories of reason and even good taste.
"The trouble with the God that Jesus claimed to represent is that
he loves too much,"[5] and becomes a scandal and embarrassment
to the good, solid, righteous, law-abiding members of the con-
gregation. "Never, I repeat, NEVER fuck with the Lord God,"[6]
Blackie advises Red Kane. Shocking? Definitely. Poor taste?
Not in context. Effective? Most assuredly. And that is precisely
the point. With Peter Pan contrariness and leprechaun irrever-
ence, Greeley uses *any* expression, *any* image, *any* story which
might conceivably serve to break through the safe categories of
conventionally dead piety and spread the "Good News" of the
implacably loving, passionately pursuing androgynous Deity.
By linking God, Woman, and Sex, and sprinkling the resulting
mixture generously with both violence and tenderness, he arrived at the magic formula: whether infuriated or delighted,
offended or enthralled, people will be forced to listen and

think—about themselves, their friends and family, their love lives, their Church, and their God. For ultimately, the *real* protagonist of all of Greeley's stories is—Herself.

She appears in many archetypal incarnations, as Mother Goddess, the womb-tomb source and goal of physical life, the tender fountain of nourishment and protection; as Virgin, aloof and independent, untouched by man, the eternal promise of spring and youth; as Spouse, passionately alluring and implacably pursuing, at once strong and gentle, active and yielding, mysteriously concealed even in her nakedness, a perfect sacrament of gifted-ness and coiled erotic passion. She is the the "Eternal Feminine," the Jewish Mary and the Irish Brigid, Wolfram's Condwiramurs, Petrarch's Laura, Dante's Beatrice, Teilhard's Beatrix. She manifests Herself in the clear and yet unfathomable depths of the Lake, at once mysteriously alluring and profoundly threatening, and She metamorphoses into the Boat which allows the faithful to immerse themselves into Her essence. As Boat She is an ambivalent fusion of the occasion of Ninlil's rape by Enlil, the crystal vessel which carried the ancient Irish to the Island of the Immortal Women, Jesus' boat on the Lake of Galilee, the Ship of Fools, and St. Peter's Ark. She lurks in the House which is also Home, its interior warmly lit by the twentieth-century equivalent of Hesta's hearth, a "lighthouse" beacon of sorts, inviting, reassuring, comforting. "And once you went into its light you never left," realizes Hugh Donlon, "Mason Avenue, Lake Geneva, Bethlehem."[7] She lies in wait within the protectively captivating walls of the fascinating, dazzling, ever-changing and surprising City, at once the *civitas diaboli*, Las Vegas and the *civitas Dei*, Chicago-Camelot.

She both operates through and is reached by the path of Eros, the primal force of love and life, the highest and most potent form of fusion energy. The new birth (of ourselves as individual, actualized, God-related human beings, *and* the "community of the faithful") cannot occur until the real demons of sexuality (the flesh *denied* as enemy) have been exorcised, and sexuality is accepted as positive sacrament of creation and generation. The nuptial meaning of the body, the sacramentality of the flesh, must be recognized and affirmed. Properly understood, sexuality represents an invitation to physical *and* spiritual intimacy, which in turn demands that we overcome our pessimistic dread of dependence and vulnerability, rooted in suspicion of others (including the cosmos) and self-hating self-pity which insist that we can't be lovable. The empirical datum of sexual attraction and attractiveness allows us to approach ultimate reality as fundamentally loving and gracious.

The journey toward psychic wholeness involves the awareness of alienation and despair, the romantic descent into the libidinal underworld of chaotic instincts and violent, often deadly passions, the recovery of archetypes in the depths of the unconscious, a turning point (symbolized by Dante as literally passing through the Satanic anus), and the ascent toward renewed and consciously appropriated psychic integration.

The literary form of the Romance thus emerges as the perfect medium for Greeley's message. It is the "secular scripture" which, particularly in its courtly troubador incarnation rooted in Celtic non-dualistic worship of the Fully Feminine, celebrates the "Redemptive Female" left out of the officially redacted Scriptures of the androcentric, authoritarian, dualistic Church. It represents, literally, "the rest of the story," anticipated by "popular demand" in the marvelously multivalent figure of Mary, Catholic goddess in function if not in name, waiting to be discovered and recovered for the present age, as she was captured for the Middle Ages by Dante in her manifestation as Beatrice, a physical, real woman whom he loved on earth. She is both the incarnation of moral goodness and an accessible, tangible human being, a woman whose love sustains him through the Inferno and Purgatory to Paradise. He is redeemed through human love, he senses the sacramentality of the world and fuses the material and the spiritual. The entire *Divine Comedy* is an analogical argument for the popular insistence that human love can indeed lead to the beatific vision, that God might lurk in a lover's glance and passionate embrace.

The post-modern period with its supposed secularism presents precisely the kind of fertile ground necessary to comprehend God in His/Her fullness and finally to allow the radical implications of the Incarnation to transform our lives, admitting both woman as analogue for God and the sacramental potential of our sexual nature. Nineteenth-century positivism unwittingly prepared the field by burning off the accumulated deadwood of the past while leaving the living root systems intact.

Our vision need no longer be obscured by the impenetrable walls constructed by the Catholic "garrison" Church or the Protestant "unchanging" Word. The analogical universes of Christianity and the Romance are free to be united.

Unlike the authors of most literary Romances, however, who because of their Hellenistic, Patristic, or Cathar dualism) derive a great deal of action out of protecting the heroine's hymen from laceration by friends as well as foes, and tend to relegate sexual consummation to a point shortly *after* the conclusion of the story, portraying it as the anticipated, secret event yet to occur, Greeley consciously uses physical passion and union as symbols for both preexisting divine love and the elemental force facilitating not only the initial consummation but possibly even more importantly, the continued renewal of existing relationships.

Greeley's Eros is not the selfish, vulgar fellow bent upon a quick and preferably adulterous roll in the hay, set up and attacked as a "straw man" by de Rougemont and countless generations of well-meaning flesh-hating celibate confessors. Instead, "he" symbolizes divine passion pure and simple, the "Love," as Blackie puts it, "that launched the universe in a vast BANG,"[8] the love to which each one of us owes our individual existence, the loyal and committed yet endlessly surprising and delightful love which lies at the base of all genuine friendship and marriage as a sacrament.

Once Eros has been recovered, despair yields to hope and death to life, as the chrysalis of the human tragedy breaks open to reveal the overarching divine comedy of grace. The journey can be continued, and a new beginning can occur (for the second or twenty-second time). Beyond the churning thunderclouds, the goal is now in sight, the clear blue summer sky, the Holy Grail, the Magic Princess, the *real* Church, the primal inspiration and the ultimate goal of the human quest. Paradise Lost is transformed into Paradise Regained, and we discover that the object of all our yearnings has been with us all along. Greeley's Celtic roots are essential at this point, for he not only portrays his Magic Princess as an implacably pursuing force, actively participating in the quest, but he also resolves the dualistic dilemma in a typically Celtic manner by positing the "Other World . . . neither above nor below, but *beside*, . . . [to be]

entered when one wishes."[9] This vision of reality is most clearly expressed in the science fiction universe of "Godgame," which literally posits an alternate, parallel cosmos connected to ours through channels of love.

The Magic Cup, the Holy Grail, thus emerges as the central and most significant symbol in Greeley's writings, for even more than the literary form of the Romance (though inseparable from it), the Grail theme allows him to combine his two loves for the Catholic Church and for his Irish heritage, while simultaneously permitting him to pursue the theological topics of the sacramentality of sexuality and the womanliness of God.

The mysterious Grail calls up countless archetypal associations, womanly as well as androgynous, pagan as well as Christian. Some of these associations include the Celtic feminine principle of birth, death, and immortality; a mysteriously ill Fisher King, evoking images of Jesus and the ichthys/fish as symbolic of nourishment, fertility, and sexually alluring and aroused women; the Last Supper; an infant descending into the Eucharistic wafer contained in the Grail; the vessel/womb being fertilized, and the Christian event of the Annunciation/Incarnation; a lance bleeding into a silver cup or cauldron, brought to France by Mary of Magdala; the Eucharistic cup, or the ciborium placed in charge of a woman, and thus Mary as *theotokos* (God-bearer), the manifestation of the nurturing, healing, maternal, passionately and tenderly loving aspects of divinity. Seen in this perspective, the Grail not only represents divine femininity in all its aspects but is also associated specifically with the redemptive passion of Christ. It is even linked to the Philosopher's Stone, symbol of alchemical transformation, eternal youth, the *coniunctio oppositorum,* and the *mysterium coniunctionis.*

In its communal manifestation the Holy Grail/Magic Princess syzygy represents the Church as Fair Bride: Blackie's ideal Church, the one symbolized by Noele, conceived at Easter and born at Christmas, and the Ryan clan, a community dedicated to fostering emotional and intellectual maturity among its members, a community which supports rather than controls, which resists envy, and puts power into the service of love, a Church formed in the image of a gracious God, of Woman God at once the lioness, fiercely protecting her young, and the Madonna, gently spreading Her mantle. The Church-as-Grail lives in priests like Blackie Ryan and is anticipated in Kevin Brennan listening to Ellen confess her "real sin." It is "a Church of First Communion and May Crownings and Midnight Mass and Community and Love . . . a damn-fool Church which says," like her damn-fool founder, "'Ellen Foley Curran Strauss [significantly, a Catholic married to a Jew], we really didn't notice you were gone, because we never let you go.'"[10]

This Church as Community of Love is contrasted to the Church as Whore, hustling for power in the name of religion, a Church of inhumane and inhuman laws and regulations, uncaring, intoxicated with the need to control, permeated by hypocrisy and envy, shaped in the image of God the Tyrant who is concerned not about people but Sacraments.

The erotic dimensions of divine love as well as the ultimate goal of the individual and humankind as the mystical marriage of Jesus and the Church are symbolically represented by the Easter Vigil Christianized pagan fertility rite of blessing the Baptismal waters by plunging the lighted Easter candle into their depths. This rite analogically links the archetypal motifs of birth, death, sexuality, and divinity. Ecstasy, in all its joy/pain ambiguity, revealed most clearly in mystical experiences and sexual union, emerges as the edge, the horizon of finitude. Mystics and lovers in the throes of passion are literally invaded by that searing, dazzling cosmic Eros which breaks into their spatio-temporal chrysalis, that Spirit of Love and Surprise which allows their true selves to emerge for an eternal instant in an indescribable experience of terrifyingly joyous transformation and radical union with the Really Real, which nevertheless preserves their selfhood intact and presents a limit-experience in the here-and-now of the Death-Which-Is-Life.

The erotic dimension of human life is shown as inextricably associated with the uniquely human struggle to wrest meaning from a reluctant cosmos, to break out of isolation and alienation and to merge with the the universal forces of life, a primal instinct mythically expressed in the nuptial imagery of Yahweh's stormy love affair with His people, and the Kabbalistic myth of God as a conjunction of all the primordial powers of being and becoming, the *hieros gamos* of the masculine *yesod* with the *Shekinah*, the feminine, providential guide of Creation. Ultimately our God, Yahweh-Wisdom-Jesus, primal Mother/

Father, Holy Grail and Magic Princess/Prince reveals Himself/ Herself to each one of us in and through those we love and by whom we are loved. We are sacraments of divine love for others, as they are sacraments of divine love for us.

And so, Andrew Greeley, man, scholar, storyteller, and priest, first and foremost priest, recalls a vision from the past, his "Eternal Feminine," Beatrice-Brigid-Mary-God, and affirms his faith in the graciousness of the Really Real.

> A still life in my memory, aflame
> As a Van Gogh blossom, radiantly fresh
> Unfaded by the claims of age and pain,
> And the first quiet hints of lurking death.
> Girl and woman in delicate suspension,
> Deft painting bathed in blue and golden glow
> Perfection, promise in one dimension
> And a self that has only begun to grow.
>
> Now, wife, mother, widow, forty years have fled
> Does your story, just begun, approach its end?
> Are your bright grace and promise already dead?
> Hope remains, distant rival, do not bend.
> By God's love at fourteen you were not misled.
> We shall be young once more, we shall laugh
> again.[11]

notes

Preface

   1. William Smith, "Brotherly Advice," *National Catholic Register*, 4 September 1983, p. 4.

   2. Cf. Ingrid H. Shafer, "Catholic Priests on Andrew Greeley," *Chicago Studies*, Fall 1986. In this article I report and analyze the findings of both the preliminary national survey and a subsequent in-depth study of Chicago Archdiocesan priests. The hypothesis of a submerged hostility-engendering factor was neatly born out. Multiple regression analysis uncovered that a "clerical culture factor" made up of the following three variables, all antecendent to reading the novels, explained well over half the variance in hostile reactions to Greeley's novels: a) the respondent's image of God, b) the respondent's image of the Church, and c) the respondent's attitude toward Greeley's financial success. Those who had a rigidly authoritarian (traditionally masculine) image of God, feared for the image of the Church, and resented the author's monetary success, were far more likely to have hostile opinions concerning the books. Those who had a more flexible and democratic (traditionally feminine) image of God, saw the Church as a relatively unthreatened institution, and did not suspect the author's motivation, tended to react far more favorably to his books.

3. Andrew M. Greeley, "Who Reads *Those* Books," *America*, 26 May 1984, p. 395.

Introduction

1. Alfred North Whitehead, *Religion in the Making: Lowell Lectures, 1926* (New York: The Macmillan Company, 1926), pp. 16-17.

2. Andrew M. Greeley, *The New Agenda: A proposal for a new approach to fundamental religious issues in contemporary terms with a foreword by Gregory Baum* (New York: Image Books, 1975), p. 17.

3. David Tracy, *The Analogical Imagination: Christian Theology and the Culture of Pluralism* (New York: Crossroads, 1981), p. 32.

4. Ibid., p. 451.

5. Elisabeth Schüssler Fiorenza, *In Memory of Her: A Feminist Theological Reconstruction of Christian Origins*, (New York: Crossroads, 1984), p. 42.

6. Cf. Bernadette Brooten and Norbert Greinacher, eds., *Frauen in der Männerkirche* (Munich: Kaiser, 1982 and Mainz: Grünewald, 1982). This excellent little volume provides a multifaceted international introduction to current feminist theological thinking concerning the role of women and attitudes toward sexuality in the Church. Contributors include Maria Agudelo, Elizabeth Carroll, Marie de Merode-de Croy, Nadine Foley, Naomi R. Goldenberg, Jacqueline Grant, Catherina J.M. Helkes, Beverly Wildung Harrison, Hans Küng, René Laurentin, Ferdinand Menne, Marie-Augusta Neal, Judith Plaskow, Ida Raming, Elisabeth Schüssler Fiorenza, and Dorothy Sölle.

7. Fiorenza, p. 35.

8. Ibid., p. 41; italics mine.

9. Cf. Herbert Biesel, *Dichtung und Prophetie* (Düsseldorf: Patmos, 1972). While Biesel's volume deals with Goethe, T. Mann, Rilke, and Kafka, his basic premise that poetry and fiction are by their very nature prophetic in the sense of illuminating the religious dimensions and meaning systems of their world and times, is relevant to the methodology of this study.

Greeley himself has discussed this point repeatedly in such nonfiction books as *The Religious Imagination* and such articles as "Films as Sacrament" (*The Critic*, Fall 1985). Also compare Richard Blake's objective, sensitive, and challenging review of Jean-Luc Godard's controversial film "Hail Mary" in *America* (November, 1985). Blake comprehends not only the ontological necessity of a fully female Immaculata (free of sin but blessed with sex), but tacitly assumes the sacramental potential of film. He vividly describes a "limit-experience," his personal encounter with "Mystery," precipitated precisely by the shock of the Virgin presented as an *erotically* appealing young woman, a self-actualizer utterly in tune with her organismic identity. I can think of no more convincing argument for the power of the Spirit lurking literally *everywhere* waiting to break through our carefully constructed self-protective shells than a priest's honest admission that by viewing the film and mulling over its implications "the Word . . . was made flesh" for him, "not an idea, but wondrously and beautifully through the cells and the fluids of a woman's body."

10. Tracy, p. 451.

11. David Tracy, *Blessed Rage for Order: The New Pluralism in Theology* (New York: The Seabury Press, 1975), pp. 135-36.

One

1. Greeley, *Lord of the Dance* (New York: Warner Books, 1984), pp. 377-78.

2. John Shea, *Stories of Faith*, (Chicago: Thomas More, 1980), p. 75.

3. Bernard J.F. Lonergan, S.J., *Method in Theology* (New York: Herder and Herder, 1972), p. 112.

4. Greeley, *Unsecular Man* (New York: Schocken Books, 1972), p. 1.

5. John Shea, *An Experience Named Spirit* (Chicago: Thomas More, 1983), pp. 12-13.

6. In the context of this study it is important to note that I am using the term "Romance" in the strict sense as a legitimate literary form to be distinguished from Harlequin-type formula

works. To accentuate that distinction the word will be capital-
ized throughout unless it is employed to include the popular
meaning. For my understanding of the Romance and its place in
popular (as contrasted with elite) literary imagination, I am
deeply indebted to the work of Northrop Frye.

7. Shea, *Experience*, p.13.

8. Greeley, *Religion: A Secular Theory*. (New York: The
Free Press, 1982), p. 33.

9. Greeley, *The Religious Imagination* (Los Angeles: Sadlier, 1981), p. 18.

10. Greeley, *Religion*, p. 34.

11. Greeley, *Imagination*, p. 17. For an original, scholarly,
and beautifully written exploration of narrative theology see
Terrence W. Tilley, *Story Theology* (*Theology and Life Series 12*,
Wilmington, Delaware: Michael Glazier, 1985). Since I did not
discover this book until after my book had been accepted for
publication, I did not use it as reference in the text. Otherwise, I
would have certainly noted his distinction between *myths* ("stories that set up worlds"), *parables* ("stories that upset worlds"),
and *actions* ("realistic stories set within worlds"). I was delighted,
however, to note Tilley make "my" point when he wrote "The
tasks of any Christian theology are to explore the traditions of,
to transform (when necessary) the formulations of, and to proclaim the meaning of the Christian faith. A Christian *propositional* theology engages in exploring, transforming, and proclaiming the stories of Christianity. A Christian *narrative* theology
undertakes exploring, transforming and proclaiming the stories
of Christianity. If stories give meaning to the metaphors/stereo-
types/codewords/doctrines which we use, then a narrative theology is more fundamental than a propositional theology." (p.
11) In other words, the religious imagination is ontologically
prior to the rational constructs of propositional theology. The
Hegelian in me notes an interesting dialectical tension between
the two types of theology. While narrative theology by its very
nature accepts ambiguity and tends toward open-ended pluralism and process, propositional theology generally sees its task as
establishing closed systems of ultimate Truth. To use the overarching metaphor of this book: the story telling religious imagination might be linked with the Great Mother feminine dimension of divinity while the proposition-making religious intellect

might be viewed as proceeding from the masculine God of philosophers and theologians. It should be remembered that each is barren apart from the other. Paradoxically (in another application of the dialectic), the very pluralism of story-telling tends to engender a lived reality of non-dualistic acceptance, synthesis, and holism.

12. Greeley, *Thy Brother's Wife* (New York: Warner Books, 1982), p. 276.

13. Greeley, *Imagination*, p. 18.

14. Greeley, *Lord*, p. 11.

15. Greeley, *Lord*, p. 67.

16. Ibid., p.59.

17. Northrop Frye, *The Great Code: The Bible and Literature* (New York and London: Harcourt Brace Jovanovich, 1981), p. 15. Within the context of literary criticism Frye deals with precisely the same intuition of a momentous paradigm shift toward non-dualistic non-mechanistic "field theories" affecting the very structure of our ways of viewing ourselves, the world, and ultimate reality which is explored by such contemporary thinkers as the economist E.F. Schumacher and the theoretical physicist Fritjof Capra.

18. Ibid., p. 16.

19. Carl Gustav Jung, *Man and His Symbols* (Garden City, New York: Doubleday, 1964), p. 89.

20. Greeley, *Strangers in the House: Catholic Youth in America* (New York: Sheed and Ward, 1961), p. 15.

21. Ibid., p. 22.

22. Ibid., p. 61.

23. Ibid., p. 64.

Two

1. Greeley, *Wife*, p. 276.

2. Angelo Roncalli, *Journal of a Soul* (London, Geoffrey Chapman, 1980), pp. 95-96; quoted in Margaret Hebblethwaite, *Motherhood and God* (London: Geoffrey Chapman, 1984), p. 136.

3. Burke, Thomas J.M., S.J., ed., *Mary and Modern Man* (New York: The America Press, 1954), p. 49.

4. Schillebeeckx, *Jesus, An Experiment in Christology* (New York: Seabury Press, 1979), p. 178.

5. Greeley, "Godgame," p. 50.

6. Karl Rahner, *Theological Investigations. Volume I: God, Christ, Mary and Grace.* Translated with an Introduction by Cornelius Ernst, O.P. (Baltimore: Helicon Press, 1969), p. 124.

7. Ibid., p.123.

8. Ibid., p.125.

9. Ibid., p. 209.

10. Revelations 14:4.

11. Carl Gustav Jung, *The Psychology of C.G. Jung*, trans. K.W. Bash (New Haven: Yale University Press, 1954), p. 162.

12. Eric Erikson, *Identity: Youth and Crisis* (New York: Norton, 1963), pp. 185-86.

13. Cf. Fiorenza, p. 233.

14. Robert M. Pirsig, *Zen and the Art of Motorcycle Maintenance* (Toronto and New York: Bantam New Age Books, 1981), pp. 69-72. The work presents a powerful argument for the fatal effects, both for the individual and a for civilization, of overemphasizing one or the other of the two modes of thinking and being. Significantly, the narrator/author finds the goal for his quest for self/God at the "bottom of the ocean," an archetype for the primal creative Matrix/Mother of all things.

15. Hajime Nakamura, *Ways of Thinking of Eastern Peoples: India-China-Tibet-Japan*, revised English translation, edited by Philip P. Wiener, (Honolulu: East-West Center Press, 1968). Cf. Wendy Doniger O'Flaherty, *Dreams, Illusion and Other Realities*, The University of Chicago Press, Chicago and London, 1984, which offers evidence for and explores the Indian tendency to blur the boundaries between dream and waking, subjective and objective, psychic and material reality.

16. Gershom G. Scholem *On the Kabbalah and its Symbolism*, trans. Ralph Manheim (New York: Schocken Books, 1965), p. 105.

Three

1. Greeley, "The Final Planet," p. 156. My quotations from "Planet" are based on an early unpublished manuscript (Greeley's first lengthy story written even before *The Magic Cup*), which Greeley is currently expanding and revising. In the most recent version, a more virtuous or possibly more threatened Seamus stops short of total sexual surrender. While I am generally citing from the most recent manuscript versions of works in progress, I have made an exception in this instance because the passage presents a powerful and undisguised descent into the demonic libidinal underworld of chthonic passion and serves as thematic prototype for such parallel "baptized" images as Red Kane's "swamp" in "The Patience of a Saint."

2. Greeley, *The Magic Cup* (London: Futura Publications, 1984), p. 29.

3. Greeley, "Rite of Spring," p. 175.

4. Greeley, *Ascent Into Hell* (New York: Warner Books, 1984), p. 18.

5. Frye, *The Great Code: The Bible and Literature* (New York and London: Harcourt Brace Jovanovich, 1981), p. 68.

6. Hebblethwaite, *Motherhood*, p. 21

7. Conrad Pepler, "The Great Mother" in Burke, *Mary and Modern Man*, p. 35.

8. Hesiod, *Theogony*, v, p. 126, quoted in Mircea Eliade, *Patterns in Comparative Religion*, trans. by Rosemary Sheed (Cleveland and New York: The World Publishing Company, 1963), p. 239.

9. Mircea Eliade, *Patterns*, pp. 239-62.

10. Pepler, p. 40.

11. N.J.A. Williams, ed., *The Poems of Giolla Brighde Mac Con Midhe* (Dublin: Irish Texts Society, 1980), p. 223.

12. Ibid., p. 217.

13. Marina Warner, *Alone of All Her Sex: The Myth and the Cult of the Virgin Mary* (New York: Alfred A. Knopf, 1976), p. 205.

14. Anselm Schott, O.S.B., *Das Messbuch der heiligen Kirche. Mit liturgischen Erklärungen und kurzen Lebensbeschreibungen der Heiligen* (Freiburg: Herder, 1957), p. 879.

15. Warner, p. 155.

16. James P. Preston, *Mother Worship: Theme and Variations* (Chapel Hill: The University of North Carolina Press, 1982), pp. 95-122.

17. Fiorenza, pp. 227-32.

18. Preston, p. 113.

19. Frye, pp. 33-34.

20. Nor Hall, *The Moon and the Virgin: Reflections on the Archetypal Feminine* (New York: Harper and Row, 1980), p. 10.

21. Teilhard de Chardin, *Writings in Time of War* (New York: Harper & Row, 1968), pp. 191-204.

22. Ecclesiastes 24:9.

23. Greeley, *The Mary Myth: On the Femininity of God.* (New York: The Seabury Press, 1977), p. 71. It should be noted, however, that Ramakrishna, the gentle 19th century Hindu sage and champion of religious toleration, dedicated himself to the service of the terrible Kali (after forays into Christianity and Islam), whom he managed to transform into a tenderly affectionate "Mother Divine," insisting that the love of God resembled woman, and She the ocean into Whom all the streams of rival religions flow. Many of his passages sound (even in translation) like love poetry.

24. Greeley, *The Cardinal Sins* (New York: Warner Books, 1982), pp. 40-42.

25. Ibid., pp. 39-40.

26. Hermann Hesse, *Gesammelte Werke in zwölf Bänden. Werkausgabe edition suhrkamp*, vol. IX: *Das Glasperlenspiel*, pp. 466-70.

27. G. L. Anderson, ed. *Masterpieces of the Orient. Enlarged Edition* (New York: W. W. Norton, 1977), p. 747.

28. Hall, p. 25.

29. Jean Markale, *Woman of the Celts,* Trans. by A. Mygind, C. Hauch and Peter Henry. (London: Gordon Cremonesi, 1975), p. 66.

30. T.S. Eliot, "Ash Wednesday" in *Collected Poems 1909-1962* (New York: Harcourt Brace Jovanovich, 1963).

31. Rosemary Radford Ruether, *New Woman New Earth: Sexist Ideologies & Human Liberation* (New York: The Seabury Press, 1975), p. 40.

32. Jerome *Adversus Jovinianum* 1.3 (PL 23.224) cited in Fiorenza, p. 113.

33. Jung, *Answer to Job*, trans. R.F.C. Hull (London, 1954), cited in Warner, p. 132. Cf. Jung, *Memories, Dreams and Reflections*, recorded and edited by Aniela Jaffe, translated from the German by Richard and Clara Winston, revised edition (New York: Vintage Books, 1965), p. 202, and Ruether, *New Woman*, pp. 151-59. Warner to some extent, and feminist theologians such as Ruether in general, tend to regard Jung and Jungians with suspicion as introducing patriarchal misogynism in a tantalizingly beguiling form. Jung, after all, connected the masculine archetype with consciousness and reason, and the feminine archetype with unconsciousness and intuition. One might argue that this criticism of Jung represents itself as a tacit acceptance of traditional Western dualism which tends to represent reason in positive or superior and intuition in negative or inferior terms. Jung, on the other hand, never grew tired of emphasizing the central importance of the unconscious. His self, the goal of individuation, is the dynamic process of its own becoming, the mysterious center which contains the whole, entirely beyond the categories of logic and reason, and "accessible" by such unorthodox means as consulting the *I Ching*, meditating on Zen *koans*, and exploring one's dreams. In *The Collected Works of C.G. Jung*, Bollingen Series XX, vol. 11: *Psychology and Religion: West and East*, 2nd. ed., trans. R.F.C. Hull (Princeton: Princeton University Press, 1969), p. 490, he writes: "Because the unconscious is the matrix mind, the quality of creativeness attaches to it. It is the birthplace of thought-forms such as our text [the Tibetan Book of the Great Liberation] considers the Universal Mind to be. Since we cannot attribute any particular form to the unconscious, the Eastern assertion that the Universal Mind is without form, the *arupaloka*, yet is the source of all forms seems to be justified." Thus, while Jung ultimately

insists on the complementary nature of masculinity and femininity, he appears to incline towards the archetypal feminine which represents the self-liberating power of the introverted mind and exists, literally, beyond the boundaries and strictures of the rationally imposed space-time continuum.

34. Warner, pp. 31-32.

35. Most of the material concerning the early "career" of Mary in Catholic consciousness is based on Warner, pp. 3-67.

Four

1. Greeley, *Sins*, p. 40.

2. Greeley, *Planet*, p. 127.

3. Ibid., p. 133.

4. Greeley, *Death in April* (New York: Dell Publishing, 1984), p. 74.

5. Greeley, *Ascent*, pp. 22-23.

6. Isak Dinesen, *Winter's Tales* (New York: Vintage Books, 1961), pp. 265-66.

7. Ibid., p. 285.

8. Greeley, "Planet," p. 130.

9. Greeley, *Death*, p.64.

10. Ibid., p. 99.

11. Wing-Tsit Chan, *A Source Book in Chinese Philosophy* (Princeton: Princeton University Press, 1963), p. 157.

12. Greeley "Rite of Spring," pp. 195-96.

13. Carl Gustav Jung, *The Collected Works of C.G. Jung*, Bollingen Series XX, vol. 14: *Mysterium Coniunctionis*, 2nd ed., translated by R.F.C. Hull (Princeton: Princeton University Press, 1963), p. 42.

14. Ibid., p. 43.

15. Ibid., p. 359.

16. Ibid.

17. Greeley, *Cup*, p. 202.

18. Greeley, *Death*, pp. 41-42.

19. Greeley, *Wife*, p. 294.

20. Greeley, *Ascent*, p. 54.

21. Greeley, "Rite," p. 148.

22. Frye, p. 102.

23. Markale, p. 73.

24. Samuel Noah Kramer, "Mythologies of Sumer and Akkad," in Kramer, ed. *Mythologies of the Ancient World* (Garden City, New York: Anchor Books, 1961), p. 96.

25. Ibid.

26. John P. McKay, Bennet D. Hill, and John Buckler, *A History of World Societies* (Boston: Houghton Mifflin, 1984), p. 96.

27. Greeley, *Ascent*, p. 209.

28. Mary G. Durkin, *Feast of Love: Pope John Paul II on Human Intimacy*, (Chicago: Loyola University Press, 1983), pp. 171-80.

29. Greeley, *Ascent*, p. 243.

30. Ibid., p. 211.

31. "Godgame," pp. 204-5.

32. Mircea Eliade, *Patterns in Comparative Religion*, translated by Rosemary Sheed (Cleveland and New York: The World Publishing Company, 1963), p. 148.

33. Markale, p. 49.

34. Greeley, "An Injudicious Affair," pp. 121-22.

35. Ibid., p. 278.

36. Greeley, *Ascent*, p. 486.

37. Greeley, *Death*, p. 79.

38. Greeley, *Lord*, pp. 397-98.

39. Erich Neumann, *The Great Mother: An Analysis of the Archetype*, translated by Ralph Manheim, Bollingen Series XLVII (Princeton: Princeton University Press, 1963), p. 283.

40. Kathryn Allen Rabuzzi, *The Sacred and the Feminine: Toward a Theology of Housework* (New York: The Seabury Press, 1982), p. 44.

41. Ibid., p.81.

42. Ibid., p.87.

43. Ibid., p. 89.

44. Greeley, *Ascent*,p.123.

45. Ibid., pp. 471-72.

46. Greeley, *Death*, p. 124.

47. Greeley, *The Great Mysteries: An Essential Catechism*, (New York: The Seabury Press, 1976), p. 58.

48. Greeley, "Planet," p. 26.

49. Ibid., p. 149.

50. Greeley, *Death*, pp. 244-45.

51. Greeley, *Ascent*, p. 83.

52. Greeley, "The Patience of a Saint," pp. 15-16.

53. Ibid., pp. 341-42.

54. John Ruskin, *The Queen of the Air, Being a Study of the Greek Myths of Cloud and Storm* (Chicago: Donohue, Henneberry & Co., 1869), pp. 80-81.

55. Eliade, p. 371.

56. Ibid., p. 38.

57. Greeley, *Strangers*, p.64.

58. Greeley, *Death*, p. 60.

Five

1. Genesis 1:26-27.

2. Greeley, *Sins*, pp. 59-62.

3. Karl Kerenyi "Kore," in C.G. Jung and C. Kerenyi, *Essays on a Science of Mythology: The Myth of the Divine Child and the Mysteries of Eleusis*, translated by R.F. Hull, Bollingen Series XXII (Princeton: Princeton University Press, 1971), p. 109.

4. Ibid., p. 123.

5. Henri de Lubac, S.J., *The Eternal Feminine: A Study on the Text of Teilhard de Chardin*, translated by René Hague (London: Collins, 1971), p. 56.

6. Anderson, *Masterpieces*, p. 410.

7. Karl Rahner, *Theological Investigations. Volume III: The Theology of the Spiritual Life*, translated by Karl H.—and Boniface Kruger (Baltimore: Helicon Press, 1967), p. 60.

For a fascinating discussion of the Augustinian roots of Catholic magisterial teachings concerning original sin and the horrors of concupiscence, see William A. Herr, "Augustine Reconsidered" (*The Critic*, Spring 1986, pp. 33-47). Herr argues that Augustine scripturally justified his (ex-fornicator and not quite ex-Manichaean) hatred of the flesh by (unknowingly) appealing to a *mistranslation* of Romans 5:12 into the Latin equivalent of "in whom all (of us) have sinned" (referring to Adam) instead of the correct "so death has passed to all because of this (fact), that all have sinned," and that he along with Ambrose and Jerome "introduced into Christianity an element of pessimism and despair which, although it was completely alien to the gospel message, continued to pervade Christian thinking from his day until at least the Renaissance." (p. 35)

8. Ibid., p. 59.

9. Ibid., p. 85.

10. Andrew M. Greeley and Mary G. Durkin, *How to Save the Catholic Church*, Preface by David Tracy (New York: Viking, 1984), p. 119.

11. Greeley, *The Jesus Myth* (Garden City, New York: Doubleday, 1971), p. 117.

12. Greeley, "Patience," pp. 135-41.

13. Evelyn Underhill, *Mysticism*, 12th ed. (London: 1930; reprint ed., New York: E.P. Dutton, 1961), p. 169.

14. Ibid. The transient (yet ego-transforming) nature of the mystical experience is emphasized among others by William James whose empathetic analysis of the phenomenon in *The Varieties of Religious Experience* provides the paradigm for Greeley's illustration. The four standard Jamesean marks of mystical experiences (ineffability, noetic quality, transiency, and passivity) are all present. In a sense Greeley invests Red Kane with the characteristics of an "average" American mystic, the kind one might see step out of the chapter "Mysticism" in his *The Sociology of the Paranormal: A Reconnaissance* (Beverly Hills and London: Sage Publications, 1975) based on a study conducted by himself and William McCready. On p. 66 Greeley writes: "In summary, the data we have presented in this section indicate that ecstatic interludes are widespread in the population and that they are described by those who have experienced them in terms

not unlike those used to describe the "classic" mystical episodes with which we began this section. No evidence was found in our data to confirm the image of the mystic as someone who is escaping from reality or as a quasi-schizophrenic. Mystics (unlike psychics) are more likely to be male; they are also likely to be better educated than nonmystics, more sucessful economically, less racist, and substantially higher on scores of psychological well-being."

15. "Patience," p. 136.

16. Greeley, *Sexual Intimacy* (Chicago: Thomas More, 1973), p. 173.

17. Rahner, *Theological Investigations III*, p. 58; italics mine.

18. Greeley "Patience," p. 138.

19. Robert Blake, "The Garden of Love," in Mary Lynn Johnson and John E. Grant, eds., *Blake's Poetry and Designs. Authoritative Texts. Illuminations in Color and Monochrome. Related Prose. Criticism* (New York: W.W. Norton, 1979), p. 51.

20. Greeley, *Virgin and Martyr* (New York: Warner, 1985), pp. 116-17.

21. Greeley, *Angels of September* (New York: Warner, 1986), pp. 231-32.

22. Fiorenza, *Memory*. She presents scriptural evidence for the exegetical tendency to assume a generic inclusive meaning when passages refer to the Christian community in general and a gender specific meaning when leadership titles are discussed (p. 47). In Romans 16:1-3,for example, Phoebe is referred to as *diakonos* and *prostasis* of the church at Cenchrae. The term *diakonos* is translated as deacon when it is applied to men, but "servant" or "helper" in connection with a woman. Fiorenza notes: "Since exegetes of the New Testament take it for granted that the leadership of the early Christian communities was in the hands of men, they assume that those women mentioned in the Pauline letters were the helpmates and assistants of the apostles, especially of Paul. Such an androcentric interpretative model leaves no room for the alternative assumption that women were missionaries, apostles, or heads of communities independent of Paul and equal to him. . . . Because scholars use androcentric

heuristic models that cannot do justice to the position of influence of women like Phoebe, Prisca, or Junia, or adequately integrate them into their conception of early Christian leadership, their reconstructions serve to legitimize the patriarchal practice of the contemporary church. . . . The early Christian authors have selected, redacted, and reformulated their traditional sources and materials with reference to their theological intentions and practical objectives. . . . Since the early Christian communities and authors lived in a predominantly patriarchal world and participated in its mentality, it is likely that the scarcity of information about women is conditioned by the androcentric traditioning and redaction of the early Christian authors. This applies particularly to the Gospels and Acts since they were written toward the end of the first century. Many of the traditions and information about the activity of women in early Christianity are probably irretrievable because the androcentric selection or redaction process saw these as either unimportant or as threatening." (pp. 48-49)

23. Ibid., p.42.

24. Elizabeth Fox-Genovese, "For Feminist Interpretation," USQR 35 (1979/80), p. 10; cited in Fiorenza, p. 42.

25. Cited as Augustine's phrase in Warner, p. 58.

26. Tertullian, *Disciplinary, Moral and Ascetical Works* (New York, 1959), trans. Rudolph Arbessman, Sister Emily Joseph Daly, and Edwin A. Quain, S.J.; quoted in France Quéré-Jaumles, ed., *La Femme. Les Grands Textes des Peres de l'Eglise* (Paris, 1968), p. 138; cited in Warner, p. 58.

27. Revelation 14:4.

28. 2 Corinthians 15:22; 2 Corinthians 5:17; Romans 5:14.

29. Song of Solomon 4:12.

30. *Dialogues* of Pope Gregory I, quoted in Bertrand Russell, *A History of Western Philosophy And Its Connection with Political and Social Circumstances from the Earliest Times to the Present Day* (New York: Simon and Schuster, 1945), p. 379.

31. Greeley, *Ascent*, p. 209.

32. Monsignor Egger is apparently in complete accord with the Most Reverend Paulus Rusch, retired Bishop of his diocese of Innsbruck, who recently publicly attacked official

Roman birth control teachings as totally out of step with the lived actuality of modern life and in conflict with the opinions of the majority of moral theologians as well as the praxis of 95% of the faithful. He argues that since the ban on artifical birth control is no more a scripturally based (revealed) doctrine than the medieval prohibition of usury (which was lifted in response to changing economic conditions) or the notorious *Syllabus of Errors* which was overruled by the Second Vatican Council with its affirmation of freedom of conscience and religion. Rusch writes: "The prohibition was well justified at a time when large-scale birth control involved the genuine threat of decimating the world population. Today, thanks to medical advances, we are confronted by exactly the opposite menace of global overpopulation leading to mass starvation of humanity. This is the first change." Rusch continues: "In the past . . . children represented an economic asset. The contemporary separation of home and work-place (particularly considering the small size of apartments) presents the opposite state of affairs. What is a family to do if the parents already have three or four children by age 35? Neither floor space nor income can accommodate more." He admits that natural family planning would be ideal but insists that it represents an unrealistic solution. He states that "in keeping with the above argument the Austrian Conference of Bishops stated in 1968 that practices contrary to the official teaching of the Church must continue to remain a possible alternative for reasons of conscience with due consideration of individual circumstances." He concludes "By developing a responsive solution to this matter of conscience, moral theologians could offer the foundation for inner liberation to countless faithful and relieve the deplorable current state of affairs. At that point Church doctrine could once again coincide with Christian life." ("Hier lehrt Rom am Leben vorbei: die bedrückende Kluft zwischen Theorie und Praxis in der Sexualmoral," *Die Furche*, 30 September 1985.)

33. James Bruce Ross and Mary Martin McLaughlin, eds., *The Portable Medieval Reader* (New York: The Viking Press, 1974), pp. 75-78.

34. Quoted by Palmer, p. 137.

Six

1. Greeley, *Death*, p. 205. Jim O'Neill seems preconsciously aware of Lynnie's challenge to his semi-comfortable and stereotypically Western (and masculine) assumption that sane and responsible adults do not act out their fantasies. By taking her fantasy seriously, Lynnie represents a characteristically non-Western and specifically Indian (and feminine) perspective. On p.61 of *Dreams*, O'Flaherty writes: "In one type of romantic adventure the hero flies, or rides on a white horse, to another world, where he meets a princess. This romantic adventure becomes a specific dream adventure when the hero finds his princess after falling asleep or when he visits her magically every night. Implicitly, however, one might regard all 'other worlds' as dream worlds and all romantic adventures as paradigms of the dream of sexual adventure." In its Western incarnation the plot leads either to success or failure. "If the prince regards his experience in the other world as a real experience, he brings back his princess; if he regards it as a dream, he does not bring her back." This kind of distinction does not hold for India, where "the two themes are combined, since there is no impermeable boundary between dream and reality. Here the hero acknowledges that his dream was "just" a dream—but he still succeeds in bringing back his princess." Greeley's as yet largely preconscious preoccupation with the intersecting worlds of what Westerners call dream and reality, fantasy and truth, eventually moves from the limen of consciousness to center stage in "Godgame" in which the hero (who in a sense exists "only" in the narrator's imagination, who in turn represents a persona of the author) claims his "princess" and recognizes her as one whom he has visited frequently in his dreams, and another character is discovered by the narrator in his study, reading the O'Flaherty book I am citing.

2. Frye, *The Secular Scripture: A Study of the Structure of Romance* (Cambridge: Harvard University Press, 1976), p. 15.

3. Frye, *Code*, pp.174–75.

4. Eliade, *Rites and Symbols of Initiation*, partially reprinted in John Cafferata, *Rites* (New York: McGraw-Hill, 1975), p. 31.

5. Frye, *Scripture*, p. 157.

6. Greeley, *Cup*, p. 243.

7. Frye, *Scripture*, p. 60.

8. Ibid., p.136.

9. Ibid., p. 87.

10. Ibid., p. 87.

11. Ibid., p. 92.

12. Ibid., p. 23.

13. Ibid., p. 29.

14. Ibid., p. 97.

15. Gerhard Schulz, ed., *Novalis Werke*, 2nd edition (München: C.H. Beck, n.d.), pp. 41-53.

Seven

1. Greeley, "Godgame," p. 165.

2. Ibid.

3. Greeley, *Lord*, p. 395.

4. Henry Francis Cary, trans., *The Vision or Hell, Purgatory & Paradise of Dante Alighieri* (New York: Hurst & Co., 1844), p.600.

5. Georg Wilhelm Friedrich Hegel, *Sämtliche Werke: Jubiläumsausgabe in zwanzig Bänden*, edited by Hermann Glockner, vol.II: *Phänomenologie des Geistes* (Stuttgart: Frommann, 1927), p. 71.

6. Frye, *Code*, p. 222. Jung focuses extensively on the motifs of ascent and descent. In *Mysterium Coniunctionis* (p. 223) he writes: "Ascent and descent, above and below, up and down, represent an emotional realization of opposites, and this realization gradually leads, or should lead, to their equilibrium. . . . The [opposites] become a vessel in which what was previously now one thing and now another floats vibrating, so that the painful suspension between opposites gradually changes into the bilateral activity of the point in the centre. This is the 'liberation from opposites,' the *nirvanda* of Hindu philosophy, though it is not really a philosophical but rather a psychological development. . . . I therefore am the One and the Many within me."

7. Greeley, "Confessions of a Parish Priest," pp. 9-10.

8. Greeley, *Death*, p. 64.

9. Greeley, *Angels,* p.1.

10. Franklin Edgerton, *The Bahagavad Gita*, translated and interpreted (New York: Harper and Row, 1964), p. 57.

11. Ibid., p. 58.

12. Greeley, *Ascent*, p. 27.

13. Ibid., p. 59.

14. Ibid., pp. 338-43.

15. Ibid.,p. 409.

16. Greeley, *Virgin*, p. 380. Those who condemn Greeley for the actual gang-rapes in *Virgin and Martyr* and *Lord of the Dance* or the psychic-demonic gang rape in *The Angels of September* should turn to Judges 19 and read the hideous tale of the Levite from Ephraim who saved his own precious skin by literally throwing his wife to an angry mob (originally bent on "abusing" him!) and abandoning her to their cruel sport. "They had relations with her and abused her all night until the following dawn, when they let her go. Then at daybreak the woman came and collapsed at the entrance of the house in which her husband was a guest, where she lay until the morning. When her husband rose that day and opened the door of the house to start out again on his journey, there lay the woman, his concubine, at the entrance of the house with her hands on the threshold."

The woman was dead. He "lord and master" loaded her on his donkey and took the corpse home where he hacked it into twelve pieces. Next he sent the severed body parts to the various tribes of Israel which were thus properly inspired to kill 75,000 Benjamites.

A sickening tale from our primitive past? Certainly. But as Freud reminded us, the demon within us is only partially concealed and contained by a thin veil of civilization. This kind of outrage is as likely to occur today as it was three thousand years ago. In the ancient report one looks in vain for compassion for the woman as a person. After all she was only a piece of property whose destruction must be avenged as an offense against her husband and a violation of the sacred code of hospitality. In contrast to the biblical narrative (written from within the context of patriarchal androcentrism) and in keeping with New Testament Incarnational thinking and the contemporary democratic emphasis on human worth, Greeley's stories of demonic sexuality invariably focus on the plight of the victim who is seen as suffering a form of crucifixion. It seems significant that the anonymous woman of the above-cited Old Testament passage is identified as "concubine from Bethlehem of Juda." A female victim is debased, abused, tortured, murdered, and, like Osiris, the Egyptian symbol of resurrection, is dismembered. The female Christ analogue-prefiguration at Gabaa merges with Greeley's Cathy who "dies" and rises from the tomb at Rio Secco.

17. Ibid., pp. 384-86. Cathy's ultimate victory over the forces of evil, her ability to use deadly violence (in addition to cunning) in order to save her life give evidence to an aspect of femininity which I have largely disregarded in this study. For reasons of simplicity, I have focused on the female stereo/archetype of gentle, tender, cooperative maternity. Greeley's women characters, however, are invariably strong as well as tender, competitive as well as cooperative, passionate as well as compassionate.

18. Ibid., pp. 394-95.

19. 1 Corinthians 10:14.

20. Robert Maynard Hutchins, ed., *Great Books of the Western World*, vol. IV: *The Iliad of Homer and The Odyssey: Rendered into English Prose by Samuel Butler* (Chicago: William Benton, 1952), p. 258: Such was his story, but Minerva [Athena] smiled and caressed him with her hand. . . . "He must indeed be a shifty lying fellow," said she, "who could surpass you in all manner of craft even though you had a god for your antagonist. Dare-devil that you are, full of guile, unwearying in deceit. . . . We will say no more, however, about this, for we can both of us deceive upon occasion—you are the most accomplished councellor and orator among all mankind, while I for diplomacy and subtelty have no equal among the gods."

21. Frye, *Scripture*, p. 89.

22. Greeley, *Virgin*, p. 13.

Eight

1. Greeley, "Rite," p. 391.
2. Greeley, "Godgame," p. 86.
3. Greeley, *Ascent*, pp. 470-71.
4. Greeley *Virgin*, p. 430.
5. Greeley, "Patience," p. 127.
6. Anders Nygren, *Agape and Eros*, trans. by Philip S. Watson (Philadelphia: The Westminster Press, 1953), p. 180.
7. Robert Maynard Hutchins, ed., *Great Books of the Western World*, vol. VII: Benjamin Jowett, trans., *The Dialogues of Plato* (Chicago: William Benton, 1952), pp. 163-67. For my understanding of the Platonic Eros I am deeply indebted to countless conversations around twenty years ago with Professor Gustav E. Mueller, as well as his books, most specifically *Plato: The Founder of Philosophy as Dialectic* (New York: Philosophical Library, 1965).
8. Denis de Rougemont, *Love in the Western World* (Albert Saifer, 1940), p. 58.
9. Ibid., p. 85.
10. Ibid., p. 86.
11. Ibid., p. 64.
12. Greeley, *Angels*, pp. 359-60
13. Greeley, *Death*, p. 21.
14. Ibid., p. 44.
15. Ibid., p. 99.
16. Greeley, *Imagination*, p. 209.
17. Greeley, *Sins*, p. 465.
18. Martin C. D'Arcy, S.J., *The Mind and Heart of Love. Lion and Unicorn: A Study in Eros and Agape* (Cleveland and New York: The World Publishing Company, 1956), pp. 31-32.
19. Greeley, *The Friendship Game* (Garden City, New York: Doubleday, 1970), p. 35.
20. Nygren, p. 92.
21. D'Arcy, pp. 88-92.

22. Ibid., p. 91.

23. Ibid., p. 69.

24. Ibid., pp. 80-81.

25. Thomas Merton, *Mystics & Zen Masters* (New York: Dell Publishing, 1967), p. 77.

26. Chan, p. 171.

27. D'Arcy, p. 16.

28. Merton, p. 18.

29. Lonergan, p. 113.

30. Ibid.

31. Ibid., p. 106.

32. Ibid., p.76.

33. Jung, *Memories, Dreams, Reflections*, p. 353.

34. Ibid., pp. 353-54.

35. Hans Küng, *On Being a Christian*, translated by Edward Quinn (New York: Image Books, 1984), pp. 262-63.

36. Ibid., p. 262.

Nine

1. Greeley, *Cup*, p. 209.

2. Greeley, *Death*, p. 21.

3. Ibid., p. 64.

4. Greeley, *Sins*, p. 42.

5. Ibid., p. 62.

6. Greeley, *Ascent*, p. 482.

7. Greeley, "Rite," p. 109.

8. Ibid., p. 156.

9. Greeley, *Mary Myth*, p. v.

10. Louis Herbert Gray, ed., *The Mythology of all Races in Thirteen Volumes*, volume III: John Arnott MacCullogh, *Celtic* and Jan Machal, *Slavic* (Boston: Marshall Jones, 1918), p. 84.

11. Ibid., p.86.

12. Markale, p. 52.

13. Gray, pp. 117-19.

14. Markale,p. 199.

15. Roger Sherman Loomis, *Arthurian Tradition & Chrètien de Troyes* (New York: Columbia University Press, 1961), p. 382.

16. Greeley, "Confessions,"p.43.

17. Loomis, p. 382-83.

18. Ibid., p. 363.

19. Ibid., p. 91.

20. Ibid., pp. 63-64.

21. Wolfram von Eschenbach, *Parzival: Mittelhoch-deutsch/Neuhochdeutsch*, vol. 2 *Buch 9-16* (Stuttgart: Philipp Reclam Jun., 1981), p. 82 (479, 8-12): "durch die heidruose sin."

22. Loomis, p. 65.

23. Ibid., p. 379.

24. Ibid., p. 381.

25. Ibid., p. 376.

26. Ibid., p. 372.

27. Ibid. Considering this citation and my subsequent discussion, it seems highly significant to note that popular and poetic fascination with the Grail burst forth at exactly the time in history when the most hotly debated doctrinal issue concerned the Mystery of the Eucharist, a controversy which culminated in the promulgation of the dogma of transubstantiation by the Fourth Lateran Council in 1215. In my paradigm of the double tradition, the "high clerical" and the "low popular," the Grail ("Magic Cup"-pregnant womb) image would provide a perfect *popular* anticipation of the subsequent elite dogma.

28. Greeley, *Cup*, p. 29.

29. Greeley, *Death*, p. 64

30. Ibid., p. 21.

31. Ibid., p. 206.

32. Sarvepalli Radhakrishnan and Charles A. Moore, eds., *A Source Book in Indian Philosophy* (Princeton, New Jersey: Princeton University Press, 1957), p. 80.

33. Greeley, *Sins*, p. 465.

34. Ibid., p. 505.

35. Greeley, *Wife*, p. 167.

36. Ibid., p. 302.

37. Greeley, *Ascent*, p. 471.

38. Ibid., p. 486.

39. Ibid.

40. Greeley, *Lord*, p. 394.

41. Ibid., p. 396.

42. Greeley, *Virgin*, p. 425.

43. Ibid., p. 437.

44. Ibid., p. 438.

45. Greeley "Patience."

46. Ibid., p. 416.

47. Ibid.

48. Greeley, "Rite," p. 109.

49. Ibid., p. 156.

50. Ibid., p. 175.

51. Loomis, pp. 337-38.

52. Greeley, "Godgame," p. 243.

53. Greeley, *Sins*, p. 62.

54. Greeley, *Virgin*, p. 13.

55. Greeley, *Cup*, p. 168.

56. Greeley, *Death*, p. 247.

57. Ibid., p. 250.

58. Greeley, *Angels*, p. 415.

59. Ibid., p. 417.

60. Greeley, *Ascent*, p. 295.

61. Greeley, *Sins*, p. 505.

62. Greeley, *Wife*, p. 276 and *Lord*, p. 378.

63. Greeley, *Ascent*, pp. 471-72.

64. Greeley, "Patience," p. 138.

65. Greeley, *Happy are the Meek* (New York: Warner, 1985), p. 242.

66. Greeley, "Happy are the Clean of Heart," p. 355.

67. Greeley, "Godgame," p. 67.

68. Ibid., p. 14.

Ten

1. Greeley, *Cup*, pp. 167-68.
2. Greeley, *Sins*, pp. 348-49.
3. Nora's nurturing and cherishing Woman God and Church roles have paradoxically gone almost entirely unnoticed by reviewers and critics, such as James E. Johnston in "Priests, Prose, and Preachments," *Theology Today* (July 1984), pp. 161-70.
4. Austin P. Flannery, ed., *Documents of Vatican II: A new authoritative translation of the Conciliar documents—including Post Conciliar papers and commentaries*, rev. ed. (Grand Rapids, Michigan: William B. Eerdmans, 1984), p. 351.
5. Ibid., pp. 353-54.
6. Ibid., p. 354.
7. Ibid.
8. Ibid., p. 358.
9. Ibid., p. 357.
10. Ibid., p. 66.
11. Ibid., p. 358; italics mine.
12. Greeley, *Sins*, pp. 349-50.
13. Greeley, *Lord*, p. 19.
14. Ibid., p. 89.
15. Ibid., p. 88.
16. Greeley, *Virgin*, p. 276.
17. Greeley, *Death*, p. 136.
18. Greeley, "Confessions," p. 724.
19. Greeley, "A Star for Christmas: A story of love and loyalty," in *Family Circle*, 11 Dec. 1984, p. 17.
20. Greeley, "Confessions," p. 724.
21. Greeley, *Virgin*, p. 191.
22. Ibid., p. 183.
23. Ibid., p. 182.
24. Ibid., p. 197.
25. Ibid., p. 350.

26. Ibid.

27. Ibid., pp. 75-76.

28. Greeley, *Angels*, p. 309.

29. Ibid., p. 360.

30. Ibid., p. 444.

31. Ibid., p. 446.

32. Greeley, "Patience," p. 409.

33. *Sermo Super Cant.* 9, 7 quoted in Ulrich Köpf, "Bernhard von Clairvaux in der Frauenmystik," in Peter Dinzelbacher and Dieter R. Bauer, eds., *Frauenmystik im Mittelalter* (Ostfildern bei Stuttgart: Schwabenverlag, 1985), p. 56.

34. Greeley, *Wife*, pp. 303-4.

Eleven

1. Greeley, *Death*, p. 100.

2. Greeley, *Lord*, p. 394.

3. Greeley, "Patience," pp. 15-16.

4. Ibid., pp. 135-41.

5. Jung, *Mysterium*, p. 25.

6. *Missale Romanum ex decreto sacros. Concilii Tridentini restitutum S. Pii V. Pontificus Maximi jussu editum Clementis VIII. Urbani VIII. et Leonis XIII. auctoritate recognitum* (Ratisbonae, Neo Eboraci et Cincinnati: Fridericus Pustet, 1884), pp. 199-200.

7. Greeley, *Intimacy*, p. 195.

8. Jung, *Memories, Dreams, Reflections*, p.294.

9. Ibid.

10. Ibid.

11. Ibid., p. 295.

12. Lefkowitz, *Heroines and Hysterics* (New York: St. Martin's Press, 1981). The story of Zeus and Io may serve as an example. After Zeus has impregnated Io and turned her into a comely heifer to deceive his jealous spouse, she wanders miserably about the globe until she is finally returned to human form

and gives birth to a son. Having fulfilled her function she disappears from the mythological stage. This contrasts sharply with the Catholic insistence on continuing to focus attention on Mary as *theotokos* while possibly explaining her relatively minor role in the New Testament which, after all, was written within the androcentric cultural context of the Hellenic world. Lefkowitz also points to the mythological motif of withholding/destruction in which virginity is preserved while the woman runs the risk of preserving her individuality by being transformed into an essentially static, non-human form, incapable of arousing the passion of the pursuing male. Again, the Catholic imagination, at least in its popular form, continued to envision Mary as active, vital, and supremely attractive nubile young woman, an inspiration for poems such as Hopkins' celebration of vernal fertility in his "May Magnificat."

13. Greeley and Durkin, *Church*, p. 156.

14. Greeley, *Intimacy*, p. 64.

15. Scholem, *Kabbalah*, p. 95.

16. Ibid., p. 108. Scholem points out that the related formula "for the sake of the reunion of God and His *Shekhinah*" was found in (orthodox) Jewish prayer books until the nineteenth century when it was eliminated as irreconcilable with reason, which provides additional evidence for my contention that the concepts of divine androgyny and Woman God are deeply embedded in the Hebraic tradition.

17. *Sexual Intimacy*, p. 65.

18. Greeley, "Patience," p. 134.

19. Ibid.

20. Ibid., p. 6.

21. Cf. section "City."

22. Greeley, *Intimacy*, p. 101.

23. Greeley, "Patience," p. 135.

24. Ibid., p. 137.

25. Ibid., p. 139.

26. Ibid.

27. Ibid., p. 140.

28. Ibid., p. 141.
29. Greeley, *Intimacy*, p. 198.
30. Greeley, "Amazing," p. 217.
31. Ibid., pp. 182-83.
32. Ibid., pp. 222-23.

Conclusion

1. Greeley, "Count the Ways," p. 11.
2. Greeley, *Angels*, p. 2.
3. Greeley, "Patience," pp. 442-43.
4. Frye, *Code*, p. 221. Frye points out that genuine reading involves making further discoveries within the same structure of words, allowing their "polysemous" meaning to unfold organically through a dialectical process which was schematized by medieval theorists such as Dante as beginning with the literal sense and proceeding from there to a series of further levels in a movement from the immediate to the allegorical. Discovering or uncovering polysemous meaning is analogous to the process of Hegel's *Phenomenology* which involves increased understanding through a process of appropriating opposites.
5. Greeley, *Jesus Myth*, p. 45.
6. Greeley, "Patience,"p. 524.
7. Greeley, *Ascent*, p. 486.
8. Greeley, *Virgin*, p. 438.
9. Markale, p. 209.
10. Greeley, *Sins*, p. 350.
11. Greeley, "Confessions," p. 103.

BIBLIOGRAphy

Texts

Greeley, Andrew M. *The Magic Cup*. London: Futura Publications, 1984.

_____. *Death in April*. New York: Dell Publishing, 1984.

_____. *The Cardinal Sins*. New York: Warner Books, 1982.

_____. *Thy Brother's Wife*. New York: Warner Books, 1982.

_____. *Ascent Into Hell*. New York: Warner Books, 1984.

_____. *Lord of the Dance*. New York: Warner Books, 1984.

_____. *Virgin and Martyr*. New York: Warner Books, 1985.

_____. *Happy are the Meek*. New York: Warner Books, 1985.

_____. *Angels of September*. New York: Warner Books, 1986.

Unpublished Manuscripts

_____. "The Final Planet."

_____. "Happy are the Clean of Heart."

_____. "The Patience of a Saint."

_____. "The Rite of Spring."

_____. "An Injudicious Affair."

———. "Godgame."

———. "Amazing."

———. "Count The Ways."

———. "Confessions of a Parish Priest."

Other Sources

Anderson, G.L., ed. *Masterpieces of the Orient. Enlarged Edition* (New York: W.W. Norton, 1977), p. 747.

Burke, Thomas J.M., S.J., ed. *Mary and Modern Man.* New York: The America Press, 1954.

Capra, Fritjof. *The Tao of Physics: An Exploration of the Parallels between Modern Physics and Eastern Mysticism.* Berkeley: Shambala, 1975.

Cary, Henry Francis, trans. *The Vision; or Hell, Purgatory, & Paradise of Dante Alighieri.* New York: Hurst & Co., 1844.

Chan, Wing-Tsit. *A Source Book in Chinese Philosophy.* Princeton: Princeton University Press, 1963.

Dante, Alighieri. *The Vision; or Hell, Purgatory, & Paradise of Dante Alighieri.* Translated by Henry Francis Cary. New York: Hurst & Co., 1844.

D'Arcy, M.C., S.J. *The Mind and Heart of Love. Lion and Unicorn: A Study in Eros and Agape.* Cleveland and New York: The World Publishing Company, 1956.

Dinesen, Isak. *Winter's Tales.* New York: Vintage Books, 1961.

Dinzelbacher, Peter and Bauer, Dieter R. *Frauenmystik im Mittelalter.* Ostfildern bei Stuttgart: Schwabenverlag, 1985.

Durkin, Mary G. *Feast of Love: Pope John Paul II on Human Intimacy.* Chicago: Loyola University Press, 1983.

Edgerton, Franklin. *The Bahagavad Gita.* Translated and interpreted by Franklin Edgerton. New York: Harper and Row, 1964.

Egan, Harvey D. *Christian Mysticism: the future of a tradition.* New York: Pueblo Publishing Company, 1984.

Eliade, Mircea. *Patterns in Comparative Religion.* Translated by Rosemary Sheed. Cleveland and New York: The World Publishing Company, 1963.

_____. *The Sacred and the Profane: The Nature of Religion*. Translated by Willard R. Trask. New York: Harcourt, Brace & World, 1959.

_____. *Cosmos and History: The Myth of the Eternal Return*. Translated by Willard R. Trask. New York: Harper and Row, 1959.

Eliot, Thomas Stearns. *Collected Poems 1909-1962*. New York: Harcourt Brace Jovanovich, 1963.

Flannery, Austin P., ed. *Documents of Vatican II: A new authoritative translation of the Conciliar documents—including Post Conciliar papers and commentaries*. New Revised Edition. Grand Rapids, Michigan: William B. Eerdmans, 1984.

Fiorenza, Elisabeth Schüssler. *In Memory of Her: A Feminist Theological Reconstruction of Christian Origins*. New York: Crossroad, 1984.

Frye, Northrop. *The Great Code: The Bible and Literature*. New York and London: Harcourt Brace Jovanovich, 1981.

_____. *The Secular Scripture: A Study of the Structure of Romance*. Cambridge: Harvard University Press, 1976.

Gaster, Theodore H. *Myth, Legend, and Custom in the Old Testament: a comparative study with chapters from Sir James G. Frazer's Folklore in the Old Testament*. New York and Evanston: Harper & Row, 1969.

Goethe, Johann Wolfgang. *Goethe's Werke*. Edited by Gerhard Stenzel. Volume II. Vienna: Buchgemeinde Donauland, 1957.

Gottfried von Strassburg. *Tristan. With the surviving fragments of the Tristran of Thomas*. Translated by A.T. Hatto. New York, 1982.

Grau, Joseph A. *Morality and the Human Future in the Thought of Teilhard de Chardin: A Critical Study*. Rutherford: Fairleigh Dickinson University Press, 1976.

Gray, Louis Herbert, ed. *The Mythology of All Races in Thirteen Volumes*. Volume III: *Celtic Slavic*. Boston: Marshall Jones Company, 1918.

Graves, Robert. *The White Goddess: A historical grammar of poetic myth*. Amended and enlarged edition. New York: Farrar, Strauss and Giroux, 1976.

Greeley, Andrew M. *Strangers in the House.* New York: Sheed and Ward, 1961.

———. *The Friendship Game.* Garden City, New York: Doubleday, 1970.

———. *The Jesus Myth.* Garden City, New York: Doubleday, 1971.

———. *The Sinai Myth.* Garden City, New York: Doubleday, 1972.

———. *Unsecular Man.* New York: Schocken Books, 1972.

———. *Sexual Intimacy.* Chicago: Thomas More, 1973.

———. *The New Agenda: A proposal for a new approach to fundamental religious issues in contemporary terms with a foreword by Gregory Baum.* New York: Image Books, 1975.

———. *The Sociology of the Paranormal: A Reconnaissance.* Beverly Hills and London: 1975.

———. *The Great Mysteries: An Essential Catechism.* New York: The Seabury Press, 1976.

———. *The Mary Myth: On the Femininity of God.* New York: The Seabury Press, 1977.

———. *The Religious Imagination.* Los Angeles: Sadlier, 1981.

———. *Religion: A Secular Theory.* New York: The Free Press, 1982.

Greeley, Andrew M. and Durkin, Mary G. *How to Save the Catholic Church.* Preface by David Tracy. New York: Viking, 1984.

Hall, Nor. *The Moon and the Virgin: Reflections on the Archetypal Feminine.* New York: Harper and Row, 1980.

Hebblethwaite, Margaret. *Motherhood and God.* London: Geoffrey Chapman, 1984.

Hegel, Georg Wilhelm Friedrich. *Sämtliche Werke: Jubiläumsausgabe in zwanzig Bänden.* Edited by Hermann Glockner. Vol. II: *Phänomenologie des Geistes.* Stuttgart: Frommann, 1927.

Hesse, Hermann. *Gesammelte Werke in zwölf Bänden: Werkausgabe edition suhrkamp.* Vol. IX: *Das Glasperlenspiel.* Frankfurt am Main: Suhrkamp, 1970.

_____. *Gesammelte Werke in zwölf Bänden: Werkausgabe edition suhrkamp*. Vol. XII: *Schriften zur Literatur II*. Frankfurt am Main: Suhrkamp, 1970.

Hutchins, Robert Maynard, ed. *Great Books of the Western World*, vol. IV: *The Iliad of Homer and The Odyssey: Rendered into English Prose by Samuel Butler*, and vol. VII: Benjamin Jowett, trans., *The Dialogues of Plato*. Chicago: William Benton, 1952.

James, William. *The Varieties of Religious Experience: A Study in Human Nature. Being the Gifford Lectures on Natural Religion Delivered at Edinburgh in 1901-1902*. Foreword by Jacques Barzun. New York: New American Library, 1958.

Johnson, Mary Lynn and Grant, John E. *Blake's Poetry and Designs. Authoritative Texts. Illuminations in Color and Monochrome. Related Prose. Criticism*. New York: W.W. Norton & Company, 1979.

Jung, Carl Gustav. *The Collected Works of C.G. Jung*. Bollingen Series XX, vol. 11: *Psychology and Religion: West and East*. 2nd ed. Translated by R.F.C. Hull. Princeton: Princeton University Press, 1969.

_____. *The Collected Works of C.G. Jung*. Bollingen Series XX, vol. 14: *Mysterium Coniunctionis*. 2nd ed. Translated by R. F. C. Hull. Princeton: Princeton University Press, 1963.

_____. *Man and his Symbols*. Garden City, New York: Doubleday, 1964.

_____. *Memories, Dreams, Reflections*. Recorded and edited by Aniela Jaffe. Translated from the German by Richard and Clara Winston. Rev. ed. New York: Vintage Books, 1965.

Jung, C.G. and Kerenyi, C. *Essays on a Science of Mythology: The Myth of the Divine Child and the Mysteries of Eleusis*. Translated by R.F.C. Hull. Bollingen Series XXII. Princeton: Princeton University Press, 1971.

Kotre, John N. *The Best of Times, the Worst of Times: Andrew Greeley & American Catholicism, 1950-1975*. Chicago: Nelson-Hall Company, 1978.

Kramer, Samuel Noah, ed. *Mythologies of the Ancient World*. Garden City, New York: Anchor Books, 1961.

Küng, Hans. *On Being a Christian*. Translated by Edward Quinn. New York: Image Books, 1984.

———. *The Church—Maintained in Truth: A Theological Meditation*. Translated by Edward Quinn. New York: Vintage Books, 1982.

Lefkowitz, Mary R. *Heroines and Hysterics*. New York: St. Martin's Press, 1981.

Lonergan, Bernard J.F., S.J. *Insight: A Study of Human Understanding*. New York: Philosophical Library, 1970.

———. *Method in Theology*. New York: Herder and Herder, 1972.

Loomis, Roger Sherman. *Arthurian Tradition & Chrétien de Troyes*. New York: Columbia University Press, 1961.

Lubac, Henri de, S.J. *The Eternal Feminine: A Study on the Text of Teilhard de Chardin*. Translated by René Hague. London: Collins, 1971.

McKay, John P., Hill, Bennet D. and Buckler, John. *A History of World Societies* (Boston: Houghton Mifflin, 1984).

Markale, Jean. *Women of the Celts*. Translated by A. Mygind, C. Hauch and Peter Henry. London: Gordon Cremonesi, 1975.

Martin, Ernst, ed. *Wolfram von Eschenbach Parzival und Titurel*. Part I. Halle: Verlag der Buchhandlung des Waisenhauses, 1900.

Matarasso, Pauline M., translator. *The Quest of the Holy Grail*. New York: Penguin Books, 1984.

Merton, Thomas. *Mystics & Zen Masters*. New York: Dell Publishing, 1967.

Missale Romanum ex decreto sacros. Concilii Tridentini restitutum S. Pii V. Pontificus Maximi jussu editum Clementis VIII. Urbani VIII. et Leonis XIII. auctoritate recognitum. Ratisbonae, Neo Eboraci et Cincinnati: Fridericus Pustet, 1884.

Mueller, Gustav Emil. *Plato: The Founder of Philosophy as Dialectic*. New York: Philosophical Library, 1965.

Nakamura, Hajime. *Ways of Thinking of Eastern Peoples: India-China-Tibet-Japan*. Revised English translation. Edited by Philip P. Wiener. Honolulu: East–West Center Press, 1968.

Neumann, Erich. *Amor and Psyche: The Psychic Development of the Feminine—A Commentary on the Tale of Apuleius.* Translated by Ralph Manheim. Bollingen Series LIV. Princeton: Princeton University Press, 1973.

_____. *The Great Mother:An Analysis of the Archetype.* Translated by Ralph Manheim. Bollingen Series XLVII. Princeton: Princeton University Press, 1963.

Nygren, Anders. *Agape and Eros.* Translated by Philip S. Watson. Philadelphia: The Westminster Press, 1953.

O'Flaherty, Wendy Doniger. *Dreams, Illusion and Other Realities.* Chicago and London: The University of Chicago Press, 1984.

Pirsig, Robert M. *Zen and the Art of Motorcycle Maintenance: An Inquiry into Values.* Toronto and New York: Bantam New Age, 1976.

Preston, James P. *Mother Worship: Theme and Variations.* Chapel Hill: The University of North Carolina Press, 1982.

Rabuzzi, Kathryn Allen. *The Sacred and the Feminine: Toward a Theology of Housework.* New York: The Seabury Press, 1982.

Radhakrishnan, Sarvepalli and Moore, Charles A., eds. *A Source Book in Indian Philosophy.* Princeton, New Jersey: Princeton University Press, 1957.

Rahner, Karl. *Theological Investigations. Volume I: God, Christ, Mary and Grace.* Translated with an Introduction by Cornelius Ernst, O.P. Baltimore: Helicon Press, 1969.

_____. *Theological Investigations. Volume III: The Theology of the Spiritual Life.* Translated by Karl H.—and Boniface Kruger. Baltimore: Helicon Press, 1967.

Ross, James Bruce and McLaughlin, Mary Martin, eds. *The Portable Medieval Reader.* New York: The Viking Press, 1974.

Rougemont, Denis de. *Love in the Western World.* Albert Saifer, 1940.

Ruether, Rosemary Radford. *New Woman New Earth: Sexist Ideologies & Human Liberation.* New York: The Seabury Press, 1975.

Ruskin, John. *The Queen of the Air, Being a Study of the Greek Myths of Cloud and Storm.* Chicago: Donohue, Henneberry & Co., 1869.

Russell, Bertrand. *A History of Western Philosophy And Its Connection with Political and Social Circumstances from the Earliest Times to the Present Day.* New York: Simon and Schuster, 1945.

Schillebeeckx, E., O.P. *God and Man.* New York: Sheed and Ward, 1969.

_____. *Mary Mother of the Redemption.* Translated by N.D. Smith. New York: Sheed and Ward, 1964.

Scholem, Gershom G. *On the Kabbalah and its Symbolism.* Translated by Ralph Manheim. New York: Schocken Books, 1965.

Schott, Anselm, O.S.B. *Das Messbuch der heiligen Kirche. Mit liturgischen Erklärungen und kurzen Lebensbeschreibungen der Heiligen.* Freiburg: Herder, 1957.

Schulz, Gerhard, ed. *Novalis Werke.* 2nd edition. München: C.H. Beck, n.d.

Shea, John. *An Experience Named Spirit.* Chicago: Thomas More, 1983.

_____. *Stories of Faith.* Chicago: Thomas More, 1980.

Teilhard de Chardin, Pierre. *Writings in Time of War.* Translated by René Hague. New York: Harper and Row, 1968.

_____. *The Heart of Matter.* Translated by René Hague. New York: Harcourt Brace Jovanovich, 1979.

_____. *Human Energy.* Translated by J.M. Cohen. New York: Harcourt Brace Jovanovich, 1969.

_____. *Entwurf und Entfaltung: Briefe aus den Jahren 1914-1919.* Edited by Alice Teillard-Chambon and Max Henri Begouen. Freiburg: Karl Alber, 1963.

Tracy, David. *Blessed Rage for Order: The New Pluralism in Theology.* New York: The Seabury Press, 1975.

_____. *The Analogical Imagination: Christian Theology and the Culture of Pluralism.* New York: Crossroad, 1981.

Tilley, Terrence W. *Story Theology.* Theology and Life Series 12. Wilmington, Delaware: Michael Glazier, 1985.

Underhill, Evelyn. *Mysticism.* 3rd ed. 1930. Reprint. New York: E.P. Dutton, 1961.

Warner, Marina. *Alone of All Her Sex: The Myth and the Cult of the Virgin Mary.* New York: Alfred A. Knopf, 1976.

Whitehead, Alfred North. *Religion in the Making: Lowell Lectures, 1926.* New York: The Macmillan Company, 1926.

Williams, N.J.A., ed. *The Poems of Giolla Brighde Mac Con Midhe.* Dublin: Irish Texts Society, 1980.

Wolfram von Eschenbach. *Parzival: Mittelhochdeutsch/Neuhochdeutsch* 2 vols. Stuttgart: Philipp Reclam Jun., 1981.

Index

F

Faith, redemption through, 8
Fall from grace, 127, 135
Faust, 184
Feminine cunning, motif of, as
  means of salvation, 143
Femme fatal, motif of, 176
Fertility goddesses, 35
Fiction, writing of, ix-x
"Final Planet, The," 80, 132
  quotes from, 37, 57-58, 78
Fiorenza, Elisabeth Schüssler, xxv,
  43-44, 109
Fire-water symbolism, 7, 51, 92,
  169, 204, 213-26, 236
Flaubert, Gustave, 125
Fosse, Bob, 144, 159
Francis of Assisi, 154
Frau Welt, 10
Freud, Sigmund, 128
Friendship Game, The, 160-61
Frye, Northrop, 12, 15, 34, 44, 65,
  123, 124, 126-27, 231

G

Garrison Church, 5, 200, 234
Geoffrey, archbishop, 113
Gilson, Etienne, 183-84
Gnosticism, xxvi, 155
God
  androgyny of, 17-29, 220, 229,
    230
  as creator, 19
  as Father, 19, 20-21, 28
  fullness of, 29, 121, 230
  images of, 19, 29, 236-37
  as judge, 19, 20, 107
  of laughter, 8, 18, 52
  as lord, 19, 20
  of love, 20-21, 52, 188, 228-29
  as Mother, 18-19, 29
  personhood of, xix-xx, 20, 24
  revelations of, 20
  stories of, 3-15
  will of, 106-7

"Godgame," 68, 133, 193, 196
  quotes from, 19-20, 69, 131-32,
    147
Goethe, xiii, 133
Golden Ass, The, 137
Gospels, dualism in, xxiii, 94
Great Code: The Bible and Literature,
  The, 12
Greeley, Andrew
  novels of, xi-xii, 5-6, 230; See also
    novels by name
  religious paradigm of, 6-7, 230
  separation of as author from
    sociologist, 5
  as sociologist, 5
Gregory I, 111-12
Gulik, Robert van, ix

H

"Happy are the Clean of Heart," 81,
  205
Happy are the Meek, 195-96, 209
Healing, theme of, 141-42
Hebblethwaite, Margaret, 36-37
Hegel, xxvii, 133, 150
Heliodorus, 136, 143
Hellenistic dualism, 108, 150
Heraclitus, 97
Heroism, 124
Hesiod, 38
Hesse, 50
Hieratic language, 12
Hieroglyphic language, 12
Hinayana Buddhism, 65
Holy Grail, archetype of, 56, 93-94,
  104, 121, 173-96, 199, 211-12,
  220, 224, 235-36
Holy Week, liturgy of, 120
House, feminine archetype of, 71-77
Hugo, Victor, 125
Humanae Vitae, 206
Human consciousness, and the need
  for order, 7
Human love, theme of, 165
Huxley, Aldous, ix

I

Immaculate Conception, feast of, 115
Imagination, quotes from, 9, 159
Inbolc, festival of, 39
Incarnation, xxvi, xxvii, 20, 55, 56, 94, 95, 98, 107-8, 112, 138-39, 150, 157, 169, 230
Injudicious Affair, An, 64, 194
quote from, 70, 71
Innes, Michael, ix
Intercourse, symbolism of, 50-51, 213-14
Ishtar, goddess of, 144

J

Jacobi, Jolande, 25
Jainism, 150
James, apocryphal Book of, 54
James, William, 6
Jesus
expression of womanliness of God as, 121-22
revelations of God through, 19, 20-21
Jesus Myth, The, 98-99
John of the Cross, 18
John Paul II, Pope, 67
John XXIII (pope), 18
Joseph of Arimathea, 180, 183
Jovinian, 54
Judaism, 28, 219-20
Julian, Dame, xiv, 29
Julian of Norwich, 18
Jung, Carl Gustav, 13, 24, 25, 54, 61, 133, 167, 216-17, 222, 226
Jungian psychology, 60

K

Kabbalism, xxvi, 29, 155, 220, 230
Kerenyi, Karl, 89
Kerygmatic language, 15
Kramer, Samuel N., 65-66
Küng, Hans, 168

L

Lake, feminine archetype of, 57-62
Lao-tze, 60, 164, 165
Laughter, theme of, 8, 18-19
Lefkowitz, Mary R., 218
Lent, liturgy of, 118-19
Leo XIII, Pope, 208
Levi-Strauss, Claude, xii
Lewis, C.S., ix-x
Liturgical year, cycle of, 118-19
Lombard, Peter, 115
Lonergan, Bernard, 166
Loomis, Roger, 179, 181-83
Lord of the Dance, 7, 8, 9, 77, 190, 195, 199, 202, 204, 205
quotes from, 3-4, 9, 11, 72, 132, 202, 214
Lourdes, springs at, 51
Love
power of, 4-5
symbol of, 156-57
unconditionalness of, 21-22
Loyola, Ignatius, 187
Lugnasad, feast of, 38, 185
Lumen Gentium, 199

M

Madonna of the Arch cult, 43, 44
Magic Cup, The, xxx, 39-40, 121, 132, 139, 177-78, 185-86, 191-92, 194
quotes from, 32, 62, 173, 177-78, 185-86, 187-98
Magic Princess, symbolism of, 82, 104, 121, 173-96, 199, 211-12, 234, 235
Mariolatry, Catholic, xxvi
Markale, Jean, 65, 69-70, 176-77
Marriage, sacramentality of, 157, 158
Martin I, Pope, 55
Martyr, Justin, 111
Marx, Karl, 208
Mary
ascendancy of, 156

Thanatos, 158
Theological message, use of novel
  to convey, 5-6
Therapeutae, 95
Theravada Buddhism, 150
Thomism, 157
Thy Brother's Wife, xiii, 8, 9, 189,
  195, 199, 203, 204, 211
  quotes from, 17, 63, 211-12
Tillich, Paul, xxii, xxvi, 24, 34, 188,
  202
Tracy, David, xxii, xxvi, 231
Trent, Council of (1545-63), 158

U

Underhill, Evelyn, 103
Undset, Sigrid, xiii
Unsecular Man, 5
Unspelling quest, motif of, 179

V

Values, Christian, 20-23
Vatican Council II, 5, 42, 44, 157-
  58, 199, 207, 210
Virgin and Martyr, 53, 139, 144, 184,
  190, 193-94, 203, 205, 206, 207,
  208-9
  quotes from, 106-7, 140-41, 149,
  191, 207
Virgin archetype, 11, 45-46, 89, 232
Virginity, essence of, 45-57, 53-54
Vitalis, Ordericus, 113, 114, 115

W

Warner, Marina, 41
Water, symbolism of, 50-51, 52, 59-
  62; *See also* Fire-water symbolism

Werfel, Franz, xiii
Whitehead, xxvii
Wilde, Oscar, 91-92
Wing-Tsit Chan, 164
Womanliness of God, xx-xxi, xxvi,
  20
  expression of
    in figure of Jesus, 121-22, 229
    in figure of Mary, 229
  as Magna Mater, 31-45, 102, 112
  houseboat as symbol for, 68
  and sexuality, 122
  theme of, 7, 10, 120, 121, 122,
    124, 155, 159, 192, 196, 229
  as Virgo, 45-56
Wu, John C.H., 165

X

Xenophon, 143

Y

Yahweh
  jealous deity, 19, 168
  as masculine, 28, 219-20
  relationship of, with Bride, 95,
    102, 108, 195, 222
  revelations of, through Jesus, 20
Yin/Yang, 29

Z

Zen *satori,* mystical concept of, 165-
  66